Postdisciplinary Studies in Discourse

Series Editor
Johannes Angermuller
University of Warwick
Coventry, UK

Postdisciplinary Studies in Discourse engages in the exchange between discourse theory and analysis while putting emphasis on the intellectual challenges in discourse research. Moving beyond disciplinary divisions in today's social sciences, the contributions deal with critical issues at the intersections between language and society.

More information about this series at
http://www.palgrave.com/gp/series/14534

Mohamed Douifi

Language and the Complex of Ideology

A Socio-Cognitive Study of Warfare Discourse in Britain

palgrave
macmillan

Mohamed Douifi
English Department
University of Algiers-2
Algiers, Algeria

Postdisciplinary Studies in Discourse
ISBN 978-3-319-76546-4   ISBN 978-3-319-76547-1   (eBook)
https://doi.org/10.1007/978-3-319-76547-1

Library of Congress Control Number: 2018939179

© The Editor(s) (if applicable) and The Author(s) 2018
This work is subject to copyright. All rights are solely and exclusively licensed by the Publisher, whether the whole or part of the material is concerned, specifically the rights of translation, reprinting, reuse of illustrations, recitation, broadcasting, reproduction on microfilms or in any other physical way, and transmission or information storage and retrieval, electronic adaptation, computer software, or by similar or dissimilar methodology now known or hereafter developed.
The use of general descriptive names, registered names, trademarks, service marks, etc. in this publication does not imply, even in the absence of a specific statement, that such names are exempt from the relevant protective laws and regulations and therefore free for general use.
The publisher, the authors, and the editors are safe to assume that the advice and information in this book are believed to be true and accurate at the date of publication. Neither the publisher nor the authors or the editors give a warranty, express or implied, with respect to the material contained herein or for any errors or omissions that may have been made. The publisher remains neutral with regard to jurisdictional claims in published maps and institutional affiliations.

Cover image © Glenn Harper / Alamy Stock Photo

Printed on acid-free paper

This Palgrave Macmillan imprint is published by the registered company Springer International Publishing AG part of Springer Nature.
The registered company address is: Gewerbestrasse 11, 6330 Cham, Switzerland

To my parents

Acknowledgements

This book was made possible with the encouragement, assistance and critique of many scholars whom I had the opportunity to meet during the last few years. Portions of this research have been discussed in some international conferences and informal meetings with a number of discourse studies scholars. I would like to thank Pierre Ratinaud and Andre Salem for permission to use their software.

Contents

1 Introduction 1

2 Basic Theoretical Insights on Ideology and Discourse Analysis 17

3 Contemporary Orientations in Discourse Studies 55

4 The Anglo-Iraqi Relationships: A Historical Overview 81

5 Blair's Foreign Policy Discourse on Iraq 105

6 The Discursive Construction of the Iraq War in the British "Quality" Press 161

7 Conclusion 203

Appendix: List of Speeches by Former Prime Minister Anthony C.L. Blair (CPS) 213

Index 215

Abbreviations

APOC	Anglo-Persian Oil Company
CDA	Critical Discourse Analysis
CDS	Critical Discourse Studies
CNA	Corpora of News Articles
CPS	Corpus of Political Speeches
DHA	Discourse Historical Approach
IPC	Iraqi Petroleum Company
ISIS	Islamic State of Iraq and Syria
NATO	North Atlantic Treaty Organization
NPT	Non-Proliferation Treaty
NRS	National Readership Survey
OPEC	Organization of the Petroleum Exporting Countries
PDA	Political Discourse Analysis
SFL	Systemic Functional Linguistics
UNMOVIC	United Nations Monitoring, Verification, and Inspection Commission
UNSC	United Nations Security Council
UNSCOM	United Nations Special Commission
WMD	Weapons of Mass Destruction

List of Figures

Fig. 3.1	Cross-disciplinarity in critical discourse analysis	62
Fig. 3.2	Macrostructures. This figure maps out the theory of macrostructures and its most important elements in van Dijk's socio-cognitive model	76
Fig. 5.1	Relative frequency distribution of "Iraq", "weapons" and "terrorism" in the CPS	148
Fig. 5.2	Concordance of "Iraq" in the CPS	149
Fig. 5.3	Concordance of "Saddam" in the CPS	150
Fig. 5.4	Dendrogram of DHC	151
Fig. 5.5	Descending hierarchic classification of the CPS vocabulary co-occurrences	153
Fig. 6.1	Dendrogram of classes drawn from the corpus of *The Independent* using descending hierarchical classification	195
Fig. 6.2	Dendrogram of classes drawn from the corpus of *The Daily Telegraph* using descending hierarchical classification	196
Fig. 6.3	Dendrogram of classes drawn from the corpus of *The Guardian* using descending hierarchical classification	197
Fig. 6.4	Concordance of terrorism in the news corpora	199

1

Introduction

This study addresses the discursive legitimization strategies in the controversial discourse of Blair on the Iraq War (2003) and demonstrates how this was reproduced in the British "quality" press. The ramifications of the war are still unfolding in the Middle East and raising serious questions about the jurisdiction and role of the United Nations (UN). As the qualitative and empirical findings indicate, there was much emphasis on moralism in Blair's discourse to justify his interventionist policy in Iraq and elsewhere. The ethical claim was subsequently embraced by the press as a legitimate cause for war when the military machine crossed the borders of Iraq. Recurrent references were also made to the threat of Saddam's "nuclear weapons" and his support of international terrorism. The empirical illustration provided in this book not only consolidates the qualitative interpretations I advanced on how ideology permeates the threads of discourse, but also solves some issues that relate particularly to the cognitive analysis of language.

At an abstract theoretical level, I argue that behind the surface language structure lies another highly complex socio-cognitive web of structures that define and assign particular meaning to events and social objects. In this sense, language itself cannot adequately express such intricacy, and hence, much of what people want to convey through language remains partly incomplete or fragmented. Understanding such metalevel of discourse would necessitate a multifaceted method of analysis that meticulously scrutinizes many aspects of language use. This is why I opted to conduct this study within the Critical Discourse Studies (CDS) framework, which is less reductionist and rich, both in terms of theory and in terms of methodology. As it stands, this book contributes to the field of discourse analysis and adds original insights to the contemporary CDS approaches that are more cognitively oriented. It is also relevant for other disciplines that consider the function of language in society such as social constructivism, quantitative linguistics, political science, media and communication studies.

It is worthwhile noting at the very outset that the methodological rationale of this research work is grounded within the field of CDS, which is also alternatively, but perhaps not quite appropriately, dubbed Critical Discourse Analysis (CDA). Because the latter label sounds somewhat reductionist in regard to the spacious domain of "language analysis", it is now far less used. Following Teun A. van Dijk, (Critical) Discourse Studies is an umbrella epithet that is more apt than the traditional and misleading label "Critical Discourse Analysis", which has been universally embraced since the early 1990s. This tradition of discourse critique is especially associated with the works of Teun A. van Dijk himself, Norman Fairclough, Ruth Wodak, Paul Chilton, Theo van Leeuwen, James Paul Gee and other research groups and schools.[1]

This would reduce CDA to a mere branch of inquiry or "school" under the broad realm of CDS, which includes a wide range of methods and approaches—some of which are predominantly descriptive. Indeed, such a view has recently been shared by many other leading scholars as well. Van Dijk clarifies that "this more general term suggests that such a critical approach not only involves critical *analysis*, but also critical *theory*, as well as critical *applications*. The designation CDS may also avoid the widespread misconception that a critical approach is a *method* of discourse analysis" (2009a, p. 62). He further comments that "discourse studies is often defined as the contemporary discipline of what used to be called rhetoric since antiquity, that is, the practice and study of 'good' public speaking and writing, for instance in parliament, in court or in literature" (2007, p. xxix). Amongst the very essential preoccupations of this trans-discipline is to mediate on the form–function dichotomy in language use, bringing together a broad range of disciplines from across the social sciences and humanities in one melting pot (see Angermuller, Maingueneau, & Wodak, 2014; Hart & Cap, 2014). Christopher Hart adds that "CDS is principally concerned with the communication and discursive construction of social, including political, knowledge, as well as with linguistic persuasion and manipulation. These processes, however, must ultimately be grounded in the cognitive systems of interacting social agents" (2011, p. 1).

Ostensibly, following the boom in the philosophy of language that was inaugurated by the linguistic shift of the 1960s or thereabouts, several scholars endeavoured to refine our understanding of language and its function in the social world. Shortly thereafter, their collective efforts were crystallized in a bunch of innovative conceptual frames of reference, models and theories which sought to advance a systematic and more objective critique of the various types of discourse. Thenceforth, a cluster of heterogeneous strategies were suggested which winded their way through a variety of disciplines, primarily linguistics, sociology, psychology and philosophy, to name but a few. It was inevitable, however, due to this highly intricate, and sometimes asymmetric, convergence between linguistics and social theory that discourse analysis would become a thriving subject of research in its own right. This was indeed a major leap in the general theory of language, yet there remain some unresolved theoretical issues and lacunae vis-à-vis the nature of discourse, and particularly the parameters involved in discourse processing and analysis.

In order to avoid the ambiguity that might arise from the vast literature in the realm of discourse analysis, one might need to highlight once again the fact that CDA has been defined in a myriad of ways, which were sometimes at odds with each other. The reason for such flexibility in the theory of CDA is not hard to discover. Put simply, the various schools that emerged especially from the 1970s onwards embraced different conceptualizations of discourse, and implemented strategies of critique that were congruent with their own perceptions and research objectives. Furthermore, those fundamental idiosyncratic discrepancies, both in terms of theory and praxis, were informed by the heterogeneous domain assumptions adopted by these schools that may originate from different disciplinary backgrounds. Nonetheless, they do sometimes intersect and reinforce each other.

Based on this thriving theoretical framework, I attempt to scrutinize the relationship between language use and ideology, taking the military involvement of Britain in the 2003 Iraq War as a case study.[2] At a narrow level, the goal is twofold.

First, to examine the strategies of legitimization in Blair's discourse through the analysis of the lexico-semantic structure of his language so as to link such structure with power relations, cognitive processes and structures in society. In other words, I seek in the first place to unscramble the ideological load of language which is mostly, but not necessarily, embedded in the grammar, vocabulary and style that characterized Blair's political discourse. Close attention, however, is paid to his controversial pro-war stance in relation to Iraq. The other contextual elements, the historical, socio-cognitive and political in particular, are equally discussed because they are important to make sense of the meaning of language in the situation where it is used. The term "ideology", then, designates one of the most essential concepts in this book, whose overall purpose is to comment on both the conscious and unconscious workings of ideology in society and language.

Second, the above-mentioned components are examined once more in an extended corpus of news articles (CNA) taken from some well-circulated British "quality" papers: *The Daily Telegraph*, *The Guardian* and *The Independent*. In this respect, one has to bear in mind that in a democracy such as Britain, the discourse of the press is supposed to be independent from the shackles of the official ideology and its overt political biases. This is especially so when it comes to cover a controversial issue such as a military offensive against another sovereign state, as will be exemplified in the case of Iraq.

Obviously, the study of ideology and discourse is not a totally nascent subject area of research, but genuinely rooted in the traditional disciplines of the social sciences and humanities, most plainly, perhaps, in rhetoric studies and literary criticism. What is continuously changing is the lens through which we look at the widely diverse societies, their cultural patterns, ways of seeing and ideologies, where language is still a key instrument to decipher the complexity of these social worlds.

One of the preoccupations of contemporary social theorists and linguists, amongst many other scholars, is to come up with a comprehensive and thorough account on the multiple articulations of ideology in discourse. Indeed, this is the very same concern of this research work, which is based on a cross-disciplinary methodology, giving prominence to the social and cognitive dimensions of language use. That is to say, it aims to decode ideology in discourse through a critical reading of the surface structure of language, as well as its deep structure. Such a flexible mode of analysis, it must be stressed, is handled with a description of the context of the different communicative situations addressed. In this sense, focus is to be placed upon, on the one hand, the analysis of the patterns of language in the corpora and, on the other hand, the various cultural, historical, epistemic, social and political factors that make a given language structure coherent and meaningful at a particular time, that is, the British social milieu at the first decade of the twenty-first century in this case study.

The crux of my argument rests on the belief that the discursive *manufacturing* of the pro-war ideology in Britain, as manifest specifically in Blair's hostile rhetoric towards Iraq, could be best uncovered via a systematic analysis of the linguistic, social and cognitive dimensions of language use. With reference to the proposed corpora, this research takes into account two fundamental centres of power: First, it will showcase how manipulation was carried on at the level of the "political society", which is entrusted with institutional power, authority and decision-making. Focus, however, is to be placed solely on the political discourse of Tony Blair during his campaign to rally support for the military action against Saddam's regime. This is done through a close reading of a selection of Blair's most powerful speeches in which the major tenets of his allegedly "ethical" foreign policy were presented and defended. The second level of analysis considers the discourse(s) of the press, which is supposed to be a parallel centre of power to the former because it is, as it has always been, a typical gatekeeper and a major disseminator of information in Britain.

Basically, my choice of the Iraq War of 2003 as an instrumental case study to explore the link between ideology and discourse is due to its controversial nature and thus the ramifications that it left on the world stage and the Middle East in particular. The hasty move to military action against Saddam's Iraq, though its regime was dictatorial *par excellence*, enthralled the political and academic circles during the last few years. In the first place, the declaration of the war without the consent of the United Nations Security Council indicated a radical shift in power relations in today's world. The unilateral decision by the "coalition of the willing" to invade a sovereign state mirrored the fuzzy role of the UN and its inability sometimes to implement its decisions and orders. There is no doubt that the onslaught on Iraq raised perennial questions about the credibility and also the jurisdiction of international institutions in relation to conflict resolution and peacekeeping. Moreover, as is palpable in the dramatic events that are still unfolding in Iraq, which has now gripped most of the Middle East, the fall of Saddam's central government unleashed another protracted episode of disarray throughout the country. More alarmingly, sectarian tension escalated and there emerged terror groups with different allegiances and ideologies, which have found the desert of Iraq a safe haven for their aggressive activities, which are obviously crossing the borders to other countries. It is needless to add that the key local and international players are still playing a dirty game in the region to promote their geostrategic, economic and self-interest calculations, which would have far-reaching consequences on world peace and stability in the long run.

At a broad theoretical level, the dynamic intersection between ideology, cognition and society constitutes the focal point of this research. In essence, I attempt to decipher the codes of ideology in discourse which are intricately woven in the threads of language. As far as the case study is concerned, this entails a careful assessment of the vocabulary, syntactic structures and the various semantic features of the language of Blair, along with that of the print press, through the lens of a macro-discursive methodology. In this sense, it is intended to project the ways in which social reality is constructed in the language of politicians, and how such a reality is justified and ultimately challenged or reproduced in the news discourse(s). Indeed, the 2003 Iraq War has been discussed by many politicians and academics from various perspectives in the last two decades. To my thinking, there has been little serious academic criticism of the war discourse, at least, in the British academia, and the literature is still somewhat scant. It is the aim of this study to consider two major sites of power where the process of legitimization and manipulation, on the question of military intervention in Iraq, took place.

Another basic notion which I frequently refer to alongside discourse and ideology is *knowledge*. The knowledge–discourse dichotomy seems to be still problematic for many CDS critics, especially if one considers the ideological element in the analysis of this reciprocal link. How is knowledge produced and reproduced in discourse? The kind of knowledge that normalizes the status quo and power relations in order to serve an individual, group, political party or ideology over other ostracized ones. In the context of this study, attention is paid to Tony Blair both as an ordinary British citizen and as UK's Prime Minister who produces specific forms of political knowledge that address the then question of Iraq. Undeniably, the broadsheet press is another major producer of knowledge that plays, as a matter of fact, a crucial role in the education of the "mass mind" and manipulation of the public opinion.

I claim that legitimization in discourse operates, in large part, at the unconscious level, where the members of the same "epistemic community" are more likely to embrace the ideology that is produced by their elite, with little critical judgement. In this sense, the endorsement of a given ideology, which would become mainstream or a common-sense practice amongst the "in-group" social actors at a particular point in time, is substantially a passionate and emotional behaviour which is informed and sustained by the socio-cultural stock of knowledge they share. Through the analysis of how Britain enmeshed in the Iraqi puddle, I will lay bare the modes and strategies of legitimization used by Blair which frequently brought to the fore references to shared common values, cultural collective identity and belonging to promote his pro-war stance. In similar fashion, this ideological slant was reproduced by the broadsheets which implicitly embraced the in-group ideology. The press was, however, becoming more explicit in its skewed coverage to the official line as the war drew close just to follow propagandistic style in the aftermath. I advocate here that this was partly due to the impact of the socio-culturally shared knowledge which regulates the circulating discourse and imposes real restraints on the members of the community.

Though the methodology adopted is cross-disciplinary in its theory and procedures, the socio-cognitive model developed by CDS theorist Teun A. van Dijk (1988a, 1988b, 2008, 2009a, 2009b) is the mainstay that guides my analysis and interpretation. The application of a cross-disciplinary approach comes from my belief that the study of ideology in discourse, particularly in conflicting issues, is complex and manifold due to the tangled socio-cultural sources of ideology. Thus my argument, though seems controversial, suggests that ideologies are endorsed, shared and defended mostly unconsciously by the ideologues and the mass public alike. The study of language use would help us assess the embodiment of those ideologies in the fabrics of language that reflect the kind of circulating worldviews in a specific social grouping, and understand better their modes of judgement and ways of seeing.

The socio-cognitive model is perhaps one of the very few approaches in discourse studies that made systematic reference to cognition. Basically, it is designed to analyse large chunks of text and talk, with an emphasis on the cognitive aspect of language and context. The assumption that underlies van Dijk's definition of ideology stems from classic works in the sociology of knowledge which postulate that shared knowledge influences the attitudes and perceptions of individuals. With reference to cognitive psychology and other related disciplines, van Dijk made a valuable contribution to the theory of context by integrating the cognitive dimension in the analysis of discourse understanding and interpretation. However, the conceptualization of context in terms of "mental models" is perhaps still difficult to be operationalized, which is also the case for the concept of *macrostructure*. Due to these shortcomings, I opted to apply a cross-disciplinary methodology by borrowing a number of theoretical insights and analytical strategies that are not necessarily associated with the socio-cognitive model.

A critique of the legitimization of the Iraq War has been made, albeit succinctly, by van Dijk in his analysis of some political speeches by the former Spanish Prime Minister José María Aznar during parliamentary sessions held in February and March 2003 (see van Dijk, 2005). Focus has been paid to the rhetorical devices used by the Prime Minister to legitimize his controversial position that was explicitly in favour of the war on Iraq, even without the need for UN resolution. This was handled through questioning the role of what was termed as "political implicatures" in Aznar's political discourse. Van Dijk argued that the political implicatures in Aznar's speeches, taking the latter as a form of political discourse, served to function as pragmatic articulations of political cognition and action in the political process. Unlike implications which are related to the mere semantic properties of language, van Dijk devotes much importance to the implicatures of discourse which are presuppositions made under the influence of pragmatic and contextual conditions. Another contribution by van Dijk, which is the closest to this study, basically in terms of goals and strategy of analysis, is his analytical account of Blair's speech on Iraq which was delivered in the UK House of Commons on 18 March 2003 (2009b, pp. 213–247). In the examination of the dialectic relation between knowledge and discourse, the theoretical cognitive notions introduced by van Dijk were tested against the then prowar discourse of Blair. Particularly, the ways in which knowledge constructs specific "mental models" in the mind of discourse participants are explained so as to relate them to manipulation and power abuse in the political discourse of Blair.[3]

Accordingly, this research work, which lies under the heading of British Studies, aims to contribute, in some modest measure, to the discipline of (Critical) Discourse Studies in general. At a narrower level, it attempts to give a boost to the argument that calls for the integration of the findings and tools of modern cognitive science into the study of discourse, not as a complementary element but rather as a fundamental instrument of analysis. It must be highlighted once more that it is not my purpose here to elucidate why Britain supported the neoconservatives in the USA, nor to judge the legality of the war, albeit this point is briefly discussed in the fourth chapter, but rather to better fathom the underlying and unconscious processing mechanism of legitimization and manipulation in discourse in its original British milieu. Simply put, how was the pro-war ideology legitimized in Blair's political discourse and reproduced in the British press? How were the cultural, political and historical conditions exploited to normalize and sustain such an aggressive ideology towards another sovereign state?

One of the limitations of this research relates to CDA itself as an analytical approach, which could lead to unbalanced criticism of discourse. Indeed, this issue has been raised by some CDA scholars, notably those engaged in the critique of social issues that contain much "political" load. I strongly adhere to the view that discourse analysis is a complex, discursive and variegated task. A set of theoretical goals are set for assessment—some of these are the ones listed in what follows:

- To describe and analyse the structure of the official political and news discourse(s) in Britain in relation to the Iraq War through a careful analysis of the "knowledge schemata" packaged in these discourses.
- To experiment with a body of strategies in discourse analysis which are informed by the theories that fall under the umbrella of CDS. More particularly, some insights from the social cognitive theory are heavily cited. Yet, the backbone of the designed methodology is formed precisely from the tools suggested by discourse theorist Teun A. van Dijk in his socio-cognitive model.
- To critically assess and test the applicability of van Dijk's proposed notion of "cognitive interface" in the analysis of the political and news discourse.
- To trace the underlying logic behind the normalization of violence and the dehumanization of the "Other" during the zenith of a crisis, such as the engagement in war.

In broad terms, the research design of this study is based on a blend of qualitative and quantitative materials that, taken together, would produce comprehensive readings of the object. I, therefore, believe that the implementation of a quasi-approach in the analysis of an extended corpus of texts is quite valuable for a thorough analysis of discourse production, understanding and interpretation. As will be clarified in some detail in the first chapter, the rationale of this methodology is non-linear, but rather systematic and substantially influenced by a diverse set of theoretical orientations that are not necessarily within the bounds of the social sciences and humanities.[4] Hence, this methodology resides at the cutting edge of a number of research fields and also some more empirical branches of inquiry. Partly, in the qualitative textual analysis of the data, I emulate van Dijk's ways of analysis through direct reference to his socio-cognitive model. The quantitative instruments implemented in the exploration of the corpora are taken from French lexicometry (see Benzécri, 1980; Lebart, Salem, & Berry, 1998).

In brief, the major part of the discourse critique offered here is based on a qualitative analysis of numerous political and news items. Thus, the analytical account of this object is deemed to be process oriented, systematic and less intuitive. Therefore, those selected texts were handled separately so as to be able to consider the context of each text individually, and also compared against each other at a later stage. Because qualitative analysis requires relatively much space, a few texts were chosen from the corpus of political speeches and were examined at the linguistic and non-linguistic levels. Moreover, the remainder of the corpus is also subjected to an exhaustive quantitative analysis. The same procedures are applied on the news corpus, with slight differences due to the heterogeneous nature of the political (speeches) and news texts (articles), at least in terms of form, goal and structure.

To reiterate, the socio-cognitive model of Teun A. van Dijk is the mainstay of the methodology adopted, whose roots date back to the early 1980s. A major positive feature of this theoretical model is its multidisciplinary nature, where it draws from a variety of disciplines and sub-disciplines of the social sciences and humanities, and also from cognitive science. A further elaboration on the linguistic properties of the corpora is also handled through some sophisticated lexicometric programmes.[5] Therefore, the second part of this study is more formalized and empirically driven using a quantitative strategy in the analysis of the corpora. The function of the software is to dismantle the various lexico-semantic patterns of the treated texts at many different levels and in a myriad of ways. Basically, the software packages are used due to the relatively large size of the news corpus and also the kind of systematic and correlation analysis I aim at, which cannot be adequately fulfilled qualitatively. Besides, these tools are customizable to some processing norms. Hence, the outcome of the different operations implemented on the textual input would result in the form of graphical forms and visual illustrations such as tables of word frequency and co-occurrences that best account for both macro and micro lexico-semantic structures of a single and multiple texts.

Indeed, computer-assisted analysis of text corpora has been widely used recently in literary criticism, discourse analysis and many other disciplines in the social sciences and humanities. In the case of this research, the quantitative findings are not there only to reassess the qualitative interpretations, but rather, they relate to its main argument which integrates the cognitive aspect of discourse processing. Moreover, since the corpora used are somewhat large in size, they do require a condensation process to produce different partitions that would equally lend themselves to a narrow qualitative reading. The resulting tables, charts and figures exhibit in much clarity and accuracy the linguistic repertoire around which a specific topic is grounded; that is, how is such a given theme or "discourse topic" described, defined and explicated by the speaker (Blair). Consider, for example, the descending hierarchic classification (DHC) figure which shows a top-down lexicometric classification of different lexemes and their associated vocabulary in Blair's speeches. This signals the order and connection between the themes in the linguistic repertoire of Blair that he relied upon in constructing and justifying specific attitudes, beliefs and opinions towards many political issues such as education, local economy, Britain and Europe, and the Iraqi dossier (see the last section of Chap. 5). Further clarification on the logic of this software-based textual analysis will be expounded thoroughly.

Undeniably, the application of a mixed methodology in the analysis of discourse would enable us to compare the findings and maximize their validity. As has been just mentioned, the samples that constitute the unit of analysis are divided into two parts: First, a small corpus containing 30 official speeches of Tony Blair while serving as Prime Minister. The corpus (corpus of political speeches—abbreviated as CPS) includes formal speeches only (listed in the Appendix) and does not consider other declarations, official documents, interviews or conference notes delivered elsewhere which might be equally pertinent to the overall understanding of Britain's policy on Iraq. Despite the accuracy of the statistical representations, there are still some caveats that require further comment and clarification, as is the case for the cognitive explanation made based on the statistical output.

The second corpus includes various news articles from three well-circulated broadsheets: *The Daily Telegraph* (June 2000–May 2003), *The*

Guardian (January 2000–May 2003) and *The Independent* (January 2000–May 2003). Relevant texts (1000 texts from each title) were manually tracked based on the search for specific key words in the headlines, such as Iraq War, WMD (weapons of mass destruction), Saddam and Blair.[6] The selected newspapers are amongst the most widely circulated during the first decade of the century,[7] and they represent a spectrum of political and ideological affiliations in Britain. For example, *The Telegraph* has been largely conservative and pro-capitalist, *The Guardian* is more liberal and progressive, while *The Independent* is centre-left, with a noticeable socialist touch.

One needs to acknowledge some of the cracks and gaps in this research strategy, which is, in fact, part of the problem investigated, that is, the cognitive analysis of discourse. One of the hindrances of the socio-cognitive methodology as a whole, regardless of the model or theory followed, is the difficulty to operationalize some of its abstract concepts, which are nonetheless still valid theoretically. In the second and third chapters, I intend to provide a comprehensive introduction to the conceptual framework that underpins the methodology of discourse analysis utilized. It is worth noting, however, that the practical intricacies of the socio-cognitive paradigm demand much space for a thorough explanation. Partly, this complexity arises from the constraints imposed by the other related disciplines. Moreover, the exact meaning of a cluster of technical terms that are used solely in this methodology needs further elaboration, which would definitely exceed the limit of this book, yet brief marginal annotations and references are given only when necessary.

The second chapter succinctly reviews the literature in the field of CDS that is germane to my topic and describe the theoretical correlation between ideology and discourse, which are sometimes defined in relation to each other. I trace the development of each term historically and introduce adequate definitions, which are subsequently operationalized in the chapters that follow. In the third chapter, I exhibit the fundamental concepts and strategies of the adopted methodology which cut across the trio of the socio-cognitive model: discourse, society and cognition.

The fourth chapter surveys some major events in the profile of the Iraqi crisis with the key Western powers by breaking into the flow of history to comment particularly on the fickle relationship between Iraq and Britain. This serves to provide a glimpse of the historical, legal and political contextual dimensions that led to the war of 2003. From another perspective, I would showcase the deep-rooted involvement of British imperialists in the making of the modern state of Iraq and also the diplomatic influence that followed.

Chapter 5 analyses Blair's foreign policy discourse on Iraq during the period that preceded the invasion, as mirrored in his political speeches. The critique of this discourse is based upon a selection of a few essential speeches to reveal how the concept of ethics was exploited in the justification of the pro-war ideology. Due to its salience in the political discourse of Blair, the modern issue of international terrorism is also discussed. It is argued, therefore, that the rise of terror in the post-9/11 world has pervasively impinged on the policy of Britain in Iraq. Furthermore, a quantitative analysis of the corpus of political speeches is made through the use of lexicometric software (Lexico3 and IRaMuTeQ). The sixth chapter is devoted to the analysis of the news discourse to assess not only how the question of Iraq was represented, but also whether the press critiqued or merely reproduced Blair's interventionist rhetoric. I first provide a comment on some socio-economic and political factors that accompanied the evolution of the news culture in Britain. It will be demonstrated how the concentration of ownership in the information industry made the press what it looks nowadays, and how it guides its ideological orientation. Finally, a close reading of the news corpora is carried out at the micro and macro levels of language structures using the aforementioned tools and strategies.

Notes

1. See Wodak and Meyer (2009) for a detailed literature review on CDA, its genesis, development, goals and agenda.
2. Many different labels were used by politicians, the media and academics to refer to the 2003 US-led invasion of Iraq. Each given label reflected, to some extent, a specific ideological stance in relation to the war. "Iraqi Freedom

Operation" reverberated in the US official documents, army sources and rhetoric of politicians. The Iraq War and the Second Gulf War were also frequently used. Yet, other anti-war proponents preferred the phrase "War on Iraq" to emphasize that the military act was aggressive and illegal.
3. The concept of mental models and thus the role of knowledge, as prescribed by the socio-cognitive model of discourse analysis, are explained in some detail in the third chapter.
4. One of the most important remarks that should be highlighted is the emphasis on the cross-disciplinary nature of method and theory in CDS—not only within the domain of traditional disciplines of the social sciences and humanities, as this intersection might extend to newborn arenas of research that are much more *scientifically* oriented and less speculative, such as the empirically based logic of cognitive psychology.
5. I used the latest version of IRaMuTeQ and Lexico3, which are high-performance software tools for data mining and textual analysis.
6. The word-frequency illustrations of each of these newspapers clearly show the centrality of Iraq as a main theme in the texts retrieved.
7. For more information about the circulation and readership estimates of the British newspapers and other related details, check the official website of the Audit Bureau of Circulation (UK): abc.org.uk

References

Angermuller, J., Maingueneau, D., & Wodak, R. (Eds.). (2014). *The discourse studies reader: Main currents in theory and analysis*. Amsterdam/Philadelphia: John Benjamins Publishing Company.

Benzécri, J. P. (1980). *Pratique de l'Analyse des données* [Practice of data analysis]. 3 vols. Paris: Dunod.

Hart, C. (Ed.). (2011). *Critical discourse studies in context and cognition*. Amsterdam: John Benjamins Publishing Company.

Hart, C., & Cap, P. (Eds.). (2014). *Contemporary critical discourse studies*. London: Bloomsbury.

Lebart, L., Salem, A., & Berry, L. (1998). *Exploring textual data*. Dordrecht, The Netherlands: Kluwer.

Van Dijk, T. A. (1988a). *News as discourse*. Hillsdale, NJ: Erlbaum.

Van Dijk, T. A. (1988b). *News analysis: Case studies of international and national news in the press*. Hillsdale, NJ: Lawrence Erlbaum.

Van Dijk, T. A. (2005). War rhetoric of a little ally: Political implicatures and Aznar's legitimatization of the war on Iraq. *Journal of Language and Politics, 4*(1), 65–69.

Van Dijk, T. A. (Ed.). (2007). *Discourse studies*. London: Sage.

Van Dijk, T. A. (2008). *Discourse and context: A sociocognitive approach*. London: Cambridge University Press.

Van Dijk, T. A. (2009a). Critical discourse studies: A sociocognitive approach. In R. Wodak & M. Meyer (Eds.), *Methods of critical discourse analysis* (2nd ed., pp. 62–85). London: Sage.

Van Dijk, T. A. (2009b). *Society and discourse: How social contexts influence text and talk*. Cambridge, UK: Cambridge University Press.

Wodak, R., & Meyer, M. (2009). Critical discourse analysis: History, agenda, theory and methodology. In R. Wodak & M. Meyer (Eds.), *Methods of critical discourse analysis* (2nd ed., pp. 1–33). London: Sage.

www.abc.org.uk

2

Basic Theoretical Insights on Ideology and Discourse Analysis

2.1 Highlights on the Genesis and Development of the Concept of Ideology

2.1.1 Destutt's *idéologie*

It would perhaps be sufficient, at this starting juncture, to exhibit a constellation of basic theoretical notions that are germane to the study of ideology and its processing in language use. Primarily, this is made through recurrent references to a mosaic of Marxist and a few other language-oriented perspectives from the structuralist paradigm. But first and foremost, there is a need to closely pinpoint the meaning of the, somewhat vague, concept of "ideology" in the existing literature, and thus its implications on the language critique tradition. Nevertheless, the aim herein is not to redefine or dilute this concept, which is by no means value laden, but rather to account for ideology and its processing as a highly discursive socio-cognitive phenomenon whose workings in the social milieu would eventually be crystallized in language and its structure.

Discourse is another central concept which likewise requires careful consideration due to the wide array of connotations that have been assigned to it, and thus its theoretical intersection with ideology. In doing so, I intend to stimulate a thorough reflection on the ways in which individual and collective ideologies are "manufactured", legitimized and reproduced in a given "epistemic community" with reference to the linguistic, social and cognitive aspects of these processes. It should be emphasized in this respect that I endorse the assumption that ideology is not arbitrary and does not always manifest itself in discourse, but it is often implicit and encoded in the threads of language.

Throughout this chapter, a succinct critical overview is given of some basic issues in the theory of ideology and the criticism that arose by the modern academia. For the sake of clarifying the original meanings of the term *idéologie*, attention is drawn first to its roots, which lay in the philosophical and political transformations that occurred in Europe during the last 200 years or so. I start with tracking the term's etymology and the political context where it was first used, and then follow up its subsequent metamorphosis. Nonetheless, one has to bear in mind that it is out of reach to consider all perspectives related to ideology as a concept and also as a process in the formulation of discourse(s). As previously highlighted, with reference to the selected case study, I seek to illustrate the manifestations of ideology in two types of discourse. First, the official British political discourse on the then pending question of Iraq as enacted by the former Prime Minister Tony Blair. Second, the subsequent narratives in the British quality press starting from the year 2000. Accordingly, this investigation, which takes language as an object of analysis, aims to uncover how Blair endeavoured to legitimize the 2003 military attack on Iraq, and how the pro-war official stance permeated the discourse of some of the best-selling national dailies. This is a potentially controversial point because the press in Britain is a separate centre of power that is subject to no statutory control whatsoever. This makes ideology and how it functions in communication and interaction a central theoretical concern worthy of critical scrutiny. I assume, therefore, that ideology, as conceptualized in this chapter, would make it relatively easier to fathom the exercise of power, with a close focus on language use.

Many CDS scholars and theorists, from across a range of schools of thought and traditions, held a firm belief that ideology could be reflected in a myriad of ways in the linguistic behaviour of those who produce a given dominant or marginalized discourse (Fowler, Hodge, Kress, & Trew, 1979). Teun A. van Dijk advocates that "ideologies of speakers or writers may be 'uncovered' by close reading, understanding or systematic analysis, if language users explicitly or unwittingly 'express' their ideologies through language and communication" (1995, p. 135). In this sense, to describe and carefully analyse the ensemble of lexical, syntactic and semantic structures of language in a specific communicative situation or event, with systematic attention to its context, is to project the underlying and embedded ideologies that lie behind the surface structure.

It must be stressed, however, that formal textual description of the language components is just one preliminary stage of analysis in the critique of discourse that is fundamental yet not sufficient per se. The context under which the language is used is also seminal to make sense of the function of the linguistic form and its link with the speaker's or writer's ideological affiliations, intentions, worldviews, the distribution of power relations among the interlocutors and so on.[1] Textual analysis, as Norman Fairclough declares, "is a valuable supplement to social research, not a replacement for other forms of social research and analysis" (2003, p. 16). As will be shown in the closing part of this chapter, the very early version of Critical Linguistics, as the forerunner of contemporary versions of CDA, investigates the manifestations of ideology in the text via a detailed examination of the form of language, with, little if any, attention to the contextual dimensions of discourse, leading, as a consequence, to major shortcomings and lacunae. Besides, ideology is often intermingled and used along with other complex social issues that relate particularly to power abuse, social oppression, dominance, iniquity and hegemony. Each of these constitutes a concept that could also be examined separately, as they are, in their own right, central themes in other disciplines and areas of inquiry. Doing discourse analysis via textual analysis, Fairclough goes on to suggest, "should not be seen as prior to and independent of social analysis and critique – it should be seen as an open process which can be enhanced through dialogue across disciplines and theories, rather than a coding in the terms of an autonomous analytical framework or grammar" (p. 16).

Indeed, the terms "discourse" and "ideology" designate two discrete concepts which have acquired a number of connotations and meanings. Clearly, the perusal of the existing large literature would show a noticeable lack of consensus amongst scholars who did not share a specific perception on the concept of discourse and ideology alike and, therefore, embraced various views on discourse analysis. Yet, despite the theoretical heterogeneity between these two concepts, they do overlap and might be used interchangeably throughout this book, but the distinctions are still quite important.

There is a lengthy body of literature that incorporated the term "ideology" as a central element in the study of several issues in economy, history, politics, art, literature, drama and the like. Some ambitious studies sought to demonstrate how the discourse of the intelligentsia, throughout the last two centuries, tailored its tone with the ideological agendas of the dominant political forces. Even the more formal and empirically based disciplines whose tools of validation are, arguably, more systematic and reliable were not immune from the influence of ideology and political indoctrination. This was the case, for example, in Nazi Germany and the Communist Soviet Union, where the ideology of the state and its interests were bound up with the objectives of science. Indeed, the impact of hegemonic ideologies on science has been debated by a number of prominent scholars, for example, Mark Walker in *Science and Ideology* (2003), which provides a comparative historical analysis of the impact of ideology on the scientific discourse under different political systems. The criticism provided by some leading philosophers of the twentieth century, such as Karl Popper and Thomas Kuhn, on the intersection of ideology and science is also of seminal importance to the debate on the discursive manifestations of ideology in discourse.

In his sharp attack on the universality of science in what he termed "epistemological anarchism", the Austrian philosopher Paul Karl Feyerabend (1975) argued against the objectivity and neutrality of science by emphasizing the ideological character of the scientific discourse, as he claims that there is always a possibility that science would turn out to be a mere ideology. Mihai Spariosu expands on Feyerabend's critique of scientific inquiry as follows:

Basic Theoretical Insights on Ideology and Discourse Analysis 21

> It is precisely from this Nietzschean agonistic standpoint that Feyerabend conducts his vigorous critique of modern science as an expression of a totalitarian mentality. He consistently shows how, in the guise of ideological neutrality (which presupposes a dispassionate pursuit of Truth, objective and universally valid standards of knowledge, fair play, and scrupulous professional honesty), the modern institutions of science impose a dogmatic ideology not only upon their own members but also upon society at large, in our schools, hospitals, free economy, government and so forth. (1989, p. 300)

It is fairly reasonable to raise similar questions and scepticism vis-à-vis the other circulating genres of discourse, common-sense assumptions, social norms, beliefs and worldviews that are usually, but not necessarily always, taken for granted to be valid and acceptable. Ideology, then, does not seem to be an ordinary term that is used arbitrarily in the academia, but a concept denoting an intricate social practice that continuously shapes our social worlds, ways of thinking and perceptions. Obviously, power, knowledge and the various information channels are amongst the instruments that "manufacture", legitimize and normalize ideologies. In this process, language comes to the fore as the vehicle through which those ideologically constructed social realities are entrenched and reproduced over space and time.

A cursory look at the historical development of the term "ideology" is of particular importance at this stage. One might claim that even at its inception, the French term *idéologie* was encased with much flexibility in meaning, and sometimes misuses and ambiguity. Nowadays, with the rapidly changing environment and the accelerated motion towards a seemingly shapeless globalized world, ideology, both as a concept and as a process, is likely to receive more idiosyncratic interpretations and contestations, which would add another layer of complexity. In what follows, I proceed with a succinct historical account about the genesis of the term and its usage. It is also worth at this point to connect this concept with the object of this study; that is, what is meant by ideology in the context of the British military involvement in Iraq, and more specifically, how it is expressed, justified and reproduced in the political and news discourses. This could be handled through a myriad ways of analysis and critique. However, I solely reflect upon the structures of language in the process of ideological production and comprehension in this bounded case, taking into account the socio-cognitive perspectives of these processes.

In retrospect, the term "ideology" was introduced by the French philosopher Antoine Destutt de Tracy (see Head, 1985). The literal translation of the word into English would be the "science of ideas" or alternatively "theory of ideas". Because language is the medium through which ideology is transmitted, de Tracy's major philosophical contributions were put on language and its relationship with thought and cognition. Without going into much detail, the term "ideology" was used to signify a branch of science that was concerned mainly with the study of *ideas* out of the orthodox metaphysical forms of thought which prevailed amongst the pre-Renaissance thinkers. As a scientifically based new offspring, this discipline was not a totally new invention but, in some extent, a further developed phase coming out of the philosophical debates of the Enlightenment era that started to drift away from the theological modes of thinking towards more secularism, rationalism and empiricism.[2] This is indeed the very same definition adopted in the context of this book in order to eschew the negativity and complexity that accompanied the term up to date.

From another angle, Destutt de Tracy, as an economist and rational philosopher, played an active role in promoting liberalism and the secular movement in France and other countries in Europe as well. This movement was at its early beginnings in France when de Tracy coined the term *idéologie*. The term, according to Tracy, was a scientific branch that sought to study ideas as abstract forms without any reference to the metaphysical and theological interpretations. The objective was, as he put it, to grasp the workings of "our intellectual faculties, their principal phenomena, and their most evident circumstances" (cited in Williams, 1977, p. 56). This school critiqued a number of issues in politics, economy, philosophy and theology. Tracy's views about the human nature and its intellect were based on a deductive approach that sought to explain the social and political behaviour from a materialist perspective. At the same time he deliberately criticized the then dominant dogmatic and religious traditions which pervaded the French culture (see Eagleton, 1991).

Within the European context of the nineteenth century that witnessed a shift from the passion with artistic excellence to scientific discovery and territorial expansion, the term "ideology" had a special glamour for many intellectuals and philosophers. It was employed in a myriad of disciplines, each of which encapsulated the term with a mosaic of meanings, leading therefore to a considerable conceptual flexibility (Barth, 1976). Indeed, the dawn of the nineteenth century was a turning point in the history of Europe, and France in particular. De Tracy and his associates sought to secularize the French society and restrain the influence of religion. Their efforts were made to foster a purely secular morality in society during a time of political turmoil and uncertainty created by the upheavals of the French Revolution.

The meaning of ideology changed from the "science of ideas" to the "ideas" of the then contesting political factions and groups when Napoleon Bonaparte opposed the "abstract" philosophy brought up by Destutt and his colleagues (Krieger, 2013, p. 553). Thenceforth, the term "ideology" acquired a firmly negative connotation. Srikant Sarangi clarifies that the negativity of the term "lies in the ways in which the word has been used historically, although this cannot be supported with purely linguistic or etymological evidence" (Garzone & Sarangi, 2007, p. 13). In the course of time, there emerged a number of philosophical approaches that attempted to unveil the dynamics of ideological processing in a variety of domains, yet most of these were not eminently sufficient to properly account for the intricate nature of ideology and its function in society. Taken as a whole, it could be claimed with little hesitation that most of these traditional approaches produced a partial explanation and were, to some extent, unbalanced, if not paradoxically ideological themselves. Marxism, for example, exploited the concept of ideology to serve its dogmatic principles calling for the eradication of the dominant capitalist mindset. The arguments offered within this framework were sometimes speculative and even contradictory with an ostensible inclination to promote its own radical ideology through revolutionary means.

2.1.2 Ideology in the Marxist Tradition

Marxism was the first philosophy to endorse the concept of ideology in the promulgation of its anti-class stance. It is easily discernible that the term was in use in the somehow "utopian" Marxist discourse to promote a new radical agenda so as to challenge the domination of the capitalist mindset, notably during the second half of the nineteenth century. The orthodox proponents of Marxism were politically committed to revolutionary change in the first place via the change of the then existing economic relations and property of the means of production. In this context, ideology was exploited to legitimize the righteousness of the Marxist worldview and justify its disdain for capitalism and the bourgeoisie culture. In this sense, ideology did not indicate simply the cultural codes associated with the privileged wealthy class, but also a complex process of manipulation, deception and "false consciousness" that developed under such unbalanced structure of economy and power.

One could claim that Marxism is, in its own right, an ideological programme with explicit political agenda just like those liberal and progressive ideologies which it vehemently criticizes. Nonetheless, its dogmatic ideas have never been seriously questioned by its followers, except perhaps for the case of Gramsci, Althusser and a few post-Marxist thinkers. This is simply what makes the Marxist logic as embodied in the *Communist Manifesto* (1848), and perhaps even the subsequent versions of it, unable to calibrate its evaluative analysis. Marxists resorted to the use of concepts such as mystification, false consciousness, manipulation and ideological bias, which were all exclusively attributed to the "Other", non-Marxist, mainly pro-capitalist, ideologies.

It is well known that the Marxist thought emerged out of what was nicknamed "left Hegelianism" and relied upon a historical–materialist approach to tackle various philosophical, socio-economic and political issues. In the course of the nineteenth century, the Marxist philosophy turned out to be a credo for the impoverished working classes in Europe. Karl Marx and his advocates called for the eradication of the bourgeoisie culture and promotion of the idea of a classless society where the "proletariat" shares the wealth and ownership of the means of production. On the plight of the working classes and how the capitalist ideology became dominant, Marx and Engels write in *The German Ideology*:

> The ideas of the ruling class are in every epoch the ruling ideas: i.e. the class which is the ruling material force in society is at the same time its ruling intellectual force. The class which has the means of material production at its disposal has control at the same time over the means of mental production, so that thereby, generally speaking, the ideas of those who lack the means of mental production are subject to it. (Arthur, 1970, p. 64)

I would advocate that the process of "ideology manufacturing" in a given society is not exclusively achieved by the coercive power of the dominant group or established authority, but it regularly nourishes itself from the consensus as well as the passivity of the public in challenging its domination over them. This is an important point to keep in mind due to the subliminal role played by the circulating customs, conventions and cultural modes in community on the consciousness of the mass public. The ingredients of ideology are of course accumulated through a long period of time, most of which become common-sense practices that are generally accepted and only occasionally disputed. It becomes clear that *culture* is an essential element in this regard that should also be incorporated in this analysis, as it sometimes serves as the vehicle of ideology. In her book *Language and Culture* (1998), Claire Kramsch comments on this theme by claiming:

> Discourse communities, constituted, by common purpose, common interests, and beliefs, implicitly share a stock of prior texts and ideological points of view that have developed over time. These in turn encourage among their members common norms of interaction with, interpretation of, texts that may be accepted or rejected by the members of these communities. (p. 62)

In broad terms, any ideology establishes itself primarily from a spectrum of structural factors that are moulded, in essence, by the cultural milieu of society, which might well be contested, challenged and eroded at a particular point in time. The final stage in the manufacturing of ideologies is the institutionalization of a set of political values that would be presented as symbols to indicate the distinctive identity shared amongst the "in-group" members of a given social group or community. It is customary in the modern era, for example, that each independent state or political entity has a charter or a constitution which lists the most essential principles shared amongst its citizens. Western liberal democracies promote individualism and civil liberty with less institutionalized intervention in the economy, unlike the eastern communist countries, such as North Korea or to a lesser extent China, which undermine the individual liberty in case it is conceived to engender a possible threat to the well-being of the public or the moral conformism of society.

It is suggested that the claim of promoting freedom for people and safeguarding their natural rights, be it in the democratically minded or non-democratic communities, is, to some extent, controversial and might not be understood without having sufficient knowledge about the underlying cultural modes circulating in these societies. Since this research considers the British community as a sample, I can claim, with a modicum of hesitation, that the mainstream ideology tends to celebrate capitalism and debunk the socialist mindset. This ideological preference is not a matter of coincidence, neither of geography nor of race, but it was massively manufactured and distributed by consent, and only rarely through coercion and physical violence. The cultural codes that are continuously promoted in a particular social environment over a period of time would turn out, in the long run, to be common-sense assumptions and no longer the ideology of those in power.

Much obfuscation was brought into the feverish debates on politics and economy by the Marxist views which encased ideology with cynical connotations. However, the contributions of the British Marxist critic Raymond Williams are, perhaps, one of the very few that took a more critical and positive stance on ideology, and also the mechanisms of social change and revolution. Ostensibly, Williams attributed a neutral sense to the term, going beyond the conservative rhetoric to consider ideology as a "relatively – formal and articulated- system of meanings, values and beliefs, of a kind that can – be abstracted as a 'worldview' – or 'class outlook'" (1977, p. 109). In other words, it is seen as a belief system that produces certain worldviews and perceptions about, inter alia, political order, economy and social life, maintaining at the same time the consumption and circulation of these worldviews in society (see also, Berger & Luckmann, 1966). With reference to the underlying assumptions of the socio-cognitive model, Teun A. van Dijk seems to hold the same attitude. He postulates that the ideological stances people embrace are the outcome of complex social and cognitive phenomena. These would eventually manifest themselves in interaction and communication and language use in general.

Further elaboration on this topic, within the neo-Marxist framework, was also produced by the Italian Antonio Gramsci, whereby ideology was bound up more with consensus and less with coercion. This claim was best articulated in his famous notebooks, where he advocates that the dominant bourgeois class did not resort to physical violence to maintain the supremacy of its ideology, but was preoccupied more with how it can "depend in its quest for power on the 'spontaneous' consent arising from the masses of the people. This consent is carried by systems and structures of beliefs, values, norms and practices of everyday life which unconsciously legitimate the order of things" (Holub, 1992, p. 45). This conceptualization of ideology is quite similar to the one I endorse in the analysis of the pro-war ideology in Britain which recognizes the subliminal impact of the shared stock of knowledge on the cognition of individuals and consciousness of the public.

To comment on the ways in which a given ideology is privileged among others and, more particularly, how it is presented and justified is indeed a difficult task. This is due to at the least the following factors: First, the discursive nature of the mechanisms and processes involved in the *manufacturing* of ideology requires references to history, culture, politics, economy, society, to name but a few. Second, ideology itself is, often but not always, tacit and therefore hard to be noticed in the structures of language. Last but not least, ideology could elevate to the level of a "common sense" when it is universally endorsed within a particular community, which makes it impossible to demarcate the lines between the ideological and the non-ideological.

British linguist Roger Fowler states that the syntactic and vocabulary choices we make to express our views and opinions about the happenings around us are not value-free. With the assistance of his colleagues at the University of East Anglia, he developed further this idea and suggested a number of linguistic devices that could be quite helpful to deconstruct the ideological trappings in the language of the news in particular (1991). On this controversial point Fowler argues that "there is no neutral representation of reality, events, processes, objects and people are always meditated for us. It is not simply a question of objectivity on the one hand, and bias on the other" (in Zavala, van Dijk, & Diaz-Diocaretz, 1987, p. 67). There can be no doubt that awareness about the ways in which ideology is embedded in the grammar of language would "enlighten" the people and raise their consciousness about how power is played out in interaction and communication.

What has been said about the impartiality of the news discourse could also be relevant to the other genres of political discourse, which are undoubtedly much more ideologically biased. It is vital to stress again that my chief concern is to examine these two parallel types of discourse in separate ways by applying the methods of analysis appropriate to each type. Thus, a comparative investigation, at an advanced level, might provide us with more clues vis-à-vis the production and consumption of ideologies. Moreover, aspects and features of the political and news discourse, and their peculiarities in term of structure and form, will be discussed in some details in the remainder of this chapter.

It should be clear by now that the term "ideology" refers to a rather fuzzy concept that has been (re)shaped by the antithetical debates of Enlightenment in Europe. During the last 200 years or so, it acquired a range of connotations that were put into practice by politicians, social reformers and many other "ideologues", to maintain or challenge the status quo and power relations. It was quite evident with regard to the Marxist worldview that the term was connected with deception, oppression, manipulation, false consciousness and the like, which became eventually established traits of ideology. And it seems to retain such negative attributions to date.

In connection with what has been said earlier, it is relevant to assign a neutral value to ideology as a process so as to proceed in an objective analysis of this topic, which is substantially fraught with much controversy. I will seek to attain this through a multifaceted strategy of language analysis that is informed by up-to-date contributions of leading discourse specialists. This will be handled on the premise that the analysis of ideology through a mixed approach would put forward a constructive critique and analysis of the object of this research. This section introduces us to the next question about the intersection between ideology and language, which is the concern of the theoretical approach and thus constitutes, at the same time, an integral part of the research question as a whole; that is, how is ideology expressed in language? In brief, the historical overview I present in this chapter serves to trace the evolution of the term *ideology* and how it drifted away from its original "value-free" meaning just to acquire scratched connotations—which will be discarded in the analysis of this topic.

I would like to emphasize the fact that providing a critique about ideology and how reality is socially constructed requires, in the first place, a meticulous analysis of the lexical and grammatical features of language. As has been mentioned earlier, understanding the cognitive processes involved in making sense of the structure of language is equally important. This point will be elaborated in the next section of this chapter, though with much simplification and brevity.

2.1.3 The Gramscian Turn: From Dogmatic Ideologies to Hegemonic "Articulatory Practices"

It has been commonplace for contemporary social theorists and linguists to advocate that discourse is a social practice that could not be reduced to designate a mere "text" in isolation from the natural context in which it was produced. Moreover, it is well known that Michel Foucault, for example, inaugurated a new trend in the study of discourse which far exceeds the linguistic bounds, where social scientists started to talk about the discursive construction of various types of discourses as manifestations of myriad forms of knowledge and power hierarchies (Foucault, 1970, 1972). Thus, other subsequent scholars have developed multiple methodologies of discourse analysis, such as CDA, to examine the linkage between the social structures and the structure of discourse, namely that the analysis of discourse in a given community could bring to the fore the distribution of power relations and ideological affiliations amongst its individuals and institutions (Fairclough & Wodak, 1997). This new conceptualization of discourse as a social practice that is constituted discursively opened the door to other theories on context, from politics to history, sociology, psychology and many other disciplines in the social sciences.

A few decades before the Foucauldian shift, an in-depth analysis was already made with regard to the nature of authority, dictatorship, legitimacy, dominance and ways of exercising power within the neo-Marxist theory. Through the scattered notes collected by his followers, which were drafted during his prison days, the Italian Antonio Gramsci provided a rich and detailed account on the struggle over power between the dominant discourse of the centre (political society) and its proponent peripheral discourses (civil society). From the Gramscian perspective, which attributes a fundamental role to the "cultural superstructure", the exercise of power is based mainly on two pillars: First, the political coercion of the State or the "political society", or State as "the organ of one particular group" which acts to ascertain that its interest and conditions of survival are secured (Forgacs, 2000, p. 205). Second, the consent of the masses or "civil society", which is achieved through complex and protracted processes that continuously formulate and (re)shape the public mind, widely known as *hegemony*. It is the second element in Gramsci's theory that underwent much elaboration, whereby he gave much attention not to the "economic base", but rather to the impact of education, the formulation of alliances and the role of intellectual leadership in the production and promotion of a given ideology to the level of class consciousness.

It is widely believed that the concept of hegemony is deeply rooted in the history of the socialist movement in Russia and has been best incarnated in, and also informed, the revolutionary philosophy of the Bolshevists (Jones, 2006, p. 42). The literature shows a close affinity between ideology and hegemony, and sometimes the latter is seen by some as a mere extension of the former. Peter Ives declares that "before Gramsci, the term 'hegemony' was more or less limited to meaning the predominance of one nation over others" (2004, p. 2). Whilst some scholars consider hegemony as a continuous struggle for power and domination (Nye, 2011; Schake, 2009), others account for hegemony as a discursive phenomenon and extend their outlook to incorporate, inter alia, the impact of domination on the formation of history and individuals' attitudes and, ultimately, behaviours (Morton, 2003).

Gramsci's critics believe that his original ideas on the concept of hegemony have been interpreted in different manners, some of which were, to a lesser or greater degree, scratched understandings. What matters, however, is that unlike his Marxist predecessors, who reduced hegemony to the classic class struggle over economic systems and relations, Gramsci developed the concept into a much more complex theory that dialectically scrutinized several issues related to the correlation between the state and civil society. Raymond Williams again writes: "[W]e have to emphasise that hegemony is not singular; indeed that its own internal structures are highly complex and have continually to be renewed and defended; and by the same token, that they can be continually challenged and in certain respects modified" (1980, p. 38). The subsequent neo-Marxist and poststructuralist scholars have extended the scope of hegemony from the national to the international level in an attempt to better grasp the intricacies and functions of global politics and economy of today's world (see, e.g., Cox & Sinclair 1996; Keohane, 1984).

As suggested earlier, the leading power in society promotes its legitimacy through exploiting the potential of various social institutions, most specifically by monitoring the information industry. The norms, values, attitudes and customs that serve to sustain the dominant ideology are encouraged and preserved, whilst rival ones are downplayed and made less visible in the public sphere. Those "articulatory practices" are particularly manifest in education, the media and the legal system. It is in this way that the bourgeoisie successfully achieved its hegemony over the other classes because it creates alliances and absorbs the resistance of the opposition based not only on crude force, but rather on social consensus. In Britain the liberal progressive ideology survived for a long period of time in proportion to many other alternative economic and political models elsewhere. Although the left political parties have had their presence in the country since the beginning of the twentieth century, they failed to achieve much progress, and lately seem to have abandoned their socialist ideals. This is indeed the very same condition for Europe and the USA, where the capitalist ideology, despite minor differences in the form of capitalism espoused by each political system, remained hegemonic over many opposing models and rival alternative ideologies.

The distribution of power relations in a particular society is controlled by the dominant class/group that wins the battle of consent-manufacturing in the first place and only secondary by physical coercion. The "soft power" is therefore the means of hegemony which is contained, in essence, within the hands of an intellectual leadership that maintains the discourse of the ruling class/groups as the dominant discourse. Working within the Hegelian and Marxist tradition, Gramsci provided a critical account of the industrial capitalist society and its liberal philosophy by reconsidering the Marxist concept of ideology and class struggle over "the means of mental production". An important remark in this regard is Gramsci's rejection of the deterministic outlook that featured the traditional Marxist thought and its excessive adherence to historical materialism. Gramsci was a theorist "who did not reduce the 'political' to a mere reflection of economic forces, and who gave due attention to the phenomena of political leadership and organization" (McNally & Schwarzmantel, 2009, p. 10).

Ancient and modern scholars debated the notion of power in terms of its agency and the nature of association between the social actors, producing a constellation of interpretations about its sources and instruments, and how it functions in society. For Gramsci, power "is constituted by a dual or dyadic opposition: force and consent, violence and persuasion" (Howson & Smith, 2008, p. 85). Special importance was given to the role of intellectual leadership, where Gramsci insisted upon its fundamental role and ability to fuse the diverse interests in society into a single "collective will". He also argued that the so-called organic intellectuals have the potential to control the political behaviour of the masses and, conversely, could urge the various heterogeneous segments of the public into resistance and authentic revolutionary change. The traditional intellectual leadership as "educators" and "organizers" has a seminal social role in subsuming the interests of the leading group with those of the subalterns (Cammett, 1967). Therefore, intellectuals are, as Gramsci put it, "the dominant group's 'deputies' exercising the subaltern functions of social hegemony and political government" (1971, p. 12).

In his *Prison Notebooks*, Gramsci distinguishes between two types of intellectuals: the organic versus the traditional (1971, pp. 3–23). Following Stuart Hall (1996), the organic intellectuals are those who tend to form new ideas and promote peripheral ideologies, whilst the traditional intellectuals bind themselves with existing structure of power relations and, therefore, resist change. In other words, the traditional intellect whose educational ideology is in conformity with the ideology of the ruling political party works, as a matter of fact, to sustain the mainstream ideology. It is clear that in a "war of position", intellectuals as the "organizers" of hegemony have a special function to perform through their activities that seek to fuse the various interests of the social players and maintain maximum consent amongst the masses, or adversely trigger the social transformation against the status quo.

Yet, one should keep in mind that the channels through which the "ideological structure" is made have witnessed a remarkable advent from the epoch of Gramsci. Then, the print newspaper was still the main medium of mass communication, with comparatively limited audiences. Without doubt, the recent boom in communication technology had further reduced the acuity of coercion and successfully relegated its potency to a secondary position. It is to be noted that over the last few years, there has been the creation of more than one possible public sphere, notably through the virtual spaces of the social media, which made political censorship, practically speaking, out of reach. Nowadays, it is quite plausible to talk about the virtual power of an extended network of invisible social activists and pressure groups who exercise power in the open virtual terrain. As a result, education and information industry are no longer under the firm monopoly of the religious centres, the academia or other social institutions, through which social control over the people was exercised by the dominant group, because the media is becoming a major "educator" of the masses.

Although not much reference was made to Louis Althusser in this book, his work on ideology cannot be ignored, as it produced a paradigm shift within the Marxist worldview by introducing a more "pragmatic" definition for ideology, power and class struggle. Just like Gramsci, he insisted on the role of social institutions in the creation of the identity of individuals endorsing a less rigid view vis-à-vis the impact of the mode of production on social relations and structures (2006). Further elaboration on Althusser's theory of ideology was made by Michel Pêcheux (1982), which brought together the then emerging "discourse analysis" and the complex theory of ideology. This is indeed the very same concern of this research work, which is nevertheless less empirical and multidisciplinary.

2.1.4 Discourse

It should be highlighted that the nature of discourse is quite complex, and thus its processing in our social worlds, as it is produced in a highly discursive manner. The large body of literature, specifically in linguistics and other related research areas, shows that this concept has been described in heterogeneous ways and with varying degrees of abstraction. A common unified consensus on how discourse functions in the social milieu and how it could be adequately analysed is hard to come due to the disciplinary variation in the definition of "discourse". Eventually, multiple definitions and contesting viewpoints have hitherto been proposed on the meaning of discourse which made it a thriving and changeable concept.

Up to this point, the ambiguity that envelops this term needs to be discussed—with some simplification—particularly on the source and implications of such polysemy, at least within the realm of CDS. It is also important is to comment on how discourse functions in society, and how to locate the elements of ideology in the various communicative situations and contexts through the instrumentality of language. In fact, the reason for this idiosyncratic divergence is not problematic per se, for each discipline has its own peculiar ways and methods of investigation which would cover, by no means, just a few facades of the intricate nature of language and its function. The second part of the question revolves around discourse analysis as a branch of critical theory that has been widely recognized by the academia as a very influential, yet still evolving sub-discipline of critique.[3] As a matter of fact, if we still have no consolidated conceptualization about discourse, discourse analysis, likewise, would mean many different things. Some valuable efforts have been made in the last few years to bring together a few disciplines as to treat language with more scrutiny and judgement. Largely, this convergence helped much to overcome the orthodox reductionist methodologies and had, presumably, a positive effect on the development of other alternatives of analysis.

As part of the methodological strategy I pursue to examine the construction of the pro-war ideology in Britain and how the reaction to the abuse of power was passive and practically unworkable, albeit opposition was strong and active at many different levels, I address, first, the following theoretical questions: What does discourse mean? What is the difference, if any, between discourse and ideology? How is reality reflected in language use? In the previous parts of the chapter I showed how ideology came into being and developed as a distinct concept from discourse. Nevertheless, it is quite plausible that the two terms would overlap to denote the very same thing. Therefore, the discourse analysis I offer in this book is, in many respects, ideology analysis.

A few epistemological concerns will be equally highlighted throughout the subsequent chapters due to their relevance to the methodology employed, specifically how knowledge production manipulates the consciousness of the mass public. Put another way, questions about what forms our social knowledge and the pivotal role of this subjective knowledge in making sense of our discourses, and therefore our realities and actions, should not be ignored. These elements, albeit very abstract and philosophical in nature, are essential constitutive properties of discourse and must be taken into account. The sources and thus channels, through which knowledge is produced and shared, would mirror the discursive formulation of discourse, how a particular ideological position dominates over others and why it is embraced by the "in-group" social members.

To properly define discourse, one needs to adequately discuss its constitutive properties and also consider how specific meanings, beliefs and opinions about a specific phenomenon in the social environment could be created, challenged and altered historically. Partly, this dynamic change in meaning is the outcome of a multifaceted socio-linguistic process that is governed by the distribution of power and shifts discursively with the shift of power. James Paul Gee defines discourse as

[a] socially accepted association among ways of using language and other symbolic expressions, of thinking, feeling, believing, valuing, and acting, as well as using various tools, technologies, or props that can be used to identify oneself as a member of a socially meaningful group or "social network," to signal (that one is playing) a socially meaningful "role," or to signal that one is filling a social niche in a distinctively recognizable fashion. (2012, p. 158)

It is a common fact in "proper" linguistics that discourse refers to the level which is above the sentence. It is the level where the grammatical and lexical patterns of a given language, when organized in a certain order, would produce a meaningful and cohesive text or talk. Certainly, this very reductionist definition of discourse, which seemingly does not account for the many other pertinent contextual elements, has been reshaped several times in the last few decades. Based on this view, the methods of textual analysis which put the text rather than context under their spotlight tend to be more descriptive and less analytical. This widely held view within the linguistic orthodoxy is not sufficient to expound the complex processes that are involved in the manufacturing of ideologies and discourses. I subsume the other social and cognitive dimensions, in particular, which have been established as essential components in defining the notion of ideology, as this also constitutes a crucial part of the conceptual framework of this research. The somehow organic link between language use and ideology, and the manifestations of ideology in communication and interaction, with reference to the theoretical model I adopt, will be illustrated more clearly in Chaps. 5 and 6, which analyse the language of Blair and that of the quality papers.

Unlike his predecessors, the French philosopher and sociologist Michel Foucault developed a genuine theoretical approach to study the notion of discourse that connected language with knowledge and power.[4] Foucault defines discourses as being the "practices that systematically form the objects of which they speak" (1972, p. 42). Though this definition sounds opaque, it clearly takes discourse to be a product of a set of "discursive practices" during a given historical moment which is substantially shaped by the structure of power relations in society. This view, which advocates for the constructivist nature of reality and discourse, illustrates how discourse is, in essence, the incarnation of a subjective knowledge in space and time.

It follows that discourse, in this sense, is an event that leaves its imprint in the form of customs, laws, social and political behaviours and the like. The correlation between discourse, knowledge and power, as Stuart Hall suggests, has made "the constructivist theory of meaning and representation" much more meaningful. Hall further comments that "it rescued representation from the clutches of a purely formal theory and gave it a historical, practical and 'worldly' context of operation" (Wetherell, Taylor, & Yates, 2001, p. 75). Many subsequent theorists have followed the same stance and applied this attitude in their methods and paradigms.

CDA founder Norman Fairclough declares that "discourse is a practice not just of representing the world, but of signifying the world, constituting and constructing the world in meaning" (1992, p. 64). Seen as a form of social practice and very concrete human act, "different discourses are different ways of representing associated with different positions" (2013b, pp. 174–75). Van Dijk adds that "discourse is not simply an isolated textual or dialogic structure. Rather, it is a complex communicative event that also embodies a social context, featuring participants (and their properties) as well as production and reception processes" (1988, p. 2). The latter definition of discourse is worked out throughout this research because it incorporates the three dimensions that are employed in the socio-cognitive methodology: First, the pure linguistic aspect of discourse which deals with the vocabulary, grammar and syntactic structures of language. Ideology is assumed to be enacted via the linguistic choices made by the interlocutors of a wide range of possibilities that the language offers. The second perspective relates to the demarcation of the existing structures of society where interaction and communication take place. The social actors are routinely engaged in exclusion and inclusion practices by drawing an imaginary boundary between those who belong to the "in-group" and those who are placed out of it. Third, the cognitive "interface" which connects the two aforementioned elements. All in all, the three components are deemed necessary to engage in a critical examination of the metadiscourse of the selected case study.

What matters is not just whether we have little or no consensus over the meaning of discourse, but most significantly to be able to identify the properties of discourse that can be possibly uncovered and critiqued by linguistic and socio-cognitive tools. Then, it should be made clear that the distribution of power relations, ways of self and other representation, and the unconscious mechanics of dominance and hegemony are among the most important aspects of discourse that are worthy of detailed consideration. For the present purpose, analysing discourse as ideology analysis, without obscuring the crucial distinction between the two in terms of usage and reference, is one of the basic aims of this book, as signalled earlier. This would entail that analysis should show how power is abused in a democracy such as Britain, and the ways in which ideological bias in the political and news centres was naturalized and unchallenged.

The now-evolving theory of context has incorporated other non-linguistic dimensions of communication, such as the social and cognitive factors that have a bearing on the way people talk and understand language, and thereby construct discourses. These and other related questions about ideology and discourse structures are highly pertinent to the research problem; that is, how specific preferred narratives and ideologies are promoted or resisted, endorsed or rejected within specific communities and social groupings. Accordingly, the definition I use brings together the three basic elements of language use so as to maximize the theoretical validity of the type of discourse analysis I conduct: (a) language at the level of its sentences, phrases and words; (b) language as a social practice that is closely tied up with society and its structure; (c) and, finally, language in relation to its function in the mind of individuals and also what is called the shared cognition of the "mass mind".

2.2 The "Manufacturing" of Ideology in the Political and News Discourse(s)

2.2.1 The Social Structure and the Structure of Language

Throughout this study, the verb "to construct" is frequently used along with discourse and ideology. The choice of this vocabulary is not random, but hints to the mainstay of my argument vis-à-vis the nature of discourse and hence the logic that I follow in the design of the adopted cross-disciplinary methodology. It is simply the idea that reality is a human product that is usually subjective, symbolic and only rarely an objective reflection of the events, happenings and objects in the social environment. Society is one crucial fragment in the evolving theory of context, as it exerts an enormous pressure on its individual members and, more importantly perhaps, its influence is unconscious and often goes unnoticed. Hence, one needs to incorporate the social dimensions that would best clarify how the existing social structures justify certain ideological stances and reinforce them. After all, the relationship between society and discourse remains one of multidimensional nature.

In the case of this research, the social context is defined as van Dijk put it, "the organized set of properties of the social situation that are relevant for the structures, strategies, and cognitive processing of discourse as interaction" (1987, pp. 345–46). As I have noted earlier, the various CDS approaches and methods examine how language conveys meaning, with systematic reference to a web of social relations where it is produced, that is, the social institutions, social strata, membership, roles, power relations and the like. In *Language as Social Action* (2002), Thomas M. Hotlgraves clarifies that "the very fundamentals of language use are intertwined with social concerns; an understanding of how language is both produced and comprehended will require a consideration of its social dimensions" (p. 4). Such a pragmatic outlook is widely held by contemporary discourse analysts, albeit the relationship between the social structures and the discourse structures is viewed rather differently. Diane MacDonnell comments that "discourses differ with the kinds of institutions and social practices in which they take shape" (1986, p. 1). She goes on further to argue that discourses differ also "with the positions of those who speak and those whom they address". This, of course, is also very much related to questions about control and power amongst the other social actors in the communicative context which reflect, after all, hegemonic ideologies and those which have less resonance.

Practically speaking, context puts a number of restraints on the interlocutors in communication and interaction, and frames their linguistic behaviour. Politicians and journalists undergo the pressure of many contextual factors that determine the tone, style, vocabulary and even grammar they use to convey a particular message to their audiences. Teun A.

van Dijk (2008) critiqued the traditional theories of context that are drawn from linguistics, for example, that of Michael Halliday. His line of argument places much emphasis on cognition to explain how the social structure influences the language structure, as he vigorously argued that the relationship between the two (i.e. language and society) is indirect (see Chap. 3).

From the point of view of pragmatics, it has been suggested that the construction of political discourse is strategically made with the intention of achieving some goals and interests by the respective writers or speakers. This process involves varying discursive patterns of persuasion and manipulation. I have also taken the assumption that most, if not all, kinds of discourses are a reflection of a matrix of ideologies largely shaped by individuals' and social groups' interests. The cluster of these ideologies will, by the end, mirror their own socio-cultural belongings, beliefs and the ways in which they justify their attitudes and thoughts vis-à-vis people, events and the objects that are there in their social environment. That is to say, the membership of a given group community, ethnic, religious, professional and so on, could be revealed through their *discoursal* behaviours which are framed under the constraints of the community's stock of knowledge.

Another important factor is the cognitive perspective of language use, which constitutes a further fundamental element in the socio-cognitive methodology, as it relates directly to the functions and features of discourse and ideological expression. Linguistics and its related disciplines have long benefited from the findings of the cognitive sciences to explore the intricacies of language and expound its processing strategies in the brain. Indeed, the relationship between language and thought is still one of the fast-growing areas of research due to its significance to other empirical sciences such as computing and artificial intelligence. Without doubt, the mechanism of language production, comprehension and interpretation is bound up with highly complex cognitive processes, which stimulated the curiosity of many scholars. A panoply of revolutionary insights were already proposed by those disciplines which aim to uncover the cognitive operations that process knowledge and information—which will eventually be represented in language. The cluster of ideas informing the theoretical approach of this research comes in essence from the findings of social cognition and social psychology, which are heavily cited in van Dijk's socio-cognitive model. It is quite useful to establish the link, albeit in very broad manner, between the social and cognitive aspects of language usage through recurrent references to the findings of the previously mentioned areas of research.

What is important to highlight at this point is the social aspect of cognition, which substantially permeates into the cognition of the in-group members and the logic they use to perceive and evaluate things. Norman Fairclough explains that language is guided by a set of cognitive processes that are socially conditioned, which he calls "member's resources". He advocates that "they are socially generated, and their nature is dependent on the social relations and struggles out of which they were generated – as well as being socially transmitted and, in our society, unequally distributed" (2013a, p. 20). That is to say, the socially shared knowledge amongst people plays a crucial role in discourse formulation and legitimization. It also guides the (re)production and expression of ideology in the political, media and public domains. There is a widespread belief, which is a fallacy, as van Dijk argues, in the interactionist paradigms on the link between the social structure and the structure of language, which is taken for granted to be direct. Discourse is held to be an observable phenomenon, but in fact, most of the fragments of the discourse people make are implicit and unseen.

2.2.2 Ideology in the Discourse of Politics

This research, as hitherto mentioned, tackles two types of discourse which react to each other but, presumably, remain mostly in two parallel positions. According to my view, it is through a combination of both these two sources of power and discourse formation that one might have some clues on the ideas and beliefs that are being instilled in the public sphere. To wit, in order to provide a critique, which is less speculative and more objective, about the circulation of dominant/peripheral political ideologies in the public discourse, I investigate both the legitimization patterns in Blair's political language and thus the major narratives of the British press that responded to the pro-war campaign. After unveiling the ambiguity that accompanies the term "political", my focus, then, will be directed first towards the identification of a proper definition of the term "news", its components and the ways in which it is being constructed. I also seek to glean light on how ideology, which sometimes elevates to the level of propaganda, is embedded in the news structure. This dual mode of analysis, I argue, will enable us to describe and then critically analyse the ways in which the divisive political decision to launch an offensive war against Iraq was legitimized and normalized in Britain.

It must be noted at this juncture that the effect of ideology on the mass public should also be incorporated because it is an integral factor in the communicative situation. I strongly advocate that it is not enough to decipher the text/talk with a toolkit of critical strategies which put the writer/speaker in the centre, but one must also be cognizant of the wide possibilities of interpretations by the respective recipients. Yet, it is difficult to assess the mood of the large audiences, except through statistics generated from opinion polls or protest activities in the physical or virtual spaces. This involves by no means references to current research findings in the cognitive sciences and social psychology. Such a mode of analysis could also be backed up by the findings of agenda-setting research, which has received serious academic interest and stimulated purposeful debates about the framing processes and their actual impact on the audience. In this respect, the following cluster of questions could be relevant and worth answering: What is meant by political discourse that is typically "political"? What are its basic characteristics? Is the official political discourse biased all time? On the other side of the coin, what makes news? And how could it be possible to decipher the implicit messages journalists convey to their audience? In brief, I seek to show and explore where and how ideologies are being encoded in the language of politicians and journalists.

The study of "political discourse" is a sub-category within the broad field of politics. I therefore need to carefully draw the limits of this study when dealing with such a fuzzy concept due, on the one hand, to its multiple references and, on the other hand, its intersection with a number of other forms and genres of discourse. It is needless to add that CDS approaches are partially endorsed by political scientists as a methodology of analysis. Hence, "political discourse" as conceptualized in the context of this research does simply refer to the political language used by political actors, that is, the type of discourse that I find in their formal speeches, official documents, declarations, interviews and so on. In my case, it is Blair's discourse on the Iraq War, which is expressed only in his own official political speeches that, directly or indirectly, addressed the Iraq problem (see the full list in the Appendix). Political discourse occurs, as political communication scholar Doris A. Graber explains, "when political actors, in and out of government, communicate about political matters, for political purposes" (1981, p. 196). The political ideology that Tony Blair espoused to rally support for a military attack was blurry and propelled unprecedented political cleavage at the local and international levels.

The term "politics", in its narrow sense, refers to a discipline that encompasses a large space within the social sciences and humanities, alternatively dubbed Political Science. Overall, this discipline is preoccupied with two major avenues: issues that relate to ways of governing and associated processes of doing politics, and those that deal with the more philosophical concerns that underlie the practice of politics itself—this is to say, topics that are related to the more abstract notions in the realm of politics such as, amongst many other things, power and ideology (Leftwich, 1983, p. 4). It is the latter theme that is pertinent to the discourse analysis offered in this research work. Paul Chilton comments that "politics is viewed as a struggle for power, between those who seek to assert and maintain their power and those who seek to resist it" (2004, p. 3). Although the symbolic boundary of politics as an independent branch with its own set of theories and perceptions is well demarcated, the consensus on what precisely the ubiquitous word "political" entails remains, to some degree, undelimited simply because, as George Orwell put it once, "all issues are political issues", at least relatively speaking. A. James Gregor suggests that "to know what a construct like 'politics' means is to study its employments, to characterize what has loosely been called its 'grammar,' to exhibit its use, role, or function with respect to other cognitive signs in the language matrix" (2003, p. 7). Hence, the usage of the term "political" in the context of this book is tightly intertwined with notions of power and power abuse, legitimization and manipulation in the construction of "biased" ideology in language.

It seems that the common purpose of all types of political discourses is to comment on conflicting issues, explain a situation, solve a problem or propose solutions to a given crisis, justify an action or consolidate a given ideology, but usually to persuade people about a controversial subject matter. Both ideology and power are constitutive components that reside at the heart of any political discourse. Thus, the expression of these elements appropriately requires high levels of language skill, argumentative strategies and a persuasive tone, at least in democracies that place no constraints whatsoever on freedom of political expression. There can be no doubt that eloquence is one of the essential qualities that determines the success or failure of a politician. On political discourse analysis Teun A. Van Dijk again writes:

> An account of the structures and strategies of, e.g., phonology, graphics, syntax, meaning, speech acts, style or rhetoric, conversational interactions, among other properties of text and talk is therefore necessarily part of political discourse analysis only if such properties can be politically contextualized. (1997, p. 24)

Unlike the other genres of discourses whose ideologies seem to be, more or less, implicit in the text and only occasionally stated in an abundant manner, the political discourse is usually—but not necessarily—overtly partisan and overloaded with ideological biases. Nonetheless, I still argue that scrutinizing ideologically driven political discourses demands both macro- and microstrategies of analysis via the treatment of a large corpus of linguistic elements, along with the assessment of a web of semantic categories and relations that are hard to be observed in the text, such as coherence, global and local structure of the themes and topics, propositions, implications and so on. A cross-direction of analysis that includes both qualitative and quantitative methods, with an emphasis on a matrix of linguistic and semantic elements, is supposed to be critically rewarding and fruitful.

In my case study, the context of political discourse revolves around the war against Iraq and all that might be germane to it during New Labour's rule. One should bear in mind, again, that any purposeful critical assessment of Blair's political discourse should be carried out with direct references to a number of contextual elements. This is so because the analysis of a political situation depends upon a set of inextricably entwined and complex historical, social and economic conditions which are finally squeezed and spelled out in language. Therefore, setting the background for a somehow brief contextual description of the causes of the war, the actors involved and their arguments, inter alia, constitutes a fundamental requisite before carrying out any critical analysis.

2.2.3 Ideology in the News Discourse

It goes without saying that political ideologies depend largely on how the media outlets get their messages across to the public spheres. Playing the role of the medium between the political and civil societies, the media is a typical information gatekeeper and also the producer of alternatives narratives. Undeniably, the press, as part of this sensitive industry, which has undergone relative regression in readership and therefore influence, still has a great share in framing events and mobilizing citizens to take action against power abuse. It could also potentially damage the reputation of politicians and put a high pressure on them. There is, indeed, a reciprocal and dynamic interplay between politics, the press and public opinion that stimulated the curiosity of a spectrum of researchers. My preoccupation in this section of the chapter is not to measure the impact of the press on the public mood, which has been a major theme in communication studies since the early 1920s. The aim, however, is to draw attention to the language patterns and practices that could influence, control and also manipulate the public mind.

Mass media and communication scholars have extensively studied the influence of the political elite on the making of news. As will be discussed in some detail in Chap. 6, this was the case for the British papers for quite a long period of time. The press went through a long phase of struggle against various forms of censorship and oppression by the royal authorities, and recently the abuse of politicians and media owners themselves. Perhaps, the freedom of speech has achieved much progress, yet the highly concentrated economic structure and the political elite still exert a tangible pressure on the media in order to sustain their interests and ideologies. For this reason it comes as no surprise that the press is not merely a channel for news reporting, but also a purveyor of political agendas. The production of news is based on the selection of only specific events, whose coverage is often embedded with subjective interpretations which eventually lead readers to ascribe such interpretations to what has been reported by the press.

In a temporal sense, the study of the news discourse is a new research area compared to political discourse. The former has emerged at the early beginnings of the twentieth century as mass readership accrued, thanks to the many structural changes in economy, technology and politics. For decades, illiteracy, the archaic means of printing, continuous political oppression and containment policies, besides the lack of professionalism in the news business, were amongst the major factors that delayed the growth of the discourse of what was labelled later as the Fourth Estate. However, the domain of political science as an autonomous discipline in the social sciences, and particularly the study of political discourse, can be traced back to ancient Greece, or perhaps earlier.[5] Further to their interest in theology and metaphysics, the intellectuals and philosophers of the Classical Age were extensively preoccupied with issues related to rhetoric, good governance, authority and social order.

Although the criticism of news discourse did not come into being as a field of academic study and research till the 1960s onwards, essential questions about the discourse of media and its impact on the public opinion and behaviour emerged as early as the 1920s. Perhaps, the publication of the *Public Opinion* in 1922 by the American journalist Walter Lippmann was one of the first serious efforts made in the study of this new emerging type of discourse, which is political in nature. The ideological manoeuvres performed by newsmakers in the legitimization or de-legitimization of polarized viewpoints are usually implicit and not squarely expressed. In this respect I assume that although the British press, in reporting the Iraq War, did not necessarily reflect the official line, yet still, it did not offer a balanced and objective representation of the events and the actors involved.

The media and the public is one of the fundamental preoccupations of the agenda-setting theory. The latter was introduced to gauge the impact of the press on its audiences through the study of the framing processes and techniques involved in news-making which are indented to create a specific script in the mind of the target public. In other words, the press could control, at least, the salience or absence of some attributes of a given subject in the consciousness of the public which would heavily influence the way the public judges the reported subject. The theoretical propositions of such a theory offered a particularly valuable tool for understanding the nature of interaction and relationships between the media outlets and the public.

A number of communication scholars have contributed to refine the claims put forth by the agenda-setting theory, which was first introduced by the American historians and theorists Maxwell McCombs and Donald Shaw in 1972. The goal was to examine the media framing techniques and how these shape the attitudes and perception of people. It sought to clearly map up the correlation between the media coverage and the possible effect of such coverage on the public perception of the events reported. Since the aim here is limited solely to the role of the press, one would ask, how can the newspaper input influence the consciousness of the mass public? Special attention is drawn on how social realities are constructed and whether they do actually influence people's comprehension and their evaluation. The agenda-setting and other related models have introduced some theories about such complex interaction between audiences and journalists. The political scientist Thomas Birkland defines agenda-setting as "the result of a society acting through political and social institutions to define the meanings of problems and the range of acceptable solutions" (1997, p. 11).

The agenda-setting theory operates at two different levels: The first level is concerned with the amount of focus given to particular events, rather than to others, as topic preference, or "priming", which is believed to orient the public's attention and their understanding of real-world events. In my case, I wonder whether the kind of coverage that addressed UK's openly hostile policy on Iraq would mould the attitudes of the British citizenry. Such topic preference started from the first Gulf War after a long "honeymoon" period between London and Baghdad. The analysis of the CNA shows clearly that Iraq has been one of the repeatedly covered topics in the British press which, according to this theory, drew people's attention to the special importance of the Iraqi dossier at the period that preceded the military attack.

The second level of the agenda-setting theory is a micro category which examines the wide range of framing patterns and techniques that are used in news-making, that is to say, the focus on some elements in coverage rather than on others. An example of this could be what van Dijk calls the "ideological square", where positive-self image is brought along with the negative-other image. Journalists may shed light exclusively on the abusive practices of Saddam's regime and its atrocities during the 1990s. It will be shown later that the negative attributes of Saddam have always been reinforced in the language of the broadsheets. Indeed, priming and framing are fundamental theories that underlie most research about media and the formation of public opinion. These provided significant insights on how the news discourse directs the political behaviour of the public.

"Priming" was first introduced in cognitive psychology as the process by which activated mental constructs can influence the perception, judgement and evaluation of the target audience. It enhances an indirect effect of the text by offering the audience a kind of prior judgement and interpretation. Mass media researchers Shanto Iyengar and Donald Kinder define priming as "changes in standards that people use to make political evaluations" (1987, p. 63). From a cognitive perspective, priming means the process by which a tacit and unconscious activation of a prior knowledge takes place to retrieve an old information basically through associations with other objects or information (Weiner, Healy, & Proctor, 2003). This process is believed to substantially mould the audience's perception when they are exposed to the primed topic in future situations.

The salience of certain topics in the press and the kind of associations made between events, objects and people will implicitly guide the interpretations of readers. This is to say, exposure to press coverage of a specific issue during a given period of time helps in making that issue more accessible in people's minds and therefore easily retrieved from memory when making judgements. For example, voters are likely to value the candidates for elections based on what they learned from previous media coverage about the qualities and performance of those candidates. In brief, through priming and framing, the newspapers predispose their audience to be involved in a pre-oriented judgement. This claim has a robust correlation with Shanto Iyengar's accessibility bias model, where the author states:

In general, "accessibility bias" argument stipulates that information that can be more easily retrieved from memory tends to dominate judgments, opinions and decisions, and that in the area of public affairs, more accessible information is information that is more frequently or more recently conveyed by the media. (Iyengar, 1990, pp. 1–15)

To rephrase the above quote, the frequency of a specific topic in the news would make it more accessible in people's memories. Thus, the associations, interpretations and explanations made by the press, which in principle reflect journalists' views and opinions, would potentially influence the public's judgement. This is so because readers will rely on a shortcut strategy in evaluation based on their previous thoughts and knowledge about the issue in hand, which had already been framed by the various media channels. When citizens are exposed to new political topics, particularly those that are controversial, they tend to retrieve only some information from their long-term memory. Journalists will attempt to drive this accessibly through certain framing techniques whereby only a few possible interpretations emerge which would suit the media narrative (Krosnick & Brannon, 1993).

In sum, the framing strategies employed by journalists may guide how people understand the happenings of the social world and thus construct judgements through the lens of the media. In a very much quoted definition, Robert Entman notes, "[T]o frame is to select some aspects of a perceived reality and make them more salient in a communication context, in such a way to promote a particular problem definition, causal interpretation, moral evaluation and or treatment recommendation for the item described" (1993, p. 52). The American political communication specialist Jim Kuypers further explains:

> Framing, then, is the process whereby communicators act to construct a particular point of view that encourages the facts of a given situation to be viewed (or ignored) in a particular manner, with some facts made more noticeable than others. When speaking of political and social issues, frames actually define our understanding of any given situation. (2002, p. 7)

Framing, as hitherto defined, is an integral part of any kind of communicative situation, most particularly in the news and political discourses which contain much ideological material. The emphasis on some aspects in reporting a given event would substantially shape the public understanding and interpretation through the encoded judgements and evaluations. At the same time, news reporting could also conceal other aspects of reality which might also be worthy of mentioning. For example, priming specific themes, and more importantly, the selection of certain lexical and grammatical constructions in covering these themes are, in fact, not made at random, but rather, they are part of a political act aiming at achieving acceptance and approval from the part of the targeted audience towards a preferred problem solution and definition—namely, they are an ideologically shaped form of representation.

Just like discourse, the notion of news as being the product of a *socially constructed reality* is the platform upon which my argument is founded. It is clear that news production is a process of selection and interpretation of events rather than a typical reflection of the realities of the world out there. This is a taken-for-granted and key assumption in this research. Hence, I stress the fact that framing is very important in conflicting issues such as wars. The case study addressed here should be very relevant example to explain and illustrate the ways in which skewed representations in favour of the powerful actors and dominant forces are framed and tacitly encoded in the language of the press.

Notes

1. Context is one of the fundamental concepts in discourse analysis which does not solely refer to space and time, but to a cluster of factors that influence the production and understanding of text and talk such as the social and cognitive structures and processes. Context as conceived in the socio-cognitive model of discourse analysis is discussed in some detail in the third chapter. A reference is made to the recent contributions by some new disciplines in the social sciences and humanities that yielded new perceptions on context and its role in discourse production and comprehension.
2. For further information about this point and thus the intellectual contributions of de Tracy on ideology, see Ulrich (1994).

3. The American linguist Zellig Harris is one of the pioneers to introduce the label "discourse analysis". The latter, in technical sense, is believed to be used first in his seminal article "Discourse Analysis" (1952).
4. Amongst his landmark publications that are widely cited in the field of discourse analysis, I can mention: *The Archaeology of Knowledge* (1969). *The Order of Things: Archaeology of the Human Sciences* (1970).
5. On the etymology of the word "politics", see: Nicolai Rubinstein, "The history of the word *politicus* in early-modern Europe," in Anthony Pagden (Ed.) (1987).

References

Althusser, L. (2006). Ideology and ideological state apparatuses (notes towards an investigation). *The Anthropology of the State: A Reader, 9*(1), 86–98.
Arthur, C. (Ed.). (1970). *The German ideology*. New York: International Publishers.
Barth, H. (1976). *Truth and ideology* (trans: Lilge, F.). Berkeley, CA: University of California Press.
Berger, P. L., & Luckmann, T. (1966). *The social construction of reality: A treatise in the sociology of knowledge*. New York: Penguin Putnam.
Birkland, T. (1997). *After disaster: Agenda setting, public policy, and focusing events*. Washington, DC: Georgetown University Press.
Cammett, J. M. (1967). *Antonio Gramsci and the origins of Italian communism*. Stanford, CA: Stanford University Press.
Chilton, P. (2004). *Analysing political discourse: Theory and practice*. London: Routledge.
Cox, R. W., & Sinclair, T. J. (1996). *Approaches to world order*. Cambridge, UK: Cambridge University Press.
Eagleton, T. (1991). *Ideology: An introduction*. London: Verso.
Entman, R. M. (1993). Framing: Toward clarification of a fractured paradigm. *Journal of Communication, 43*(4), 51–58.
Fairclough, N. (1992). *Discourse and social change*. Cambridge, UK: Polity Press.
Fairclough, N. (2003). *Analysing discourse: Textual analysis for social research*. New York: Psychology Press.
Fairclough, N. (2013a). *Language and power* (2nd ed.). London/New York: Routledge.
Fairclough, N. (2013b). *Critical discourse analysis: The critical study of language* (2nd ed.). London: Routledge.

Fairclough, N., & Wodak, R. (1997). Critical discourse analysis. In T. A. van Dijk (Ed.), *Discourse as social interaction* (Vol. 2, pp. 258–284). London: Sage.
Feyerabend, P. (1975). *Against method*. London: Verso.
Forgacs, D. (Ed.). (2000). *The Gramsci reader: Selected writings 1916–1935*. New York: New York University Press.
Foucault, M. (1970). *The order of things: An archaeology of the human sciences*. London: Tavistock.
Foucault, M. (1972). *The archaeology of knowledge* (trans: Sheridan, A.). London: Tavistock.
Fowler, R. (1991). *Language in the news: Discourse and ideology in the press*. London: Routledge.
Fowler, R., Hodge, R., Kress, G., & Trew, T. (1979). *Language and control*. London: Routledge & Kegan Paul.
Garzone, G., & Sarangi, S. (Eds.). (2007). *Discourse, ideology and ethics in specialized communication*. Bern: Peter Lang.
Gee, J. (2012). *Social linguistics and literacies: Ideology in discourses*. London: Routledge.
Graber, D. A. (1981). Political languages. In D. D. Nimmo & K. R. Sanders (Eds.), *Handbook of political communication* (pp. 195–223). Beverly Hills, CA: Sage.
Gramsci, A. (1971). *Selections from the prison notebooks* (trans. and Eds. Hoare, Q., & Nowell Smith, G.). London: Lawrence and Wishart.
Gregor, J. A. (2003). *Metascience and politics: An inquiry into the conceptual language of political science*. New Brunswick, NJ: Transaction Publishers.
Hall, S. (1996). Gramsci's relevance for the study of race and ethnicity. In D. Morley & K. H. Chen (Eds.), *Stuart Hall: Critical dialogues in cultural studies* (pp. 411–440). London: Routledge.
Harris, Z. (1952). Discourse analysis. *Language, 28*(1), 1–30.
Head, B. W. (1985). *Ideology and social science: Destutt de Tracy and French liberalism*. Dordrecht, The Netherlands: Martinus Nijhoff.
Holub, R. (1992). *Antonio Gramsci: Beyond Marxism and postmodernism*. London: Routledge.
Hotlgraves, T. M. (2002). *Language as social action: Social psychology and language use*. Mahwah, NJ: Lawrence Erlbaum Associates, Inc.
Howson, R., & Smith, K. (Eds.). (2008). *Hegemony: Studies in consensus and coercion*. New York: Routledge.
Ives, P. (2004). *Language and hegemony in Gramsci*. London: Pluto Press.

Iyengar, S. (1990). The accessibility bias in politics: Television news and public opinion. *International Journal of Public Opinion Research, 2*(1), 1–15.

Iyengar, S., & Kinder, D. (1987). *News that matters: Television and American opinion.* Chicago: The University of Chicago Press.

Jones, S. (2006). *Antonio Gramsci.* London: Routledge.

Keohane, R. (1984). *After hegemony: Cooperation and discord in the world political economy.* Princeton, NJ: Princeton University Press.

Kramsch, C. (1998). *Language and culture.* Oxford: Oxford University Press.

Krieger, J. (Ed.). (2013). *The Oxford companion to comparative politics* (Vol. 1). Oxford: Oxford University Press.

Krosnick, J., & Brannon, L. A. (1993). The impact of war on the ingredients of presidential evaluations: George Bush and the Gulf conflict. *American Political Science Review, 87,* 963–975.

Kuypers, J. A. (2002). *Press bias and politics: How the media frame controversial issues.* Westport, CT: Praeger.

Leftwich, A. (1983). *Redefining politics: People, resources, and power.* London: Methuen.

MacDonnell, D. (1986). *Theories of discourse.* Oxford, UK: Blackwell.

McNally, M., & Schwarzmantel, J. (Eds.). (2009). *Gramsci and global politics: Hegemony and resistance.* London: Routledge.

Morton, A. D. (2003). Historicizing Gramsci: Situating ideas in and beyond their context. *Review of International Political Economy, 10*(1), 118–146.

Nye, J. S. (2011). *The future of power.* Philadelphia: Perseus Books Group.

Pêcheux, M. (1982). *Language, semantics, and ideology: Stating the obvious* (trans: Nagpal, H.). London: Macmillan.

Rubinstein, N. (1987). The history of the word politicus in early-modern Europe. In A. Pagden (Ed.), *The languages of political theory early-modern Europe* (pp. 41–56). Cambridge, UK: Cambridge University Press.

Schake, K. N. (2009). *Managing American hegemony: Essays on power in a time of dominance.* Stanford, CA: Hoover University Press.

Spariosu, M. (1989). *Dionysus reborn: Play and the aesthetic dimension in modern philosophical and scientific discourse.* Ithaca, NY: Cornell University Press.

Ulrich, R. (1994). *Linguistics, anthropology and philosophy in the French enlightenment: A contribution to the history of the relationship between language theory and ideology.* London: Routledge.

Van Dijk, T. A. (1977). *Text and context: Explorations in the semantics and pragmatics of discourse.* London: Longman.

Van Dijk, T. A. (1987). *Communicating racism: Ethnic prejudice in thought and talk*. Newbury Park, CA: Sage.
Van Dijk, T. A. (1988). *News as discourse*. Hillsdale, NJ: Erlbaum.
Van Dijk, T. A. (1995). Ideological discourse analysis. *The New Courant, 4*, 135–161.
Van Dijk, T. A. (1997). What is political discourse analysis. In J. Blommaert & C. Bulcaen (Eds.), *Political linguistics* (pp. 11–52). Amsterdam: Benjamins.
Van Dijk, T. A. (2008). *Discourse and context: A sociocognitive approach*. London: Cambridge University Press.
Walker, M. (Ed.). (2003). *Science and ideology: A comparative history*. London: Routledge.
Weiner, I. B., Healy, A. F., & Proctor, R. W. (Eds.). (2003). *Handbook of psychology: Experimental psychology*. Hoboken, NJ: Wiley.
Wetherell, M., Taylor, S., & Yates, S. J. (Eds.). (2001). *Discourse theory and practice*. Oxford: Open University Press.
Williams, R. (1977). *Marxism and literature*. New York: Oxford University Press.
Williams, R. (1980). Base and superstructure in Marxist cultural theory. In R. Williams (Ed.), *Problems in materialism and culture: Selected essays* (pp. 31–49). London: Verso.
Zavala, I. M., van Dijk, T. A., & Diaz-Diocaretz, M. (Eds.). (1987). *Approaches to discourse, poetics and psychiatry*. Amsterdam: John Benjamins.

3
Contemporary Orientations in Discourse Studies

3.1 Multidisciplinarity in/and (Critical) Discourse Studies

3.1.1 A Glimpse of CDS

In retrospect, the domain of Discourse Studies has loomed in linguistics over the last 50 years out of a coalescence of a number of research areas that sought to scrutinize the nature and, precisely, the functions of language in society. The most notable of these were pragmatics, semiotics, socio-linguistics and conversation analysis. In the course of time, the study of discourse started to progressively drift from the confines of linguistics into various research domains in the social sciences and humanities, yielding therefore new, fresh and divergent insights into language and other related socio-linguistic issues that address contemporary social phenomena.

Gradually, those improvised initiatives led to the establishment of Discourse Studies as another sister branch of inquiry to the above-mentioned ones, with its own theories, tools of analysis and logic of critique. It is fairly noted that those contributions, coming particularly from psychology and sociology, have left a paramount impact on our understating of the other non-linguistic aspects of human language, interaction and communication. Through a long phase of metamorphosis, the general theory of discourse has undergone a smooth progress and generated a relatively large body of literature, most remarkably over the last two decades. It is ostensible that the terms "critical", "discourse" and "analysis" constitute, in fact, the three essential dimensions of this branch of research—each of which is substantially loaded with multiple interpretations, which led to the development of separate "programmes" and methodologies in related disciplines.

As noted earlier, CDA is the label that has recently been assigned to an assortment of analytical perspectives and strategies employed in the analysis of various types of discourses (Fairclough, 2013). It is widely agreed that the rationality that underpinned this expanding research domain has been drawn, in the first place, from the linguistic shift of the 1960s. Subsequently, many other insights were borrowed from the other social sciences, which attempted to give a boost to the analysis of language use beyond the merely linguistic frame, paving the way therefore to create bridges with other fields of research such as sociology, psychology, history and political science. Ostensibly, the multifariousness of CDA sources and CDA's synergetic link with multiple research paradigms stimulated the curiosity of researchers of diverse backgrounds. The materials designed to deconstruct the embedded messages in the written, oral and also visual items (abstract signs and symbols, cartoons, caricatures and the like) were by no means heterogeneous and diverse.

In retrospect, the labels Text Grammars, Critical Linguistics and lately Critical Discourse Analysis were used to refer to this new space of encounter between a cluster of disciplines that made cross-disciplinarity, both in theory and practice, a firmly established character of the now CDS. Yet the hybridization of other disciplines with discourse analysis is not a definite departure from conventional linguistics, but there emerged a necessity to incorporate the other socio-historical patterns of language use and change across time and place—which linguistics, in its own right, cannot adequately account for. It is widely agreed that the early fragments of this research stance can be found, for example, in Dell Hymes' *Towards*

Ethnographies of Communication (1964), Austin's landmark book *How to Do Things with Words* (1962) and a few other breakthrough contributions from linguists, literary theorists and psychologists. The latter's emphasis on context rather than the formalist preoccupation with the superstructures of language reflected a swing in the study of language and brought also new specialized areas of research with different scopes, techniques and goals. Language is held to be much more than a system of communication, but a linguistic behaviour that fulfils a gatekeeping function, where power, ideology and domination, amongst many other properties, are often, but not always, embedded rather than explicitly expressed.

Arguably, however, the sheer vastness and diversity of resources and strategies of analysis adopted by scholars proved to be a double-edged sword. That is to say, the flexibility in the theoretical background of CDS has widened the perspectives of research and inquiry; likewise, it has created a set of technical blinkers. This should behove us to consider the whole enterprise of discourse analysis as defined throughout this work and reflect about the best strategy to conduct a thorough and purposeful research through the lens of this hybrid discipline.

Eclecticism in particular, is one of the dilemmas that brought ongoing strictures from the academia. Whilst some leading critical theorists strongly prioritize the cognitive dimensions to study the complex nature of discourse, as is the case of this research, others ignore it or at least relegate it to an auxiliary position. Furthermore, some other top-level controversies might also arise from the very basic epistemological and ontological assumptions held about language use, as they have a direct bearing on the methods of language analysis. To wit, such fundamental theoretical differences would consequently lead to divergent methodological interpretations on not only how related notions are conceptualized, but also how a systematic and "critical" discourse analysis should be operationalized. In simple words, practising research is by no means rooted in the philosophical debates about the nature of valid knowledge, the reliability of the tools of investigation and how it can be properly obtained and justified (for a broad introduction, see for example, Audi, 2003).

Many scholars debated the relevance of the cognitive approaches and advocated that the "cognitive interface" should be incorporated in any serious consideration of language usage in the social milieu (Wodak &

Chilton, 2005, pp. 19–52). With the application of the socio-cognitive model in the analysis of Blair's pro-war discourse on Iraq, there emerged a few difficulties on how to integrate theory into practice and synthesize a paradigm of analysis that best accounts for the opaqueness of discourse formation (by the speakers/writers) and understanding (by the target audiences). In this respect, I am not only concerned with the case study itself, but also inclined to trigger a serious debate on the "missing link" between theory and practice within the CDS framework. It is also quite significant to comment particularly on the cognitive strategies of discourse analysis and how these could be implemented in a systematic and direct way in the examination of discourse (the political and news discourses as an example).

3.1.2 Critical Discourse Analysis

Certainly, there are a number of approaches and schools that laid the foundation to a more in-depth, explicit and systematic analysis of language use. CDA is the kind of "problem-oriented programme" that accounts for, at least, the semantic and lexical components of the text, with frequent references to the wider communicative contexts (historical, social, cultural, political, inter alia) that constitute this discourse and make it meaningful in its spatial environment. Amongst the orientations which are widely adopted by researchers are the ones mentioned in what follows:

– *Critical Linguistics* is presumably the earliest version of CDA which attempted to connect the linguistic features of language with power and ideology by emphasizing the relativity of representation (see Fowler, Hodge, Kress, & Trew, 1979). It is concerned mainly with power in society and language practices which normalize the ideological stances in the public discourse that are assumed to be unbalanced or in favour of some (powerful groups, elites and politicians) against others (marginalized groups, minorities and the general public). Roger Fowler writes, "Critical linguistics insists that all representation is mediated, moulded by the value systems that are ingrained in the

medium" (Caldas-Coulthard & Coulthard, 1996, p. 4). A toolkit of devices was advised by the proponents of this method to analyse some grammatical and stylistic aspects of language which are believed to conceal skewed representations, such as the grammar of modality, *nominalization and passivization*, and thus a careful assessment of the ideologically loaded vocabulary.
- *The Dialectical–Relational Approach* (DRA) was introduced by Norman Fairclough. As its title indicates, the DRA is a variation of CDA where language is the output of complicated social processes and systems that construct reality and meaning. Unlike the other approaches, it adopts the concept of *semiosis* as a replacement of discourse in the sense that the former is more inclusive than the latter (Fairclough, 2009). Based on this outlook, which is well grounded within critical realist epistemology, discourse analysis is not bound up with language in use only, but rather broadly with what Fairclough called "semiotic modalities."
- *The Discourse Historical Approach* (DHA) is likewise a problem-oriented and interdisciplinary version of CDA proposed by Ruth Wodak. The DHA is based on the exploitation of the historical and social to locate the embedded meaning of social events and phenomena in a specific present moment (Wodak & Meyer, 2009). The DHA is used particularly to deconstruct the anti-Semitic discourse, racism and discrimination against minorities and migrants in the West, European identity and other related topics.
- *The Socio-Cognitive Model* is another cross-disciplinary theoretical approach advocated by Teun A. van Dijk. The socio-cognitive model makes reference to the underlying cognitive perspectives in the production and reproduction of discourse and ideologies. So far, this approach has been widely implemented by scholars who are interested in the study of media and political discourses and a wide range of contemporary issues that relate specifically to racism and migration.

It is perhaps a little bit difficult to trace the first seeds that gave birth to the now-expanding field of CDS, yet there were certainly a few endeavours that left their imprints on this tradition, such as the contributions of Mikhail Bakhtin, V. N. Voloshinov, Michel Foucault, Michael Halliday, the East Anglia research group and the Frankfurt School. However, the most recent advances have come from the works of Norman Fairclough, Gunther Kress, Ruth Wodak, Theo van Leeuwen and Teun van Dijk. CDA, Ruth Wodak notes, "has never been and has never attempted to be or to provide one single or specific theory. Neither is one specific methodology characteristic of research in CDA" (Wodak & Meyer, 2009, p. 5). It is precisely this flexibility and unsettled boundaries of interest that made this "school" diverse in terms of its theoretical underpinnings and thus the tools, strategies and methods that it endorses and applies. The existing literature shows that CDA is defined in different ways by linguists and social theorists. Moreover, it is not based on one fixed methodological paradigm and its methods have no common theoretical position, but it incorporates various analytical strategies and tools. Remarkably, the field of CDA has widened in recent years to cover numerous subjects within the social sciences. Teun van Dijk comments that CDA

> studies the way social power, abuse, dominance, and inequality are enacted, reproduced, and resisted by text and talk in the social and political context. With such dissident research, critical discourse analysts take explicit position, and thus want to understand, expose, and ultimately resist social inequality. (2001, p. 352)

Unlike the traditional approaches to text analysis, CDA methodologies aim to advance a critical and objective analysis of diverse communicative situations with a meticulous description of context. In this way they tend to explain rather than merely describe how discourse structures are loaded with ideological biases.

The various CDA methods seek to bring to the fore the embedded logic that lies beneath the representation of events, people, subjects and other more abstract social constructs. By doing so, implicit ideologies and polarized viewpoints about the circulating meanings and representations in the social context are made explicit for the marginalized, the oppressed and ostracized. In other words, the distribution of power relations, the distortion in the representation of reality, issues of dominance and hegemony, racism and xenophobia are amongst the most important constitutive components of discourse which CDA practitioners aim to disclose. Hence, the function of discourse is the ultimate concern of most CDA theorists, and analysts struggle to advance positive solutions to today's social problems. Allan Luke clarifies that "CDA involves a principled and transparent shunting back and forth between the microanalysis of texts using varied tools of linguistics, semiotic, and literary analysis and the macroanalysis of social formations, institutions, and power relations that these texts index and construct" (2002, p. 100).

3.1.3 The Critique of CDA

Undeniably, CDA made a number of successful strides in applied linguistics and critical social theory alike. Throughout its progress, it gradually intermingled with other non-language–oriented research arenas, which contributed largely to make it multidisciplinary, as it is nowadays. Obviously, the junction between CDA and other disciplines is becoming manifold, so it is no longer clear where CDA would anchor its scope and limits. In fact, the boundaries of this school are difficult to be well demarcated, as it continues to draw heavily from other fields of science and scholarly inquiry that are not necessarily within the circle of the social sciences, such as cognitive sciences (see Fig. 3.1). But one must remark here that the various CDA orientations are still amply sprinkled with drawbacks and shortcomings, both as a theory and as a methodology. Some scholars argued that CDA is not truly critical and tend mostly to defend alternative propositions that are often speculative and intuitive.

Indeed, the critique of this analytical tendency came from many scholars who doubted, in particular, the critical spirit that CDA claims (see, e.g., Widdowson, 2004). In the light of the progress made in the cognitive empirical studies, there might be a need to reconsider some of the caveats of CDA with great caution as to better fathom and weigh the potential of this research attitude, and importantly to make sense of how to adequately bridge the gap between the theoretical rationale of CDA and its applied analytical strategies.

Although there has been a considerable consensus on the commitment of CDA to enlighten the oppressed, marginalized and disadvantaged through unravelling the underlying processes of normalizing social

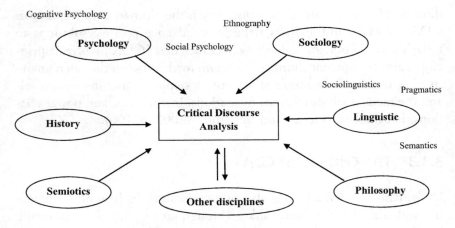

Fig. 3.1 Cross-disciplinarity in critical discourse analysis

inequalities, domination, bias, racism and the like, there have been slightly different viewpoints with regard to the very theoretical nature of CDA and its objectives. Its founding fathers disagreed whether to account for it as a method, an approach, a theory or just an amalgam of theoretical models. Accordingly, some remained within the traditional linguistic mould through their emphasis on the linguistic examination of the text, with little reference to its context. However, others broadened their scope and borrowed, to varying degrees, from the findings of major social theorists—notably, Foucault, Bernstein, Bourdieu, Giddens, Gramsci, Habermas and many others. It seems that the disparity between the mentioned views on CDA and thus its ways of analysis reflect a great flexibility in this enterprise.

According to Fairclough, CDA is a method that is preoccupied with the ways in which meaning is constructed in language with reference to a web of social variables. The "opacity" that envelops the links between the use of language, power in the social milieu and the struggle over power and thus the ideological factor that shapes, or at least, influences such intricate discursive relations requires a great deal of criticism and investigation at many different layers (Chouliaraki & Fairclough, 1999). To consider CDA as a one single and integrated approach for doing analysis would be a highly misguided view, expect perhaps for the more traditional directions, which are less systematic and more mechanistic in their adherence to pure textual analysis.

Now one may well ask what makes CDA critical. Most, if not all, discourse scholars share the assumption that CDA has an "emancipatory agenda" and seeks to lay down the foundation for constructive social change and resistance against dominant ideologies. The belief in this, somehow, idealistic stance is inferred by the fact that political and social inequalities, as well as polarized views on many different subjects, are instilled into the consciousness of individuals/groups. Therefore, to do discourse analysis is to "demystify" the implicit logic and also decipher the ideological affiliations that permeate the construction of discourse, for example, the normalization of violence during war times. CDA analysts aim to deconstruct the opaqueness of the structural relationships of power and control which are implicit and embedded in specific contexts.

Wodak and Meyer advocate that CDA "aims to investigate critically social inequality as it is expressed, signalled, constituted, and legitimized, and so on by language use (or in discourse)" (2009, p. 2). It follows that to deconstruct the medium through which people interact, and exchange information and knowledge is, in simple words, to decode the power relations involved in the process of information sharing and construction of reality. Nonetheless, it should be mentioned in passing that, although the make-up of social realities is by no means contextual, it is not always or necessarily an endeavour to manipulate, marginalize or exclude non-welcomed views, people or other relevant realities. That is why I have espoused a neutral conceptualization of "ideology" and its associated properties.

It is perhaps this "emancipatory agenda" that CDA scholars adhere to which made the whole discipline ideologically based and well placed within predetermined positions and judgements. This seems to be contradictory with the basic scientific norms of objectivity and neutrality. Widdowson claims that "CDA is, in a dual sense, a biased interpretation: in the first place it is prejudiced on the basis of some ideological commitment, and then it selects for analysis such texts as will support the preferred interpretation" (quoted in Wodak & Meyer, 2001, p. 17). One might wonder then whether the kind of criticism that CDA analysts advocate would offer a balanced critique on the topics that they tackle, or is it a justification of a set of prejudgements. It is not always true that CDA tools manage successfully to excavate the implicit meanings and inferences that the writer/speaker intends to convey to his/her audience through the deconstruction of language items (grammatical structures and lexis) and by providing a detailed description of the contextual elements that exerted a pressure on the manufacturing of the text. In simple words, there could be not just one possible "correct" analysis of the same text but many feasible readings and interpretations. Moreover, there is no sufficient evidence on how readers interpret texts and whether they do interpret the same text in similar ways.

Many methods and modes of analysis that are grounded within CDA tend to be selective. The seamlessness of CDA with the other social sciences can be fruitful, as it can be misleading, and perhaps even irrelevant. Is selectivity intended to direct research towards predetermined results which are deep-rooted personal convictions or a necessity in the treatment of the wide range of subjects that it targets? It is common among discourse analysts and practitioners to synthesize strategies and techniques from other, especially non-linguistic, disciplines to examine the intricate formulation of discourse and its function in many situations and contexts. This "shifting synthesis" that crossed the borders between the linguistic and non-linguistic approaches is becoming a norm rather than an exception. However, to pick up some techniques while ignoring others that are also germane to the analysis of a given case study might leave the impression of subjectivity and possibly bias. Eclecticism in CDA brought a wave of suspicion and scepticism about its reliability and validity. For Pennycook, most discourse analysts are involved in what he assumes to be "a strange mixture of theoretical eclecticism and unreflexive modernism" (2001, p. 76). It seems like critical analysts may produce predetermined results that are void of any systematic critique.

Yet, other scholars consider cross-disciplinarity as an asset rather than a methodological problem. James Paul Gee again advocates that "approaches to discourse analysis that avoid combining a model of grammatical and textual analysis (of whatever sort) with sociopolitical and critical theories of society and its institutions are not forms of critical discourse analysis" (2004, p. 20). Weiss and Wodak (2003), Chouliaraki and Fairclough (1999) and others advocate for eclecticism as a necessary mechanism for doing purposeful analysis. Selectivity that is not arbitrary then seems to be constructive, as it takes into account the peculiar nature of text and talk in the different communication situations and also the wide range of elements that constitute or shape them. One point that needs to be highlighted in this regard is the fact that the tools of discourse analysis should be revisited periodically as to cope with the change and refinements in the other disciplines from which it draws its inspiration and insights. The difference in the context of the discourses under scrutiny makes selectivity quite justified, if not a must. For example, the analysis of a news article would be entirely different from that of a formal political speech, and this might even apply to the study of the same text genre (a news article vs. an editorial). Texts are different considerably in their properties, structures and thus their audiences, and therefore, applying the same strategy and devices on different texts and situations might not always be relevant.

Another important remark that is worth mentioning is the possible influence of the political affiliation of the analyst, whether consciously or unconsciously, on the analysis of discourse, most importantly if he/she tackles a genre of discourse that is typically political and explicitly biased. The usage of language involves by no means politics or what James Paul Gee defines as the contestation over the "distribution of social goods" (p. 87). Hence, is it possible to have a value-free critique when it comes to applying CDA, or even other related analytical approaches, in the investigation of controversial issues (such as social conflicts and wars)? It is a truism that critical discourse practitioners investigate the ways in which language is used in its social context, yet the correlation between the two is somehow not clearly identified and explicated. Teun van Dijk levels criticism against CDA precisely on this point by calling into question the nature of impact of the social structures and roles on the composition and structure of language. He advocates that the relationship between the social structure and the structure of language cannot be established except through systematic analysis of what he calls "cognitive interface" that binds the two together.

Although the findings of cognitive psychology, which some CDS scholars utilize in their methodologies, are very much useful in describing the process of language production and understanding, they are still blurry and complex. In mundane terms, the problem of the cognitive-oriented approaches lies in the difficulty to apply their conceptual constructs in some case studies. Here, the following questions must be raised: Is it possible to integrate the findings of the cognitive sciences in the analysis of discourse? How can we, pragmatically speaking, implement the cognitive tools in the analysis of text and yield results that are observable and measurable? How can we implement the cognitive dimensions in the analysis of political discourse?

So far, the scope of CDA remains precarious and undetermined, since it borrows substantially from many other social sciences and disciplines. It also covers a number of contemporary social problems, with a particular focus on exposing how reality is constructed, disseminated and legitimized in the public consciousness. Topics that centre on racism, gender inequalities, nationalism, ethnicity, conflicts and war discourse remain amongst the most studied within this tradition. After all, there are still many patches and lacunae in terms of theory and practice that require constant update and revision. As is made clear throughout this chapter, this research project is grounded within the CDS framework, with particular interest in the use of cognitive tools in the analysis of political speeches and news discourse as a genre of political communication.

3.2 Teun A. van Dijk's Socio-cognitive Model

3.2.1 Overview and Basic Conceptualizations

As the title initiates, the second section of this chapter expounds, albeit scantily, the rationale and methodology of the socio-cognitive model in the analysis of discourse which informs the analytical strategy adopted in this research. However, due to its theoretical complexity and the multiple references from which it draws, there is a need to explain the bulk of technical terms used by van Dijk in his theory—some of which are used in other disciplines—and also the mechanism proposed to analyse the intricacies of discourse. Equally important is the underlying logic and basic philosophical tenets upon which the socio-cognitive model is founded and justified, which I shall not consider here. A detailed explication of all the notions coined or borrowed by van Dijk would definitely require more space than could well be given to it here—it is by no means necessary to be eclectic. That is to say, to select the frequently used key terms and exhibit their origins in the literature, usage and the limitations of each term in the subsequent analysis.

Thus, some of the lacunae that subsisted in the application of this theoretical model which make it extremely difficult to be fully operationalized in certain cases are also presented by the end of the chapter. This is in fact one of the conceptual preoccupations of this study. After all, van Dijk's socio-cognitive model, as will be shown, is one of the few original contributions in CDS that yielded new ways of looking at language and its interplay with the attitudes, ideologies and knowledge of a specific cultural group.

In short, this part of the chapter is, to some extent, a simplification and reproduction of van Dijk's theory and methodology in discourse studies. In order to do so, I will display the ensemble of concepts and applications of the theory by focusing on and relating together the three essential pillars of the socio-cognitive model, that is, discourse, society and cognition. This closing part of the chapter brings to the fore the positive aspects of the socio-cognitive model as well as the difficulties and the challenges that still face not only this theoretical model, but the many other theories that put the tools of cognition as the platform for its reasoning and analysis of language and ideology in society.

The socio-cognitive model, as the compound label clearly indicates, fuses the social and cognitive aspects involved in the processes of discourse formulation and understanding. The phrase "socio-cognitive" is also used in the language disciplines that are essentially preoccupied with the study of the processes of natural language acquisition and learning. In brief, the social perspective refers to the structures existing in the social milieu, the distribution of power relations between those engaged in the communicative situation, their relationships to one another and their ideologies.

In Fig. 3.1 I mentioned only some of the research areas that pulled together to give birth to the field of CDS—with the prospect of including other disciplines that are somehow a far bit in terms of scope and goals, at least for the present time. The impact of such convergence differed in its degree and influence from one discipline to another and in accordance with the toolkit and strategy of analysis embraced by the various CDS approaches, some of which were mentioned earlier.

As for the socio-cognitive model, it is by no means obvious that it has borrowed many of its assumptions from the disciplines that lay at the crossroad of sociology, psychology and the cognitive sciences, with language being at the centre of this meeting circle. The model has taken up many strategies and tools to investigate the ways in which bias, stereotypes, prejudice, negative racial attitudes, positive-self representation, legitimization and manipulation, among many other things, take place in the unconscious mind of individuals. Those embedded elements in discourse can be deconstructed if one gains sufficient understanding on how they are strategically coded in the superstructure (grammar, vocabulary, syntax) and deep structure (semantics) of the language used.

Van Dijk vigorously criticized the taken-for-granted causal relation between the use of language and the social constraints and their properties, such as gender, ethnicity, social strata, age and the like. This critique is done for good reason. In the light of the progress made recently in the cognitive sciences, the held assumption by traditional linguists about the social–discourse relationship is not a cast-iron argument, or perhaps superficially made. Instead, the impact of the social structures on the structures of discourse could be interpreted via the systematic analysis of a myriad of factors involved in discourse production and comprehension. In principle, this is what he calls *context models* of those participating in a given communicative situation, which explains the variability and diversity of discourse. This general statement about van Dijk's theory remains so unclear at this point and demands some concrete examples so as to showcase, in concrete manner, the dynamic and changing relation between discourse and the socio-cognitive contexts.

At the very basic levels of scholarly debate in discourse studies is the text–context dichotomy. Indeed, the latter has been one of the traditional objects of linguistics. The correlation between the written or spoken materials and the social environment in which they are used in received some different explanations by contemporary scholars. The ongoing debate relates particularly to how the social variables affect the use of language. What is the different between text and context? And why context matters in the analysis of discourse?

Contemporary scholarship in discourse studies views discourse as a firmly context-bound concept. Nonetheless, there are still some slight but potentially important idiosyncratic discrepancies as to what is meant by *context*, and how it could influence the processes of discourse production and comprehension. Fundamentally, apart from the spatiotemporal elements, the socio-cognitive model brings into sharper focus the role of cognitive variables involved in those processes. This makes discourse conditioned not solely by time, place, historicity, society and the like, but also by the cognition of individuals and the shared "memory" of the social group to which those individuals belong, which would add its distinctively subjective touch. Christopher Hart writes:

> Discourse is always produced and processed in context. It is always "situated" socially, spatially, temporally and intertextually, for example. This context, however, is not the context that exists out there in objective reality, but is rather the set of cognitive representations that discourse participants have of the world. Context in this sense is subjective knowledge. It contributes to meaning construction in discourse but it is also managed and maintained through discourse. (Hart, 2011, p. 1)

Cognition is not only measured at the level of the individual, but extended to what is shared amongst individuals in the social environment to which they belong. That is to say, the interaction of language users in the different communicative contexts is deemed an integral part of the language phenomenon, yet through linking this interaction with what might be called "the shared stock of knowledge". The social aspect of language use is a fundamental element in the model which, it should be mentioned, overlaps with cognition in many different respects.

It is generally accepted that Halliday's Systemic Functional Linguistics (SFL) has been one of the most influential approaches in linguistics which still informs many paradigms and methods in CDS. Although the long-established assumption on context has been drawn from SFL, the recent theoretical refinements in discourse studies and the disciplines associated with it put most of its tenets under question. Some critics claimed that the theory is bogus. Precisely, the objection to it, which relates to the point I discuss at this stage, is the reductionist conceptualization of context which ignores at least the cognitive aspect. Despite its pioneering ideas on the functionality of language and its primary insistence upon the context of language use, contemporary linguists and theorists argued against the self-contained logic of analysis and linguistic reductionism in SFL. The critique produced lately has been less to repel the instrumentality of Halliday's theory than to emphasize the need to refine the traditional conceptions about context and to adjust to the new findings in other disciplines in the social sciences that opened new avenues in looking at language and language use.

In his critique of SFL, van Dijk calls for a reconsideration of some fundamental assumptions of the theory and claims that it failed to supply an adequate analysis of many relevant semantic properties and relations involved in discourse processing. Despite the validity of Halliday's linguistic theory, it generated unbalanced explanations of language and discourse analysis; these shortcomings are, as van Dijk points out, "a function of the defects of its more general approach to language and discourse and as a paradigm of research" (2008, p. 29). Most significantly, the theory does not integrate the cognitive aspect in context and the processes involved in language use, which is, by means of recent advances in the theory of discourse, a cornerstone tool.[1] Relevant in this respect is the lack of any references to the mental processes involved in defining the notion of discourse which constitute an integral part of context and, by consequence, the processes involved in discourse comprehension and understand.

3.2.2 The Epistemics of Discourse Analysis in the Socio-cognitive Model

According to van Dijk, cognition has always been the missing link in many discourse analysis methodologies. As for the socio-cognitive model, cognition and interaction as aspects of language use are mutually dependent on each other. Arguably, though cognition is taken up to be an essential analytical element in CDS by many scholars, it remains very little exploited in an explicit manner in their paradigms. The literature displays countless references to the cognitive mechanisms and processes that relate to language and language use, most obviously in the methodologies that fall under the realm of Cognitive Linguistics. However, there has not yet been a systematic analysis of the mental strategies and processes involved in the production and interpretation of discourse.

As was previously clarified, the cognitive "interface" between discourse and society is an especially fundamental element in van Dijk's theoretical framework. Accordingly, the ensemble of mental strategies related to discourse are considered in this modest research in order to showcase the underlying unconscious processes involved in the legitimization and manipulation of the pro-war discourse in Britain during Blair's premiership—how the patterns associated with pro-war discourse were produced and reproduced in the British society during the volatile early years of the early twenty-first century.

In this respect, it is to note again that the cross-disciplinary methodology defines context not only in terms of place and time of a given communicative situation, but also in terms of the cognitive processes involved in understanding such a situation. The other aspects of discourse analysis which are based on insights from sociology and social psychology are not however neglected, but cannot be understood without reference to their cognitive bases (van Dijk, 2009). At this point, one needs to make reference to a bunch of findings from the cognitive sciences to explain what cognitive analysis of language use stands for. This might require much space for adequate simplification, yet the necessary elements are squeezed and defined—what is meant by cognitive interface and how could this be operationalized in the treatment of the unit of analysis.

In mundane terms, the cognitive aspect of the socio-cognitive model refers to the processing of discourse and information in memory and the various mental processes involved in the making of meaning. Van Dijk explains that "discourse processing, just like other complex information processing, is a strategic process in which a mental representation is constructed of the discourse in memory, using both external and internal types of information, with the goal of interpreting (understanding) the discourse" (van Dijk & Kintsch, 1983, p. 6). The meaning of a given text is only subjectively assigned to it by the various language users and cannot be found in the text itself because the meaning is represented in some specific ways in the minds of the participants. It is the aim of cognitive analysis to account for those, highly complex, mental processes involved in the making of meaning and also understanding by the respective actors.

One of the main aspects in the analysis of ideological discourse is the so-called mental models. The concept is drawn from the works of many scholars in cognitive science, neuroscience, cognitive psychology and a few other related disciplines that study the working of the human mind and precisely the multiple mental processes involved in learning and behaviour. Language as a linguistic behaviour occupies a large space in this framework. Part of this scholarly interest attributes much care to the intricacies of language and thought in the mind, including the various manifestations of language in memory. A good part of the current findings in these disciplines proved to be of vital importance to applied sciences, such as computing and artificial intelligence, which tried to emulate the human mind's functions. CDS, likewise, benefited much from these new contributions, which still change our ways of thinking about language, interaction and communication.

Van Dijk approaches the cognitive aspect in discourse processing as a form of mental model in order to expound the intricate structures of discourse. This means that mental models form an integral part of the context of the communicative situation, providing important clues to track the different fragments that constitute the whole picture of events, people and the other objects of the social world in our mind. On the nature and function of mental models, van Dijk writes:

> Mental models of contexts are subjective, but not arbitrary. After experiencing and participating in many thousands of unique communicative situations, language users tend to generalize and normalize such situations, so that also their mental models of such situations are generalized to shared, social representations of such situations. Such social representations will abstract from ad hoc, personal and other specific aspects of communicative situations, and hence reduce the subjectivity of each context model. It is in this fundamental way that (this aspect of) the social order is reproduced, how the rules of conversations and other interactions are being acquired, and how context models may be coordinated by different participants. (Fairclough, Cortese, & Ardizzone, 2007, p. 293)

To briefly paraphrase the above quote on mental models and their roles in discourse processing, it could be said that our understanding and also interpretation of the events around us are based upon some *partly* subjective and personal experiences. Those experiences are represented by mental models, which are stored in the episodic memory in the form of frames and scripts. Mental models therefore are important for future judgement and evaluations by respective participants. What is also particularly significant is the mental character of coherence and meaning-making, which entails answering at last three basic questions about (a) the production of meaning by the agent (speaker/writer), (b) the factors that determine the production of discourse and (c) how it could be comprehended and interpreted by the receptive audience? This involves, among many other things, describing the functions of memory in receiving, storing and retrieving information; the construction of knowledge and its relation with meaning; and thus the reality of the world "out there" through, of course, one of the major sources of knowledge, which is simply discourse.

What lies at the heart of the cognitive approaches to the study of language is questioning the nature of knowledge, which is a highly abstract phenomenon and hard to be described. Though this element is philosophical in essence, it is closely intertwined with both ideology and discourse in general. Besides, it is one of the regulators of power in society.

It is common sense that knowledge about the social world that humans live and interact in is a primary prerequisite for communication and a fundamental property of language, without which interaction might be non-coherent, broken or at least incomplete. It seems plausible that the more people share the same access, sources and types of particular sociocultural knowledge, the more their communication would be fluid and easy, and vice versa. This alone makes it essential to pay sufficient attention to the role of shared knowledge in making sense of the social environment humans belong to and the ways in which they understand, perceive and judge objects, people and events in their everyday life.

In *Discourse and Knowledge: A Sociocognitive Approach* (2014), van Dijk discusses in much detail the notion of knowledge and its multiple connections with the other language properties such as, inter alia, power, cognition, the shared beliefs in society and the structure of knowledge in memory (mental representation). Those ideas showcase the knowledge–discourse interconnections, borrowed also from other discourse-related disciplines, are all fused together in this short section as to re-emphasize the relevance of the *epistemics* of discourse in the analysis of our case study. This is in many different ways tied up with the cognitive aspect of discourse that informs our multidisciplinary methodology. Because knowledge is part of discourse and necessary to valid discourse analysis, it would be necessary to fathom how knowledge is manifested in meaning-making and understanding. Thus, it is vital to describe the kind of knowledge that is produced and how it is expressed and understood in language.

The epistemic assumptions espoused in the socio-cognitive model show some distinctiveness in proportion to the other traditional, and even some contemporary, views on the source, nature and expression of knowledge in communication and interaction. Social knowledge is defined as "the shared beliefs of an epistemic community, justified by contextually, historically and culturally variable (epistemic) criteria of reliability" (Van Dijk, 2014, p. 21). Such a broad definition highlights the relativity and contextual nature of knowledge, which makes meaning shifts along place and time. Knowledge in this sense cannot be isolated from the general context in which it is produced and disseminated in the public discourse, which makes it clearly subjective and context-bound knowledge. In brief, knowledge is co-textual and interactional (for a detailed elaboration, see Gee, 2012; Van Dijk, 2007, 2014).

Those questions which seem orthodox issues in epistemology are seminal, for knowledge is codified in language through not only the words and sentences, but also, mostly, what is communicated is implicit and not directly expressed, but rather inferred. In other words, knowledge could be best interpreted through specific linguistic items that are loaded with specific cultural patterns. Speakers or writers may express their knowledge (views, opinions and ideas) in an implicit manner through, for example, the use of specific grammatical structures, implications, metaphors and presuppositions, to name but a few. In close, it is to stress again that the methodology adopted in this study attempts to chart the relationship between the structure of knowledge and the structure of discourse based on a multidisciplinary perspective.[2] Precisely, it considers the kind of shared knowledge that creates the public discourse and also shapes the cognition of the individual, who belongs to a specific social group or what is called the "epistemic community."

3.2.3 Semantic Macrostructures and the Hierarchy of Discourse

The concept of (semantic) macrostructures is one of the basic analytical tools in the socio-cognitive model which, in fact, demands some simplification and elaboration. By definition, the semantic macrostructure of discourse refers to the global meaning of a text or talk. In very mundane terms, it is about the *upshot* of a given communicative situation or what is nicknamed in the model as the "discourse topic". The semantic macrostructure is also germane to the cognitive processing of discourse in memory (see a detailed explanation in Van Dijk, 1980). As indicated in the above section title, macrostructure analysis accounts for how meaning is articulated in the structure of the text through the analysis of the semantic relations and connections between the sequences of clauses, sentences and (macro) propositions. I believe that this would give us some interesting clues not only about natural language understanding and interpretation, but also about the underlying cognitive mechanisms of legitimization and manipulation that will eventually be manifest in the use of language (see Fig. 3.2).

It is advocated in the socio-cognitive model that the underlying meaning and coherence relations in a specific text or talk cannot be solely analysed and interpreted at the level of isolated words and sentences, but requires a higher-level description of the global thematic structure, both from a linguistic and from a cognitive perspective. The linguistic level refers to the semantic features of the text structure, that is, the connections between clauses, sentences and propositions, which are ordered in a hierarchical fashion. Such language structure corresponds to a particular cognitive structure that guides the processing of information and meaning in memory. Due to memory shortcomings people are not able to remember all the details about what they read in a newspaper or what they have been told by the Prime Minister in a meeting or a conference. But they still, at least, remember what the newspaper article or the political speech was about.

The preliminary stage in the analytical dissection of the various genres of discourse via the socio-cognitive model goes through a meticulous description of the structure of "global and local coherence" of the text.

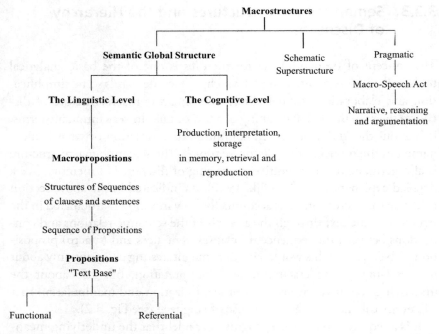

Fig. 3.2 Macrostructures. This figure maps out the theory of macrostructures and its most important elements in van Dijk's socio-cognitive model

According to van Dijk, coherence provides a text with meaning and unity just like the way grammatical rules provide meaning to a certain sequential order of words. Coherence becomes then a keyword that ought to be properly defined in the light of the adopted cognitive-oriented theoretical approach. For a long time, textual coherence and the function of cohesion have always been fundamental concerns in discourse studies and particularly in conversational discourse analysis.

However, in this context, coherence in a given communicative situation does involve both the sender and the recipient, and is not solely dependent upon the text or talk per se. In other words, the cognitive representation of the subject matter through language at a given point in time by the participants in the communicative situation should reflect some mutual and shared stock of knowledge that facilitates the understanding of this subject matter in the first place. Consequently, the text will be comprehensible and interpretable by all the interlocutors. In defining coherence in text processing, T. Givón (see Gernsbacher & Givón, 1995, pp. 59–60) listed seven different characteristic of discourse coherence. The most relevant ones to the context of this study are the ones mentioned below:

Coherence is not a text-based phenomenon but involves mental processes.
Coherence is a collaborative process that involves all the participants.
Human discourse production and comprehension involve two distinct processing channels whereby both global and local aspects of coherence are entailed.

A detailed description of the macrostructures of the political and news texts concerned here will enable us to identify the tacit knowledge and ideologies encoded in such structures at a global level. It is worth noting that macrostructures are expressed differently in the various genres of communication and interaction. While, for example, headlines and leading sentences in news articles best express the upshot of the news text, a political speech may require a *recursive* summary so as to bring to the fore the main topics and themes of the text and how they are represented. In simple words, the analysis of the macrostructures of a given piece of language is the analysis of the semantic structures and relations between the sequences of sentences and also sequences of propositions. To operationalize the notion of "macrostructure" in the analysis of the proposed corpus (CPS), the chosen texts for qualitative analysis will be the subject of a process of semantic transformation through the implementation of a set of formal *macrorules*. The latter term simply refers to the following strategies which reduce the text into few representative sentences without altering its meaning: generalization, deletion, integration (selection) and construction.

Because cognition is an essential contextual element, one needs to uncover the manifestations of knowledge that is embedded or straightforwardly spelled out in discourse. My premise is that politicians and newsmakers manipulate the consciousness of the public through the production of ideologically based forms of knowledge about social objects, events and people. In pragmatic terms, the epistemic analysis of discourse should be carried out at many different levels which put the semantic and rhetorical features of language under close scrutiny. This is to say to uncover the strategies and structures of knowledge in discourse, I need to look for the following list of elements, as suggested by van Dijk: topics, local coherence, the description of actors, levels, details and precision of description, implications and presuppositions, definitions, evidentiality, argumentation, metaphor, modalities, rhetorical devices, grammar and lexicon.

Another problem in this theoretical model, this is also the case for the other models and theories, as suggested earlier, is that the multidisciplinary nature of its sources might be a sword of double edges. The most complicated issue in van Dijk's model is its dependence upon cognitive science and the usage of some technical and specialized terminology on the functioning of the mind, memory and consciousness. All in all, the socio-cognitive model is crucial for explicit and pragmatic discourse analysis due at least to two main reasons: First, because of its focus on detailed analysis of the various properties and structures of discourse with reference to their mental representation in the memory of individuals and social groups. Second, it also pays sufficient attention to the social aspect of discourse. And, if anything else, the model follows systematic ways of analysis that are less speculative and more empirically based.

This chapter provides a succinct outline of the fundamental tenets of the socio-cognitive model and its strategies and devices in the analysis of discourse. All in all, it is plausible to hold that the integration of the cognitive aspect of language in the analysis of discourse is constructive regardless of the genre of discourse concerned. Cognitive analysis or what is sometimes labelled as "epistemic discourse analysis", as hitherto explained, aims to dissect the prevalent knowledge in a specific community. It is precisely the aim of the subsequent chapters to analyse how ideologies, worldviews, ways of seeing, cultural values and the norms circulating in the British community are manifest in the language of Blair and that of the quality press. Epistemic discourse analysis could well introduce new insights to the study of discourse in society. Discourse in this sense is reflective of the cultural patterns, ideologies, political affiliations and identity of the individuals forming a specific community.

Notes

1. Without reducing SLF to a mere speculative theory in linguistics, the critique mentioned a number of drawbacks in the ways in which the theory dealt with language and language use. A detailed critique on Hallidy's SFL is explained in van Dijk (2008), "Context and Language", pp. 28–55.
2. The disciplines which are primarily concerned with the cognitive phenomenon are heavily cited. Particular insights are taken from contemporary research findings in social neuroscience, social psychology, cognitive psychology, artificial intelligence, ethnography and anthropology.

References

Audi, R. (2003). *Epistemology: A contemporary introduction to the theory of knowledge*. Cambridge, UK: Cambridge University Press.

Austin, J. L. (1962). *How to do things with words*. Oxford, UK: Oxford University Press.

Caldas-Coulthard, C. R., & Coulthard, M. (Eds.). (1996). *Texts and practices: Readings in critical discourse analysis*. London: Routledge.

Chouliaraki, L., & Fairclough, N. (1999). *Discourse in late modernity: Rethinking critical discourse analysis*. Edinburgh, UK: Edinburgh University Press.

Fairclough, N. (2009). A dialectical-relational approach. In R. Wodak & M. Meyer (Eds.), *Methods of critical discourse analysis* (2nd ed., pp. 162–186). London: Sage.

Fairclough, N. (2013). *Critical discourse analysis: The critical study of language* (2nd ed.). London: Routledge.

Fairclough, N., Cortese, G., & Ardizzone, P. (2007). *Discourse and contemporary social change*. Bern, Switzerland: Peter Lang.

Fowler, R., Hodge, R., Kress, G., & Trew, T. (1979). *Language and control*. London: Routledge & Kegan Paul.

Gee, J. (2012). *Social linguistics and literacies: Ideology in discourses* (4th ed.). New York: Routledge.

Gee, J. P. (2004). Discourse analysis: What makes it critical. In R. Rogers et al. (Eds.), *An introduction to critical discourse analysis in education* (pp. 19–50). London: Lawrence Erlbaum Associates, INC.

Gernsbacher, M. A., & Givón, T. (Eds.). (1995). *Coherence in spontaneous text* (Vol. 31). Amsterdam: John Benjamins Publishing.

Hart, C. (Ed.). (2011). *Critical discourse studies in context and cognition*. Amsterdam: John Benjamins Publishing Company.

Hymes, D. (1964). Towards ethnographies of communication. *American Anthropologist, 66*(6), 1–34.

Luke, A. (2002). Beyond science and ideology critique: Development in critical discourse analysis. *Annual Review of Applied Linguistics, 22,* 96–110.

Pennycook, A. (2001). *Critical applied linguistics: A critical introduction*. Mahwah, NJ: Lawrence Erlbaum.

Van Dijk, T. A. (1980). *An interdisciplinary study of global structures in discourse, interaction and cognition*. Hillsdale, NJ: Erlbaum.

Van Dijk, T. A. (2001). Critical discourse analysis. In D. Schiffrin, D. Tannen, & H. E. Hamilton (Eds.), *The handbook of discourse analysis* (pp. 352–371). Oxford, UK: Blackwell.

Van Dijk, T. A. (Ed.). (2007). *Discourse studies*. London: Sage.

Van Dijk, T. A. (2008). *Discourse and context: A sociocognitive approach*. London: Cambridge University Press.

Van Dijk, T. A. (2009). Critical discourse studies: A sociocognitive approach. In R. Wodak & M. Meyer (Eds.), *Methods of critical discourse analysis* (2nd ed., pp. 62–85). London: Sage.

Van Dijk, T. A. (2014). *Discourse and knowledge: A Sociocognitive approach*. Cambridge, UK: Cambridge University Press.

Van Dijk, T. A., & Kintsch, W. (1983). *Strategies of discourse comprehension*. New York: Academic Press.

Weiss, G., & Wodak, R. (Eds.). (2003). *Critical discourse analysis: Theory and interdisciplinarity*. New York: Palgrave Macmillan.

Widdowson, H. G. (2004). *Text, context and pretext: Critical issues in discourse analysis*. Malden, MA: Blackwell.

Wodak, R., & Chilton, P. (Eds.). (2005). *A new agenda in (critical) discourse analysis: Theory, methodology and interdisciplinarity* (Vol. 13). Amsterdam: John Benjamins Publishing.

Wodak, R., & Meyer, M. (Eds.). (2001). *Methods of critical discourse analysis*. London: Sage.

Wodak, R., & Meyer, M. (Eds.). (2009). *Methods of Critical Discourse Analysis*. London: Sage.

4

The Anglo-Iraqi Relationships: A Historical Overview

4.1 Iraq Under British Conquest: The Curse of Oil

4.1.1 Britain's First Steps in Iraq and the Remaking of the Middle East

Undoubtedly, the Iraq War of 2003 was one of the highly controversial military affairs in recent history due to its blurry causes and motives. There has been, indeed, an ardent debate on the US-led war which left disastrous consequences in its wake on world politics and Middle East in particular. It is perhaps evident in the light of the now-unfolding events that Britain's engagement in the military action was a serious mistake that did not make the region safer, but apparently more vulnerable and unstable. Remarkably, the war engendered a wide discontent in Britain, the USA and elsewhere.[1] Though Britain's military involvement was relatively limited, it played a key diplomatic role in the run up to overthrow Saddam's regime.

In fact, Britain had always been present in Iraq since its early steps in the country during the First World War. I would bring to the fore the

© The Author(s) 2018
M. Douifi, *Language and the Complex of Ideology*, Postdisciplinary Studies in Discourse, https://doi.org/10.1007/978-3-319-76547-1_4

effect of such a long-dated presence and comment on some trajectories in the political history of Iraq. This, I assume, would optimally bring to light the deep-rooted intervention of Downing Street through its, usually unstated, imperialist policies not only in Iraq, but the whole disturbed region of the Middle East. Nevertheless, the basic question addressed herein revolves around the motives, whether declared or concealed, that made Blair enthusiastic about the military intervention in Iraq. To date, this question is still indeed unresolved by the privy counsellors of the Chilcot Inquiry committee. Yet, there is a need to measure the influence of Britain on Iraq's political landscape and showcase Blair's most stressed causes to declare war on Iraq.

Unlike the former Gulf War, the invasion was well covered because the media have successfully escaped the censorship of the war proponents who were struggling to legitimize their cause. This was happening at a time when the traditional means of censorship were no longer able to direct and contain the growing information flow. Arguably, the spread of communication technology and precisely the Internet and the other electronic devices, which provided many other parallel narratives to the official voice, made it impossible to mould the public opinion in favour of the war.

In 1914, as in 2003, one would ponder what was Britain's catalyst to rush for an adventurous war against a distant land like Iraq? Indeed, lengthy literature can be found in relation to the perplexing history of Iraq and its controversial relationship with the West, especially that of the last 30 years, where Iraq was brought to the UN discussion panel several times. Obviously, the political strife had been remarkable from the early announcements of the war plans following the Texas Summit in 2002. The success of the pro-war campaign and the legitimization of the military action in the eyes of a large sceptical public rested heavily on the necessity to round up the sympathy of the media. An effective communication strategy was also needed to placate the political opponents, at least at home. It is needless to add that the whole project had no legal legitimacy and was not authorized by the UNSC.

Although it has a unique geographical location and huge natural and human resources, Iraq was in a state of political instability and mayhem throughout much of the twentieth century. The American political scientist Yossef Bodansky argues that "from its inception, Iraq has remained an amalgam of hostile ethnic, national, and religious entities glued together in the early 1920s to further Britain's colonial, strategic, and economic interests" (2004, p. 242). Preserving the integrity of the Iraqi state, in such malleable conditions, was an extremely intractable task. As mentioned earlier, what made things worse is the mosaic composition of the Iraqi community, which incorporated distinct cultural groups with complex historical feud and religious grudges. Thus, these social groups held firm ideological allegiances, which made social consensus breakdowns most often. Ostensibly, the past is vividly present in the everyday life, customs and institutions of the Iraqis, which is, I would argue, a serious blinker that still hampers the making of a civil state in the modern sense. Iraq's neighbours had also posed a threat to its political stability due to some ideological and territorial disputes. In a much-quoted statement by Middle East historians, the Hashemite monarch King Faisal I, during his enduring grappling to govern the troubled Iraq territory, declares with a tone of grief and disappointment in 1933:

> There is still- and I say this with a heart full of sorrow- no Iraqi people, but unimaginable masses of human beings, devoid of any patriotic ideal, imbued with religious traditions and absurdities, connected by no common tie, giving ear to evil, prone to anarchy, and perpetually ready to rise against any government whatsoever. Out of these masses we want to fashion a people which we would train, educate, and refine .... The circumstances being what they are, the immenseness of the efforts needed for this cannot be imagined. (Quoted in Simon, 2013, pp. 3–4)

After its military clash with the Ottomans during the First World War, Britain controlled much of the Iraqi land and shortly thereafter redrew the geographical boundaries of the region and appointed the political authority of the modern state of Iraq. Its military intervention at the time was followed by a League of Nations mandate, which eventually ended up with pseudo independence and the creation of the free state of Iraq in 1932 (Tripp, 2002). Albeit less forthright as it used to be, British imperial ambition in the Middle East did not cease following its economic decline during the inter-war period. Even in the midst of the wreckage and chaos left by the Second World War, the British impact went on to mould the Iraqi political landscape to date.

The three *vilayets* (provinces) of Baghdad, Mosul and Basra were previously under the firm control of the Ottoman Empire, starting from 1638 up to the Great War (Ghareeb, 2004, p. 34). Although the late Ottoman era was marked by the continuous struggle with neighbouring Iran across the borders of Iraq, it was a period where numerous educational and administrative reforms were put into effect by the governor of Baghdad, Midhat Pasha.[2] For Britain, the dawn of the twentieth century was a turning point, where the balance of power started to shake off. There emerged other imperial rivals which truly challenged the British hegemony, yet Britain was still one of the main powerful poles in the world in terms of economic and military potentials. Following its pragmatic strategies in a hectic struggle for survival and dominance that was decorating the political atmosphere of the time, London sought to preserve its leading role as a central city in world policy-making. The British were very much concerned with the rising influence of Tsarist Russia and the new emerging power of the German Reich, especially with the relative deterioration in Britain's world status as a maritime superpower. With the "Sick Man of Europe" in its final throes of collapse, the Middle East turned out to be an open zone of contest between all these colonial powers. Under such circumstances, it was imperative for the British imperialists to accelerate their motion so as to strengthen Britain's hemisphere of influence over a large segment of the vulnerable territory left by the Ottomans.

Indeed, historians and political analysts have addressed the 1914 British occupation of Iraq from different perspectives. However, most agree on the fact that the British presence in Iraq was part of Britain's imperial thirst for expansion and the maintenance of its economic interests in Asia. From this perspective, oil had always been the driving force. The early years of the twentieth century marked the end of coal as the main source of energy and witnessed the increasing importance of oil as a much more efficient surrogate for it, although oil was still not exploited on a large scale. As the Middle East was expected to contain substantial reserves of petroleum, the British imperial officials, as well as their German rivals, put the region's promising wealth in their highest priorities, especially after the discovery of huge resources in Iran and the prospects of similar discoveries across the Iraqi lands. The materialization of this policy could be clearly seen in Britain's oil contracts with Iran, most significantly via the Anglo-Persian Oil Company (APOC), which would ultimately be one of the main shareholders of the Iraqi Petroleum Company (IPC) (Ghareeb, 2004, p. 114). The assumption concerning the ties between the British urge for military intervention and the maintenance of its economic interest, with oil being at the heart of this interest, cannot be relegated to a secondary position. Moreover, through the APOC, the British diplomacy had a privileged access to exert an influence on Persian politics and on Iraq as well.

According to Peter Sluglett, in order to maintain its vital national interests, it was necessary for Britain to secure the old trade routes, particularly with the Indian peninsula, through signing peace treaties with the territorial Gulf States. This helped also to secure the way into the heartland of Iraq. In fact, these treaties were then of particular significance, at least, to curb the French, Russian and German ambitions in the vast region of the Gulf and in the fight against the Ottomans in few years to come:

> In 1892, largely to counter what seemed to be growing French interests, Bahrain and the lower Gulf emirates were obliged to sign further agreements with Britain under which they agreed not to grant or dispose of any part of their territories except to Britain, and to conduct their relations with other powers through the British government. (2007, p. 3)

With the outbreak of the First World War, Britain sustained its efforts to confine the rich oil sources and trade routes in the region. Hence, the attack on the Ottoman forces was launched immediately on the second day of Britain's declaration of war, presumably in response to Ottoman's joining the German and Austro-Hungarian alliance. British and Indian expeditionary forces launched their attacks on the Iraqi land from the south and gradually conquered the whole country (see Barker, 2009). The geostrategic position of the Near East was necessary to the survival of what was left from the British Empire. David Fromkin also comments that "thus one thing which British leaders foresaw in 1914 was that Ottoman entry into the war marked the first step on the road to a remaking of the Middle East: to the creation, indeed, of the modern Middle East" (in Simon & Tejirian, 2004, p. 136).

To some extent, the Iraqi nationals were mutinous about the Ottoman presence, which helped the British made quick progress to isolate Iraq from Istanbul's rule. One has to bear in mind that, as the Middle East historian Judith S. Yaphe clarified, "separatism as a political goal was a result of the chauvinistic racial policies of the Young Turks, and not because of repressive Ottoman policies" (Simon & Tejirian, 2004, p. 19). The increasing tension between the local Arabs and the Ottomans was well exploited by the British, who incited the population against the Turkish officials and administrators, and in return promised the local Arabs with a fully sovereign state once the Ottoman regime is terminated. However, later war settlements made it clear that Britain's negotiations with the Sheikhs were double faced and the promises of independence were made just to gain sufficient time to defeat the determined Ottomans.[3]

As the war drew to a close, secret agreements were in place to get a firm hold of the post-war situation in the Middle East, which was divided by now into spheres of influence between traditional colonial powers, France and Britain. The so-called Arab Revolt (1916–1918) did not achieve its goal of creating a united nation; rather, there emerged a few separate states, whereby Iraq became officially under British control following the San Remo conference in April 1920. In brief, then as now, it would be wrong to assume that oil was the only driving force to mobilize the British troops to Iraq. The composition of Britain of the early twentieth century as an imperial state seeking to expand its influence over its physical territorial identity is essential in the understanding of the decision-making process and its rationale. As the military occupation was complete, the next serious challenge was how to manage the politics of the newly born offspring in the post-war chaos in Britain and elsewhere. In short, the dismemberment of the Ottoman Empire following the First World War had long-lasting consequences on the whole Middle East. As far as Britain is concerned, the campaign on the three *vilayets* of Iraq was an imperative to bridle the ambitions of its European rivals, notably to curb the German's determination to challenge the world balance of power.

4.1.2 British Imperialism, Ba'ath Dictatorship and the Creation of a "Failed State"

Britain was granted the mandate, a system approved by the League of Nations, over what is now the state of Iraq on 25 April 1920.[4] The mandate charged the British colonial authorities with the responsibility of establishing a fully independent state in a Western-like democratic style, a mission which did not attain its goal to date. Indeed, the hybrid nation-state project in Iraq, as well as the other neighbouring newborn countries, was based on more pragmatic calculations. Hence, in their "legal" task to fulfil their international commitment towards state building, British imperialist politicians, advisors and military officials were usually beset by the increasing public hostility and resistance on the ground, besides the ongoing strikes and opposition against the intervention at home. The most serious and bloody insurrection broke up on 30 June 1920, where the British resorted to brutal force to restore order. On the uprising of 1920, Courtney Hunt (2005) writes:

> The Rebellion of 1920 was led by secret societies compromised of Iraqi elites and began in Mosul. The siege, which lasted approximately three months, resulted in significant casualties for the British (estimates are as high as 2,200 dead) and massive casualties for the Iraqis … the true significance of the 1920 uprising was that the Iraqis were working together across tribal, traditional, and religious boundaries to oust the occupying British forces. (p. 63)

Other obstacles emerged out of the misunderstanding, or perhaps the negligence, of Iraqi traditions and customs, which are diverse, tribal and deeply rooted in history. The political rationale that is based on the loyalty to a central bureaucratic authority did not gain currency in the Iraqi society, where allegiance to the tribe chieftains is put above the other state institutions, which were, practically speaking, unworkable.

At a time when Britain's economic global hegemony started to regress in favour of US dominance, its foreign policy in Iraq was uncertain and changing, yet clearly indicative of retreat. In the course of the inter-war era, British enthusiasm about the unification of the Iraqis under a trusteeship system—largely perceived by Iraqis as a direct form of colonialism—went awry. Jeffrey Nadaner advocates that "their insistence at maintaining a colony in name through the fiction of a mandate system with no clear end led to the spark that ignited the revolt" (Aboul-Enein, 2012, p. 97). In that sense, the transition from the mandate to other alternatives of policy management was the only viable solution to the British. Instead of direct rule, they relied upon the assistance of tribal chieftains and land owners who were loyal to the colonial authority and were given substantial economic and political privileges in return. To some extent, this interest-based bond proved to be of great advantage in halting the frequent uprising of the population.

From another related perspective, the ongoing political strife and lack of religious consolidation amongst a spectrum of sectarian entities laid the foundation for the emergence of an Arab secular nationalist front, a remarkable and non-traditional political trend that would have long-term ramifications on the future of the state. The first seeds of this movement were laid down at the very beginning of the twentieth century, which through its slow, yet growing, motion would emerge as a political force in the early 1920s. Thus, the shocking realities of the post-war period incited the revolt of the Iraqis, who claimed for the fulfilment of British promise of full independence. Shortly afterwards, secret anti-colonial organizations were formed to resist what Iraqis considered to be a betrayal by the Allies and a direct illegitimate foreign intervention in the affairs of their newly established country, yet the process of nation-building was still not well identified and under initial construction.

At this juncture, the Cairo Conference of 1921 was held to sort out a new administrative policy to plea the public opinion in Iraq. Therefore, King Faisal I (son of Charif Hussein, who previously led the revolt against the Ottomans) was appointed as the new king of Iraq. The appointment of Faisal, who is seen as a religious symbol, thanks to his family roots, was thought to provide the Iraqis with "both a spiritual and political leadership that had been lacking under the British" (Wagner, 2009, p. 32). However, sovereignty has never been given to Iraq, and King Faisal's power was very limited and conditioned with Britain's imperial interests. In varying ways, the colonial administration was set to sustain the subordination of Iraq in economic and political matters to the British authorities and little attention was paid to the integrity of the new reforms and established institutions with the nature of the Iraqi society. Within this context, the invention of the state of Iraq, as Adeed Dawisha describes it, "was a forced and artificial creation, lacking the essential underpinnings of nationhood" (Telhami & Barnett, 2002, p. 119). The English political scientist Toby Dodge further adds that "Britain had decided to construct a 'quasi-state', one that had the appearance of a state but was in fact a façade built in order to allow Britain to disengage as quickly as possible" (2006, p. 10).

After 18 years under mandatory status, where the successive British officials struggled to implement new reforms in order to replace the long-standing Ottoman administrative regulations, power was only gradually handed to the Iraqis. Practically speaking, the transition of power to the locals was attributed to a variety of structural factors at both the regional and international levels. On the one hand, the deterioration of Britain's status, particularly in economic matters, must have been the main cause to retaliate Downing Street from sustaining a long-term presence. On the other hand, the spirit of chauvinist nationalism that spread quickly in the Middle East was also the major political feature in world politics during the 1920s and the 1930s, most noticeably in Europe, which underwent the rise of fascism. Within the rapidly changing realities on the ground, the emancipation of Iraq and the first steps towards the construction of a modern stable state were in place. However, this fragile entity went through difficult strides just to anchor in the puddle of Ba'athism dictatorship.

It is of vital importance to draw attention to the impact of the Ba'ath movement in Iraq, which shaped the political education of contemporary rulers of the country, including the most controversial Saddam Hussein. In mundane words, the Ba'athist ideology was the ultimate offspring of the nationalist movements that emerged in the early twentieth century. Officially established in Damascus in 1944 and grounded within socialist ideals and secularism, it sought to unite the Arabs into a single state, which they were denied by the former European colonizers and imperialists (see Sassoon, 2012). Dictatorship and the oppression of dissident voices constituted the dark side of the party's political ideology, which used the shining watchword of renaissance, rebirth and unity as a cover to legitimate its totalitarian and fascist orientation. It was also evident that the Ba'ath tended to put ethnicity as the axis of its dogma, relegating religion to a secondary position in the bid to consolidate loyalty of the non-Muslim Arabs and thus overcome the sectarian barriers and disputes.

Whilst Syria has been the patron of the Ba'ath party, it shared little, if any, with Iraq's Ba'athism, which in the course of time turned to be tenacious rivals. After the successful overthrew of the Hashemites during a period of political turmoil and instability in the late 1950s, the Ba'ath party of Iraq rose to power and took full control of the state by 1963 (Allawi, 2007, p. 29). Saddam Hussein was one of the active members within this movement who made his way to presidency in 1979. There is no doubt that Saddam's rule was characterized by ruthless oppression of political opponents, who were usually sentenced to death or exile. Individual or group executions without fair trials were already an established tradition that silenced any opposition to the Ba'ath leadership, which had an absolute and a firm control of the affairs in Iraq. Another perplexing issue was Saddam's unexpected and adventurous moves against his neighbouring countries which strongly opposed his pan-Arab ideology. David Malone states that "Saddam Hussein enforced national unity through terror and focused his attention on territorial expansion and other forms of aggression rather than constructive state building. On these choices hinged his absolute failure" (2006, p. 10).

Yet, the problem of Iraq could not be solely attributed to Saddam being an autocrat and a dictator, but more importantly lies in the composition of the Iraqi society, which inherited, seemingly, the burden of unsolved religious and ideological dilemmas that are still obstructing social uniformity and stability. The removal of Saddam in the last 2003 war proved once again the Western misunderstanding of the realities of Eastern societies and their traditions. In this line of argument, Lima Anderson and Gareth Stansfield note that "the regime of Saddam Hussein appears less as an aberration, and more as a logical culmination of the pathologies embedded in the state of Iraq since its creation in 1921" (2004, p. 13). As has been suggested earlier, amongst the most serious blunders of the Iraqi Ba'ath regime was the protracted military conflict with Iran that lasted eight years during which the UN interfered for the first time in the affairs of Iraq. In fact, the tension between Iraq and Iran has been continuously reproduced over a long period of time by religious, ideological or geographical disputes across their territories and the urge of both sides for regional domination by force. This crisis was also disturbing for some other international players who had either vital economic and strategic interests such as Britain, or those fearing the export of fanatic and extremist ideologies into their own territories.

4.2 The Unsafe Game of Mesopotamia

4.2.1 A Prelude to the Iraq War

It is practically useful to reflect in the remaining sections of this chapter upon the overall political atmosphere that moulded the Iraq War in order to get a better grasp of the manoeuvres that characterized the parlance of Tony Blair. It would also enable us to trace the direct as well as the less stated ideological inclinations and preferred war narratives that the broadsheets endorsed in their coverage. Particular attention, therefore, will be paid in addressing the crowded period of events that preceded the onset of the war. Thus, a sweeping analysis, with little judgements if any, of the main arguments and counter-arguments of the Iraqi crisis will be displayed to set the floor for the later detailed analysis of those themes in the corpus.

It is worth mentioning in passing that unlike the other allied states, Britain had a long historical record of direct intervention in the affairs of Iraq, both military and political. To some degree, the 2003 invasion is very reminiscent of Britain's first steps in the country during the so-called Mesopotamian Campaign of 1914. There was an array of highly intertwined factors that hastened the military action against Iraq. Whilst the coalition forces made the removal of Saddam as their main target goal, there have been slightly different modes of interpretation between London and Washington as far as the nature and scope of this controversial military engagement. The most disturbing issue was the fact that the decision of full-scale invasion was unilaterally decided by Bush's administration and its allies, most importantly Blair's inner circle, as an alternative to the containment policy.

The threat of Iraq's assumed WMD was the main argument of Blair, which he kept insisting on during his war campaign. Saddam was also accused of harbouring terrorists and attempting to transfer nuclear technology to Al-Qaeda. Regime change as such, Patrick Thornberry clarifies, "has been formally denied as a justification for the action, at least by the UK". Tony Blair asserted before the UK House of Commons on 18 March 2003 that "I have never put the justification as regime change" (Danchev & MacMillan, 2005, p. 120). However, the Bush administration was determined to exterminate the rule of Saddam and the dominance of the Ba'ath party, without the back-up of international institutions.[5]

Saddam's controversial relationship with key Western powers, on the one hand, and his unpredicted and usually hostile moves against Iraq's neighbours, on the other hand, were enveloped in great obscurity. With the end of the Iran-Iraq strife by the 1990s, the legacy of Saddam as a pitiless dictator, during more than one decade of oppressive rule as the fifth president of Iraq, came suddenly to the surface in the British media. The antiquated Orientalist stereotypes of the Middle East despots were very ubiquitous in the characterization of Saddam Hussein. He was repeatedly accused of violations of human rights through the use of poison gas and chemical weapons against his own people, yet this was totally denied and refuted during his trial. One should keep in mind that Saddam was not the only dictator in those days; however, the obsession of the British and American media with his position was salient and the threat he posed to world peace was, most of the time, highly exaggerated.

As the military option became more pronounced, a number of arguments were put forward by Blair and the neoconservatives in the USA which highly exaggerated the threat posed by the Iraqi regime on Western security and world peace in general. Since the end of war, it has become clear that Saddam's acquisition of advanced WMD technology and his alleged collaboration with the Al-Qaeda and other anti-Western terror organizations were mere false allegations. Paradoxically, however, the aggression on Iraq was framed as a humanitarian mission to liberate an oppressed nation from the despotism and tyranny of Saddam. Following the military assault of 2003, Iraq went through a long period of political, economic and security instability, which is likely to last for years to come.

An alternative interpretation—and perhaps the more important one—was the geostrategic and economic position of Iraq as a rich oil reservoir, which was largely perceived to be at the core motivation of the war. Iraq is a "swing" major oil producer with an enormous reserve capacity and a principal member in the Organization of the Petroleum Exporting Countries (OPEC). It was not, as Noam Chomsky put it, about having an access to Iraq's rich oil sources, but more essentially about controlling the oil industry (Chomsky & Barsamian, 2005, p. 6). At the same time, the overthrow of Saddam's government by force was listed as one of the major goals of the so-called War on Terror, at least by the Bush administration. The fight against worldwide networks of terrorist groups and organizations was formally shaped as one of the priorities in the US neo-conservative ideological agenda in the wake of the 9/11 assault.

Following its invasion of neighbouring Kuwait in the early 1990, Iraq was put under siege for more than 12 years. The embargo had severely damaged the economy and created a human crisis. By 2003 Iraq was already in ruin. As the Allied forces headed towards Baghdad through the Iraqi desert, they faced little resistance from the official Iraqi army. In the battle field, there had been a remarkable absence of the huge military members. The street fights and gang-like attacks against the allied forces after the occupation were mostly done by Ba'ath members and Saddam's Fedayeen force.

There was in fact a strong public opposition to the US-led invasion once the war decision was made in Britain and elsewhere. Nevertheless, the anti-war campaign started to fade away when the coalition forces started air strikes on Baghdad. Regular mass demonstrations of protest occupied the streets of big cities throughout the world, including London, particularly in February 2003. The public opinion, which was obviously against the assault on Iraq, put some pressure on the war campaigners, who relied on the support of the mass media outlets to silence opposition. Furthermore, many British politicians voiced their resentment about New Labour's unconditioned support of the US neoconservative and caused much frustration for Blair, who threatened to resign.

As the events proceeded apace, there has been a change in public's opinion.[6] An interesting question to be asked here is as follows: What makes people shift their attitudes towards an issue when they already held strong stance for or against it? This question is fundamental to the argument pursued here and in assessing the ways in which manipulation in discourse takes place at the level of what is called by sociologists "the social mind". The US media was perhaps more propagandistic in its coverage of the Iraqi dossier and thus the public opposition was less fierce. In terms of ideological attitudes, Al-Qaeda's fanatic pseudo-religious inspirations were in direct opposition to the Ba'athist ideology, which was ethnically based and secular, and therefore, the supposed link between the two, that is, Saddam and Al-Qaeda, is not grounded on any logical argument.

Although there has been a wide public discontent about the war, the US-led coalition launched its offence against Iraq on the 19th of March, without the authorization of the UNSC. Major military operations were officially ended up on the 1st of May by former US president George Bush from aboard a warship. The armed clash between the Iraqis and the Allied forces continued for several years and created a state of uncertainty about the future of the country. As expected, after more than one decade from the end of the war, the sectarian division threatens not only Iraq, but the whole Middle East, especially with the dramatic upheaval in Syria, which added another serious climax to the scene.

It was ostensible that the UNSC made strenuous efforts to settle the Iraq problem, but its role as an international institution was very limited in effect. The inability to implement the UN recommendations left profound negative implications and raised questions about the nature of the new world order where unilateralism has dismissed the multilateral grounding of decision-making upon which the legitimacy of the UN is founded. Ostensibly, the lack of consensus over the crisis of Iraq has never been a question of lacunae in law-making, but is attributed much more to the influence of the Great Powers in the Council to legalize their actions through international institutions. In the light of such obscurity about the bond between the members of the UN and the rationale over policy-making and enforcement, the UN might need much time and refinement to rehabilitate its image.

4.2.2 The Story of Iraq's Weapons of Mass Destruction

To better understand the motives behind Britain's determination to play such an essential role in the war campaign, one might reflect on a matrix of complex themes in politics, economy, ethics and, even arguably, religion. Throughout this succinct section, which is devoted solely to the question of Iraq's assumed WMD, I seek precisely to narrate the real story of Iraq's nuclear projects and their development, and to comment on the British obsession and often-hostile reaction to the armament of Iraq during Saddam's rule. How realistic is it to speak of advanced nuclear weapons projects in Iraq, particularly after the devastating eight-year-long conflict with Iran that came to close in 1988? In fact, the issue of nuclear technology is worth explaining in details due to its seminal importance at different levels. First, Saddam's determination to acquire WMD was ostensibly the chief reason and justification of the invasion, at least from the official British point of view. Second, the debate on this topic will also provide the necessary background to exhibit the controversy, and sometimes inconsistency, that might arise from the use of technical terms when referring to those weapons in diplomacy and political discourse. Third, a glimpse of the international conventions with regard to WMD fabrication, development and usage will shed some light on the legal perspective of the issue.

Broadly speaking, the label WMD stands for one of the following types of conventional and non-conventional arms: the nuclear and atomic bombs, chemical weapons (poisonous products with varying genres of toxic materials), the biological weapons (bacteriological products) and, finally, radiological weapons. What do they all have in common is the fact that they can wreak instant mass casualties and long-lasting damage. The facilities and delivery utilities through which those weapons can potentially reach distant locations, such as missiles and rockets, are by consequence prohibited. The containment of the property and use of atomic technology in warfare via international institutions was first recommended in the "Declaration on Atomic Bomb" issued on 15 November 1945 by Britain, Canada and the USA (Hashmi & Lee, 2004, p. 16).

However, the sanctions and restrictions made on the use of conventional chemical and biological arms can be traced back to the Geneva Protocol of 1925 (Graham & LaVera, 2003, p. 7). Once introduced, the meaning of the label WMD was open to contestation and, in the course of time, received much varying interpretations and disagreement. Whilst a number of states, notably the former Soviet Union and key Western powers, did approve the treaties proposed on the reduction of armament, they did not fully abide by their propositions. The term "WMD" is still used to denote a wide range of explosives that would possibly include other types of weaponry, especially with the rapid advance in war technology and nuclear engineering in particular.[7]

From a legal perspective, there had been many treaties and conventions that sought, with varying degrees and conditions, to curb the proliferation and block the property of nuclear and biological war technology. This was managed through numerous bilateral and multilateral negotiations and settlements on arms trade under the care of international institutions. Notwithstanding the progress made since the Second World War till date to thwart the widespread circulation of lethal arms, there has always been a lack of consensus. A number of problematic issues are, practically speaking, inherent in the incomplete and vague definition used to denote these weapons, and the contention about whether they are intended for defence or aggressive purposes, which bring us to the question of who owns the right and who does not?

The ideological fissure and undeclared struggle between the major players in world politics might be another underlying watershed in the question of WMD, since most of the states that ratified or approved the treaties to ban the use of WMD still have large supplies that seriously put world peace in danger.

Indeed, the international concern about the proliferation of WMD facilities dates back to the Second World War, following the indiscriminate and catastrophic devastation of Nagasaki and Hiroshima by the USA. In the few years to come many countries were highly motivated to acquire the tools of mass destruction for deterrence, offensive or defensive purposes. In the context of the Iraq War, a cluster of other types of biological, chemical and poisonous arms that inflict destruction at a large scale were already added on the prohibition list. In the wake of the

Iran-Iraq War and the subsequent withdrawal of Iraq's forces from Kuwait, the disarmament of Iraq from its chemical and biological weapons was the focus of an active diplomacy in the corridors of the UN. Lifting the then economic sanctions imposed was conditioned with Iraq's complete and unconditional compliance with UN recommendations to abandon its chemical and biological weapons stockpile.[8] It is worth remembering that the preoccupation with the development and use of those weapons by the Ba'ath regime was not deliberately expressed during the enduring conflict with Iran that resulted in huge human loss due to the use of biological arms.

It was assumed that Iraq under the Ba'ath regime had been looking for the development of nuclear energy facilities from the late 1950s onwards and was about to have nuclear weapons by the 1980s, yet its programmes were very limited in motion (Hashmi & Lee 2004, p. 321). Thus, within the turbulent atmosphere of the Cold War, the course of armament was in its peak, not only amongst the Great Powers, but also for the smaller states, which, regardless of their communist or liberal Western ideological affiliations, sought to have their share of the advanced warfare utilities. Iraq was not an exception—under the oppressive dictatorship of the Ba'ath, which had an expansionist ideology, there had been a dynamic weaponization and the armament activity was given a high priority in their political agenda.

Notwithstanding the ideological fissure between the former Soviet Union and the Western powers in general, the two blocs showed a mutual concern over the necessity to inhibit their enemies and allies alike to acquire the essential tools of nuclear technology. Edward Spiers suggested that "the negotiation of the Non-Proliferation Treaty (NPT) in 1968 and its entry into force in 1970 established an international norm against the wider dissemination of nuclear weapons" (2000, p. 9). Although the treaty came under criticism, other updates and further additional restrictions followed during the years to come, bringing more members to approve it. It could be said that the active diplomatic and intelligence endeavours to contain the widespread of WMD and its related facilities did not succeed in effectively halting the clandestine trade of those weapons. This is best exemplified in the case of Pakistan and India, which successfully escaped the international pressure and economic blockade that Iraq suffered from for more than a decade. Iraq, amongst many other states, embarked in secret programmes for the production and development of a wide range of chemical and biological weapons. The early suspicions about Iraq's plans to develop nuclear weapons were announced in March 1986 by the then UN Secretary-General Javier Perez de Cuellar, who deliberately accused Iraq of using chemical weapons during the Iran–Iraq War (Pearson, 2005, pp. 19–20). There was no doubt about Saddam's penchant for WMD, yet there was no ample evidence or signs of an advanced nuclear programme.

Saddam Hussein used to be a close ally to the USA and Britain, especially after the downfall of the Shah of Iran in the wake of Ayatollah Khomeini's revolution. This revolutionary adventurism in Iran coincided with Saddam Hussein's seizure of power in Iraq. Obviously, Saddam's secular and pan-Arabism ideology was in sharp contrast to its neighbouring newborn Iranian Shi'ite-based state, a clash in ideology which afterwards would contribute to an eight-year destructive warfare, starting from 1980. With the end of the conflict, Saddam's honeymoon with the Western powers came to its final stage, especially after his unexpected military aggression against Kuwait in August 1990 following some territory- and oil policy–related disputes with the Kuwaiti ruling class. The subsequent Iraq's occupation of Kuwait brought a wide international condemnation and had lasting negative repercussions displayed in the immediate economic and military blockade issued by the UNSC. Furthermore, the purpose of the policy of containment against Iraq was to subdue Saddam Hussein to an unconditioned and full compliance with UN inspections investigating Iraq's nuclear constructions, and its probable possession of WMD.

The official authorization of investigation on the Iraqi territory started shortly after the end of Iraq's occupation of Kuwait, which came under the pressure of the US-led coalition. By now, the UN had set up a special commission (United Nations Special Commission, UNSCOM) to investigate Iraq's programmes in the production of WMD. The commission recommended that Iraq "unconditionally not to acquire or develop nuclear weapons or nuclear-weapons-usable material or any subsystems, components or any research, development, support or manufacturing facilities" (Tolfree, 2016, p. 59).[9] It should be mentioned that the task of conducting a search for weapons was an intricate one that was not solely related to the track of facilities and plants, but also concerned with the identification of a huge amount of chemical products and biological agents. Those agents can be used in non-military fields, notably in medicine and agriculture, and might possibly be suspected to be in employed in developing lethal chemical weapons as well. Another obstacle that hobbled the progress of investigation was the near-complete absence of trust between Iraqi leadership and the assigned investigation personnel. The working teams were usually accused of spying to the US intelligence and therefore were given limited and restricted access to many sites, which further delayed the inspection timetable. Iraq complained particularly about UNSCOM chief inspector Scott Ritter, who did not follow the requirements set by the UN. After his resignation, Scott himself declared "in writing that the United States had placed CIA agents in UNSCOM" (Krasno & Sutterlin, 2003, p. 102).

A few months prior to the war of 2003, the UN inspectors working under the United Nations Monitoring, Verification, and Inspection Commission (UNMOVIC) affirmed the absence of any programme of weaponization on the Iraqi territory. From an Anglo-American standpoint, the non-compliance of Iraq with the UN resolution 1441 was sufficient to engage in a whole-scale military assault. Yet, it has to be emphasized that there had been no official UN authorization to use force by the majority of the members, which made the act of war illegal. Though Iraq was by now labelled as a part of the so-called Axis of Evil by American President George W. Bush, the inspectors resumed their work and made agreements with the Iraqis. However, the investigation work had come to an end, opening the way for the air strikes against Iraq on the 19th of March. Following the invasion, new military teams were assigned the specific mission of searching the stockpile of weapons over the country. Failure of US and British intelligence, which supplied inaccurate and flawed information, brought unrelenting critique at a time when weapons were never found.

The assault on Iraq had left an immense impact on world politics and reflected the deep structural changes in the world of today. At the institutional level, it posed a serious question about the credibility of the UN as a world peacekeeper and international organizational body that is potentially able to enforce its recommendations and resolutions through consensus. Indeed, this was the very same question that had already been raised about the significance of the League of Nations at the end of the Second World War. One recent particular problem is the Syrian crisis, which adds another major setback in the performance of the UN, at least at the humanitarian level.

With the pyrrhic victory over Saddam's Iraq, the country descended into a period of political corruption and sectarianism, which might lead to another protracted phase of violence and ferment. The eclectic benchmark in imposing laws was also another watershed in the profile of the UN vis-à-vis the containment of WMD, as was best seen again in the Syrian case. As it has been made clear, neither nuclear weapons nor chemical and biological arsenals were found. Therefore, the reports about Iraq's nuclear capabilities were, most of the time, exaggerated and used as political utility to legitimate the invasion of Iraq. The economic blockade, the no-fly zone and the frequent aerial bombardments had hampered Saddam's efforts, if any, to re-embark in nuclear weapons construction. One might ponder whether those who still acquire and develop much more destructive weapons might not be themselves another serious threat to international peace and stability in the future.

In brief, the engagement of imperial Britain in the Middle East affairs during the First World War was, without doubt, a turning point in the history of the region which left a peculiar and far-reaching impact on Iraq. It was ostensible, after all, that the Western democratic values have never been fully integrated into the intricate cultural affiliations of the Iraqi society, which date back hundreds of years ago, where the past is still very present in the conscious of the people. The commitment to democratic institutions gained relative subordination by the locals in proportion to the tribal and religious allegiances upon which the legitimacy of the social institutions is based on. Lastly but most importantly, the invasion shook off the balance of power, paving the way for the emergence of various militia groups and mafia. Hence, in the grip of sectarian violence and as tension mount up within the Sunni and Shi'a communities, prospects of a regional war that far exceeds the territory of Iraq are in the horizon.

Notes

1. For a detailed analysis on the British public reaction to the war and the factors influencing the public opinion, see Clarke, Sanders, Stewart, and Whiteley (2009).
2. For more details about the administrative organization of Iraq and the reforms implemented by the Ottoman governors, see Ceylan (2011).
3. The British pledges were overturned in the secret arrangements to divide the Middle East with France into the sphere of influence. The negotiations were collectively known as the Sykes–Picot Agreement, which was a serious blow to the inhabitants of the region, since the British pragmatic calculations did not take into account the interests of the locals.
4. Unlike what was anticipated from the Arab nationalists who fought with the Allied powers, Iraq was put under the British mandate by the League of Nations, including Jordan and Palestine, in the Paris Peace Conference held in 1919. This mandate was reaffirmed on the 25th of April at the San Remo Conference held in Italy and was ratified many times. See Ghareeb (2004).
5. The goal of regime change was made clear in a document under the title "Rebuilding America's Defenses: Strategies, Forces, and Resources for a New Century" in September 2000.
6. See, for example, the surveys and polls of *The Guardian*: "Guardian Opinion Poll – Fieldwork: March 14th–16th 2003," March 2003 http://image.guardian.co.uk/sysfiles/Politics/documents/2003/03/18/17303ICM_poll.pdf
7. For further information about the term and its alternative uses as well as international conventions and treaties of disarmament, see Carus (2004).
8. The UN economic sanctions against Iraq were put into effect from 6 August 1990 due to its invasion of neighbouring Kuwait. For further details, see Freedman (1993).
9. See also the UN Security Council Resolution 687, adopted on 3 April 1991.

References

Aboul-Enein, Y. H. (2012). *Iraq in turmoil: Historical perspectives of Dr. Ali Al-Wardi, from the Ottoman Empire to King Feisal*. Annapolis, MD: Naval Institute Press.

Allawi, A. (2007). *The occupation of Iraq: Winning the war, losing the peace*. New Haven, CT: Yale University Press.

Anderson, L., & Stansfield, G. (2004). *The future of Iraq: Dictatorship, democracy, or division?* New York: Palgrave Macmillan.

Barker, A. J. (2009). *The first Iraq War 1914–1918: Britain's Mesopotamian campaign.* New York: Enigma Books.

Bodansky, Y. (2004). *The secret history of the Iraq War.* New York: Harper Collins Publishers, Inc.

Carus, W. S. (2004). *Defining weapons of mass destruction.* Centre for the Study of Weapons of Mass Destruction, pp. 1–49. Occasional paper 4. Washington, DC: National Defense University Press.

Ceylan, E. (2011). *The Ottoman origins of modern Iraq: Political reform, modernization and development in the nineteenth century Middle East.* London: I. B. Tauris.

Chomsky, N., & Barsamian, D. (2005). *Imperial ambitions: Conversations on the post-9/11 world.* New York: Metropolitan Books.

Clarke, H., Sanders, D., Stewart, M. C., & Whiteley, P. F. (2009). *Performance politics and the British voter.* Cambridge, UK: Cambridge University Press.

Danchev, A., & MacMillan, J. (Eds.). (2005). *The Iraq War and democratic politics.* London: Routledge.

Dodge, T. (2006). *The British mandate in Iraq, 1920–1932, The Middle East online series 2: Iraq 1914–1974.* Reading, UK: Thomson Learning EMEA Ltd.

Freedman, R. O. (Ed.). (1993). *The Middle East after Iraq's invasion of Kuwait.* Gainesville, FL: University Press of Florida.

Ghareeb, E. (2004). *Historical dictionary of Iraq.* Lanham, MD: Scarecrow Press.

Graham, T., & LaVera, D. J. (2003). *Cornerstones of security: Arms control treaties in the nuclear era.* Seattle, WA: University of Washington Press.

Hashmi, S. H., & Lee, S. P. (Eds.). (2004). *Ethics and weapons of mass destruction: Religious and secular perspectives.* Cambridge, UK: Cambridge University Press.

Hunt, C. (2005). *The history of Iraq.* Westport, CT: Greenwood Publishing Group.

Krasno, J., & Sutterlin, J. S. (2003). *The United Nations and Iraq: Defanging the viper.* Westport, CT: Greenwood Publishing Group.

Malone, D. M. (2006). *The international struggle over Iraq: Politics in the UN Security Council 1980–2005.* Oxford, UK: Oxford University Press.

Pearson, G. S. (2005). *The search for Iraq's weapons of mass destruction: Inspection, verification and non-proliferation.* New York: Palgrave Macmillan.

Sassoon, J. (2012). *Saddam Hussein's Ba'ath Party: Inside an authoritarian regime.* Cambridge, UK: Cambridge University Press.

Simon, R. S. (2013). *Iraq between the two world wars: The militarist origins of tyranny.* New York: Colombia University Press.

Simon, R. S., & Tejirian, E. H. (Eds.). (2004). *The creation of Iraq, 1914–192.* New York: Columbia University Press.

Sluglett, P. (2007). *Britain in Iraq: Contriving king and country.* London: I. B. Tauris.

Spiers, E. M. (2000). *Weapons of mass destruction: Prospects for proliferation.* London: Macmillan.

Telhami, S., & Barnett, M. (Eds.). (2002). *Identity and foreign policy in the Middle East.* Ithaca, NY: Cornell University Press.

Tolfree, D. (2016). *The Iraq betrayals.* Leicester: Troubador Publishing Ltd.

Tripp, C. (2002). *A history of Iraq.* Cambridge, UK: Cambridge University Press.

Wagner, H. L. (2009). *Iraq: Creation of the modern Middle East.* New York: Infobase Publishing.

5

Blair's Foreign Policy Discourse on Iraq

5.1 Humanitarianism in Blair's Discourse

5.1.1 A Note on Political Discourse Analysis (PDA)

It is noteworthy to stress again that my goal at this stage is to better fathom how Blair managed to justify his aggressive policy towards an old ally to Britain, and to the West in general, in the Middle East. One part of the answer lies in the new "ethical" doctrine of New Labour and the political swing of 1997 that displaced a party that grew out of a left ideology to stand in the centre of British politics. Arguably, this would help to uncover the underlying logic upon which the military interventionist policy of New Labour, as a whole, was established. The analysis of this type of discourse is carried out through a meticulous examination of a complex composite of discursive practices in the "political" language of the ex-Prime Minister which were, as I advocate, simultaneously intermingled with a spectrum of ideological bearings far from being ethically oriented.

Accordingly, ideology analysis at this level revolves first around the quest to expose the grassroots of Blair's strategy of legitimization which lay special emphasis on the notions of "values", "humanitarianism" and "ethics" that featured in UK's foreign policy under New Labour. Hence, the question that poses itself here is, to what extent was the Labour Party committed to its ethical doctrine in the case of Iraq? This somehow naive question requires one to pry away the context of the Iraq War itself, and to focus narrowly upon the new vocabulary begotten by Blair which, in fact, heralded the profound change that eventually occurred in the ideology of the traditionally leftist party. In his speech "Mission Statement for the Foreign and Commonwealth Office", Labour's Foreign Secretary Robin Finlayson Cook declared:

> Our foreign policy must have an ethical dimension and must support the demands of other peoples for the democratic rights on which we insist for ourselves. The Labour Government will put human rights at the heart of our foreign policy and will publish an annual report on our work in promoting human rights abroad. (Cook, 1997)

Given this framework, the frequent reference made to morality, and the other specific shades of meanings associated with it, was not random or accidental. It will be demonstrated by the quantitative output by the end of this chapter that the ethical dimension was amongst the most silent thematic categories which anchored New Labour's political philosophy, and by extension Blair's ideological outlook. Blair did not seem too far off from Robin Cook, as he was keenly assiduous to introduce new wording to the party's rhetoric to highlight the ethical dimension, if with less clarity, and put the concept of human "values" in the centre of this doctrine. In his "acceptance speech" in 1997, Blair gave a brief talk to an audience in Downing Street where he defined the "values" that would guide the actions of his government as follows:

> It shall be a government rooted in strong values, the values of justice and progress and community, the values that have guided me all my political life. But a government ready with the courage to embrace the new ideas necessary to make those values live again for today's world – a government of practical measures in pursuit of noble causes. That is our objective for the people of Britain. (Blair, 1997)

Such morally based argumentation was often exploited to assert an aggressive interventionist policy that would not otherwise be justified. Yet this, at the same time, threw the burden of proof on the proponents of morality and humanitarian militarism, as many critics come close to arguing.

Although Blair's constant appeal to humanitarianism to normalize military intervention overseas was perhaps less disputed in some other cases of conflict, such as Kosovo in 1999, where Britain was a major player, it was not a persuasive explanation for the occupation of Iraq in 2003. I attempt to approach this controversial theme through the analysis of the semantic and lexical structures in Blair's political speeches, some of these did not explicitly address the issue of Iraq. My premise here is that Blair fails to particularly specify the meaning of "values" in the context of foreign policy, as it was expressed inconsistently and flagrantly tied up with national interests. Accordingly, it is intended through the multi-faceted language analysis of the CPS to reflect, in particular, on the three major claims that were made by Blair to legitimate the "illegitimate" military onslaught on Iraq.

First, I comment on Blair's appeal to ethics and morality to justify the war cause, which, as just mentioned, was one of the basic tenets of New Labour's foreign policy, and perhaps all the more ironic. What requires some scrutiny in this respect is the conceptualization of the doctrine of "humanitarian militarism" and the highly contentious vocabulary associated with it, which constructed the military strike as a humanitarian act to liberate an oppressed nation. Second, the issue of international terrorism was another central theme, notably the allegations about Saddam's cooperation with international networks of terror. Third, and closely related to this, was Iraq's assumed breach of the UN conventions by its acquisition of prohibited WMD. This claim demands likewise some elucidation due to the inherent ambiguity of the phrase "weapons of mass destruction", at least in this case. One has to keep in mind that the WMD frame was Blair's most-voiced argument during the build-up to the war, which turned out to be false in the aftermath. A historical account on the issue of WMD has already been given in the previous chapter. Once again, this sensitive point should be examined a little bit more closely by demonstrating how it was exploited to create a crisis and wrongly represented as an imminent threat to world peace and stability that necessitated an urgent solution.

However, before doing so, there is a need to further expound the theoretical framework, and at the same time identify the nature of "political discourse" and neatly delimit what is meant exactly by "political discourse analysis" (abbreviated henceforth as PDA) in the emerging discipline of Discourse Studies. The closing part of this chapter is devoted to an exhaustive quantitative description and analysis of the CPS. The output resulted from the treatment of the corpus is compared against the qualitative interpretation, and likewise against the news corpora at a later stage.

At this level, it is worth noting that the type of political discourse addressed in this chapter is produced in a democratic environment in one of the leading Western countries whose mature democratic political institutions evolved at least in the last 400 years or so. Despite the controversies that are sometimes obvious and striking in Blair's discourse, I shall not consider the ideological reasoning of the Prime Minister in isolation from the overall political landscape in Britain. That is to say, Blair is, pragmatically speaking, a participant and political actor who is effectively engaged in an intricate political process that is being fabricated under the influence of multiple socio-political and cultural conditions. In essence, he designs the local and foreign policies of Britain from his position as the Prime Minister, representing the supreme political force, but not the only one, that determines the final say about a major event such as declaring war against another sovereign country.[1]

From the time of Sir Robert Walpole, London placed greater weight on an imperial policy to stretch its influence and physical territory across the globe. As for the Middle East, the early roots of British interventionism, particularly its well-established ties with the Gulf States, date back to the beginning of the twentieth century. An overview about the British political mindset is quite important to the context of this case study; however, I do not intend here to trace the evolution of the British political thought and philosophy due to space limit.

Amongst the most important ingredients in the discourse of politics, which is quite at the core of this research, is the concept of power and how it is expressed in language, that is, the power to maintain or challenge people's attitudes and beliefs, to control decision-making and exert an influence on the political elite and public discourse so as to transform specific ideological convictions into a real political behaviour. Critical PDA, in Van Dijk words, "deals especially with the reproduction of political *power, power abuse* or *domination* through political discourse, including the various forms of resistance or counter-power against such forms of discursive dominance" (1997, p. 11).

Despite the terminological flexibility that encrusted the word "politics", a simple comment on its usage and derivatives is essential at this point. Indeed, politics, as a natural human activity in its most simplistic forms, has accompanied the earliest urbanized societies that emerged first on the shores of the Tigris and Euphrates. For quite a long time, the word "politics" was used to designate a variety of collective human behaviours and activities that would ultimately determine, among many different things, the ideological, institutional, legal, and social identity of a group of people. The British jurist Edward Jenks takes the term to simply mean the "business of *government*: that is to say, the control and management of people living together in a *society*" (1900, p. 1). In the Western tradition, the earliest records of the term date back to the ancient Greek period. Particular reference is usually attributed to the contributions of prominent Greek political philosophers and intellectuals, such as Aristotle's landmark book *Politics* and Plato's *Republic*. The *polis*, citizenship, justice, law and the ideal form of government were amongst the frequently debated subjects in the philosophical writings of the ancient Greek intellectuals.

Put succinctly, then as now, the practice of politics is a social act that results from the interaction of individuals within the community that they identify themselves with in negotiating notions of power, authority, social order and good governance. The contemporary doctrines of liberalism, socialism, communism and the like could all be seen, to a greater or a lesser degree, as idiosyncratic understandings of the political "state of affairs" for different social groupings across various geographical spaces. The progression of such political preferences, which are inexorably informed by relativist philosophical and cultural strands, had been moulded by a long, complicated political process that is continuously supported by consensus, coercion or both. Language in this respect is the driving force for ideological domination and hegemony. In contemporary liberal democracies, for example, the pursuit of political power requires, at least, a substantial engagement with and influence on the public sphere via a convenient usage of language and the mastery of the art of rhetoric and persuasion. As Paul Chilton put it, "[P]olitical activity does not exist without the use of language. It is true that the other behaviours are involved: for instance, physical violence. But the doing of politics is predominantly constituted in language" (2004, p. 6).

It is a truism that the subtle use of language is the most effective means by which political beliefs, opinions and ideologies would gain social consensus and, ultimately, institutionalization. Political actors recognize the strong interplay between language and politics to get a minimum consent of a specific group or community without resorting to physical coercion and violence, especially insofar as those issues tend to be conflicting by their nature. Whilst many political leaders have failed to maintain the circulation of their own worldviews for long, others have been able to extend their political influence for decades across the economic, social and cultural spectrum. What might perhaps look like a privilege for politicians is the fact that they often back up their claims and arguments by references to philosophy, theology and economy without being necessarily experts or specialists in these fields. Accordingly, the discursive manner in exploiting such sources would potentially enable them to legitimate and justify their ideologically based views and convictions.

Though the concept of discourse has already been conceptualized in the second chapter, with an emphasis on its social nature, yet highlighting at the same time its multiple associative connotations and ambiguities, the term "political" adds another layer of complexity. This is so because the type of discourse that is *political*, as is the case for Blair's speeches addressed here, is overtly biased and skewed in its ideological slant.

In very broad terms, political discourse can be defined as "a complex study of human activity" (Chilton & Schäffner, 2002, p. 207). But it is quite distinct from the other genres of discourse by its overall semantic structure, stylistic features and objectives, which are intended to have an effect on the political behaviour of, generally speaking, a mass audience, as Norman Fairclough clarifies: "[A] political discourse is also working to persuade people […] as soon as political discourse goes public, it is rhetorically constructed, part of political performance" (2000, pp. 86–87). John Wilson explains that political discourse considers both the formal and informal contexts and political actors; that is, it "is suggestive of at least two possibilities: first, a discourse which is itself political; and second, an analysis of political discourse as simply an example discourse type, without explicit reference to political content or political context" (Tannen, Schiffrin, & Hamilton, 2001, p. 398). Van Dijk adds "political discourse is identified by its *actors* or *authors, viz., politician*" (1997, p. 12).

Unlike the other genres of discourse and perhaps much more than any other form of communication, political discourse is often biased and ideologically charged in more or less explicit manner. A commonplace feature in political speeches is the fact that they are overwhelmingly condensed, with multiple references to a variety of sources. They are also rich of metaphoric expressions, vocabulary of extreme bias, mockery, stereotypes, satirical jibes and, perhaps, scarcely straightforward abusive and xenophobic expressions which are used compactly to frame a given situation. Yet this is the exception rather than the norm, especially in the formal political speeches of high-rank politicians. Therefore, the analysis of this type of discourse is essentially a judgement of an already existing paradox. In mundane terms, the goal of PDA, just like the other disciplines concerned with the critique of discourse, is to disclose, at various levels, the ideological reasoning of those who speak or write and to examine how they exploit the potential of language to construct specific representations of events and manipulate the audience for the sake of achieving their own political aims.

The political discourse under study revolves around legitimating a scratched reality to promote the pro-war ideology, whose proponents needed much political skills and a good sense of persuasion. One has to keep in mind that Blair's views about the war are not only personal, but also representative of the party he belongs to, New Labour's ideology in general, though there a growing chasm has been noticed within the party over the policy on Iraq.[2] It must be emphasized again and with clarity that the study of political discourse as a genre of discourse, not as an isolated text that is loaded with political preferences, is the main concern of this chapter. Technically speaking, this entails the consideration, through meticulous macro- and microstrategies of analysis, of the medium of the political message, that is, the use of language to deliver specific embedded messages to the audience.

5.1.2 "One-Half Trojan Horse": *Jus ad Bellum* and Humanitarian Militarism

There can be no doubt that the rapidly unfolding structural changes in today's globalized world have brought new challenges to policy decision-making processes, both at the local and international levels, that have made physical territories and political boundaries practically meaningless. With the inevitable disintegration of the Westphalian nation-state spirit, one would ponder whether this motion of change is a positive progressive stride towards mutual cooperation or just another phase of neo-imperialism, where major centres of power struggle to sustain the subordination of peripheral entities. One of the manifestations of this new condition can be projected in the military interventions that occurred recently in a few disturbed regions in the world, as is the case for Iraq. What is relevant here is the legal and ethical backgrounds upon which the world's powerful players rely to legitimate interventionary practices against, mostly, the less powerful states.[3] Particularly, there is a need to elucidate on the argument of foreign intervention to thwart mass atrocities and heinous derogation of human rights, which is still a highly contested and controversial subject.

It has been noticed that over the last few years, international consensus over military intervention faltered in some unstable regions which undergo acute human crisis, best incarnated in the recent Syrian crisis, which shows a considerable lacunae and obscurity over the politics of intervention. In principle, the legitimacy of the right to intervene via international apparatuses is usually rationalized in terms of moral and ethical, rather than political or economic self-interest, calculations. This seems very a general and, perhaps, vague statement which must lead one to dig into the morality of the warfare and peacekeeping philosophy, law and politics. After all, what looks paradoxical, however, is that waging a war is per se a blatant breach to the human rights, since it would engender, by no means, all sorts of crimes amidst the chaos and hostile environment it eventually creates.

It might be necessary to sketch out the theories that addressed the philosophy of humanitarian war as to be able, at a later stage, to chart its narratives in Blair's discourse. Broadly speaking, humanitarianism is an umbrella term that encompasses various meanings and connotations which, all in all, centre on the necessity to stop, or at least alleviate, damage to the well-being and dignity of human beings. Indeed, improving the human condition and the welfare of mankind regardless of the geographical space or political circumstances has been a noble goal for many international and non-governmental organizations. Yet humanitarianism, as a political concept, is not a recent phenomenon, but has gradually developed over centuries and is heavily moulded by the late imperial, postcolonial and, finally, liberal tendencies to form what Michael Barnett calls the "empire of humanity" (2011, p. 29).

Frank T. Carlton writes: "Humanitarianism is the natural fruit of a condition of social flux and unrest. It arises in a complex society when the lower classes are struggling for better conditions; and when older dominating interests are being thrust aside by new rivals" (1906, p. 48). Whilst Carlton prioritized the economic factor, other subsequent scholars during the twentieth century incorporated other social, cultural and political demands, particularly with respect to civil liberties and political participation, which were seen as indefeasible rights in the general democratization movement.

The idealistic philosophy of philanthropy and voluntary benevolence can be found in the ancient Asian philosophies of Buddhism, Confucianism, the Abrahamic religions and the like. With respect to the Western world, it is difficult to precisely identify a specific date when humanitarianism, as is used in today's context, emerged. Yet scholars do often refer to the nineteenth-century humanists and philosophers, notably Bertrand Russell, Pierre Leroux and Auguste Comte (see Comte, 1853). The movement was, in part, the offspring of the secular Renaissance Age, which transformed the attention from divine mercy to human beings' ability and thus responsibility for the promotion of altruistic deeds. However, the most disturbing dilemma about humanitarianism is its intersection with politics.

The use of military force for humanitarian purposes, usually nicknamed as "humanitarian war", is one of the perplexing preoccupations of contemporary international politics, as it permits a foreign intervention against the physical integrity and sovereignty of other nations, and as a matter of fact, it breaches the very same ideal that it seeks to preserve. The decision-making process of such interventionist policies is usually monitored by the powerful (Western) states, which assume for themselves, in the words of the British sociologist Keith Tester, "the weight of moral superiority". This is so, she continues to argue, because "Western metropolitan centers (and therefore media centers) are postimperial nodal points in global flaws and exchange" (2010, p. Viii). The historical roots of the concept of "humanitarian war" can be traced back to the traditional just war theory.[4] There is a plethora of books that debated this subject from the time of St. Augustine. Nevertheless, the question of what is and what is not humanitarian military intervention that is justified and wholly, or at least predominantly, acceptable remains highly contested. Answering such a simple, yet cornerstone, question is notoriously debatable, for it generates multiple interpretations at many different levels. Eric A. Heinze defines humanitarian military intervention as

> [t]he use of military force by a state or group of states in the jurisdiction of another state, without its permission, for the primary purpose of halting or averting egregious abuse of people within that state that is being perpetrated or facilitated by the de facto authorities of that state. (2009, p. 7)

To paraphrase Heinze's quotation, it becomes clear that the use of force does not necessarily require the authorization of international institutions, namely the UNSC decision might not be taken into account, which puts a question mark to the legal background of unauthorized military moves. One clear example is the intervention of the North Atlantic Treaty Organization (NATO) in the Kosovo crisis (1999) following the escalation of ethnic violence. Again, what is remarkable about the mentioned case is that it was not authorized by the UN following the veto of Russia and China, yet accounts of systematic mass ethnic cleansing, torture and rape at a large scale were well documented. Is the decision-making to intervene military conceived through the law, ethics or mere political juggling? There is still a lack of consensus on the very basic notions of ethics and law when war becomes the only viable action.

Paradoxically, humanitarianism itself poses another ethical problem when it comes to be exploited to intervene for the sake of preserving or promoting national interests of the elite states, which possess a juggernaut military potential, and also the ability to silence counter-discourse through the mass media outlets. Geostrategic calculations, ideological struggles over spheres of influence and other related issues are always put into account. Indeed, there will always be a definition problem of *humanitarian militarism* and whether it is justified in the first place. Unequivocally, the policy of interventionism under the cover of humanitarian aid and ethical responsibility to relieve a segment of population from the tyranny of abusive authorities, dictatorships, sectarian violence, militia groups and the like is still, to some extent, problematic. This paradox, as I argue, is best incarnated in the Iraq War. Despite some loopholes when it comes to the interpretation of the laws and resolutions of the UN and other international institutions, there is a clear prohibition on any unilateral action or military intervention without the approval of the UN even if it is for humanitarian purposes.

As far as Britain is concerned, New Labour's commitment to the rule of international law and institutions was reaffirmed several times by ex-Prime Minister Tony Blair. This commitment was materialized in Britain's active foreign diplomacy that backed up military intervention in various zone of conflict in Africa, Asia and Europe.[5] Under New Labour Britain embraced a more active interventionist strategy since its engagement in the Boar Wars in South Africa at the turn of the nineteenth century (Towle, 2009, p. 142). Humanitarian militarism was therefore among the policies that have been prioritized in the party's foreign policy. Noticeably, it was one of the salient features of Blair's discourse not solely vis-à-vis the Iraqi dossier, but was already set as one of the basic tenets of the party's ethical pillars in foreign affairs decision-making. This part of the chapter focuses precisely on the centrality of this theme in Blair's political agenda and, particularly, how the doctrine of humanitarianism was used to promote the war cause.

As previously noted, the idea of "humanitarian intervention" is not a recent phenomenon, nor has it been endorsed or interpreted in similar fashion by the influential powers in the modern era. Both at the level of theory and at the level of practice, there has been a remarkable ambiguity which enveloped the politics of military humanitarianism in relations to its institutional and legal basis. "It can be difficult to distinguish clearly between, for example, coercive diplomacy and 'gunboat diplomacy'; armed participation in foreign civil wars, revolts, revolutions, and insurgencies; and peace-keeping, peace-enforcement, and armed distribution of humanitarian aid" (Simms & Trim, 2011, p. 2). Nevertheless, the violation of "human rights" could be easily documented via the various media outlets and cannot be plausibly denied by the participants of warfare or conflict. Whilst aggression is not ethically acceptable, the systematic torture, enslavement and ethnic cleansing that still happen around the world in regular fashion could not be thwarted except through the resort to foreign military intervention headed by international organizations and institutions.

In sum, the debate on humanitarian military intervention in international politics raises many questions rather than providing solutions. What is a justifiable action of war will always be a controversial moral issue, except for self-defence against aggression. However, this does not entail that the action of war does not make the participants unaccountable for the crimes and atrocities that the intervention would necessary engender in the long term.

Military intervention, whether for safeguarding "human rights", battling dictatorships, self-defence or defending home abroad, is usually the last option left after all peaceful means are exhausted to settle a given problem. The policy of economic sanctions and blockade is also another alternative strategy already used in Iraq, which was arguably considered to be a lesser "evil" measure of pressure. The UN-imposed trade and financial sanctions on Iraq were the longest in proportion to other cases and caused a huge economic recession and an acute human crisis with the shortage of food and medicine. Philip Hammond (2007) argued that there was a serious "crisis of meaning" in the Western concept of humanitarian intervention that was used to justify military interventions during the 1990s. The inconsistency in the humanitarian discourse, as he postulated, was not because of its undeclared motives, which are not, of course ethically laden, but in the assertion of being so. He concluded that "the attempt to discover a new sense of purpose in humanitarian action has failed – inevitably so, since the orientation towards 'values' and 'ethics' in foreign policy was an attempt to evade the consequences of the death of politics through a search for moral absolutes" (p. 37).

In brief, the military solutions in conflicts would, by no means, engender human casualties, shake off the balance of power, strengthen oppositions, create new rivals and might stimulate a protracted antagonism between the various hostile rivals. Those dilemmas, amongst other possible future economic repercussions, should also be taken into account when considering the resort to the use of force. In what follows, particular attention will be drawn to Blair's notion of humanitarianism and how it was employed in his speeches over the period that he served as Britain's Prime Minister.

5.1.3 New Labour and the Paradox of the "Ethical" Foreign Policy

It is well known that Britain, throughout much of its history, has been a typical imperial state that acted several times beyond its natural geographical territory. Therefore, it is not surprising that with the coming of New Labour into power, there has been a noticeable resurgence of the will of explicit diplomatic and military interventionism overseas. Yet such new phase of neo-imperialism, as it were, was encased with appeals to "universal" human ethics and values. Indeed, starting from his historical victory in the 1997 general election, Blair introduced a number of amendments in Labour's ideology. Chief amongst these was the sound emphasis on morality in the conduct of foreign policy, where he insisted that Britain is committed to international institutions and would actively engage in solving issues related to human rights abuse, protection of minorities, reduction of arm sales, the fight against poverty and the like.[6] However it is highly debatable whether these commitments were fulfilled and fully manifested in reality, not only in relation to Iraq, but also in relation to the many interventions that Britain supported, or was directly involved in with its military force under New Labour.

Before exploring this theme in some detail, it is worth noting that the genre of political discourse addressed here does not consider the processes of decision-making in Britain or the macro socio-political and historical conditions that formulated its foreign policy, but it is simply a kind of narratives coming out of the treatment of the political speeches (CPS). Then, it might look like a paradox that the other political actors who have a strong presence in the political landscape, such as the then Foreign Secretary of State Robin Cook and the other high government officials and bureaucrats, are systematically ignored. In principle, reference to the interpersonal aspect of foreign policy-making and development is systematically discarded due to space limit.

Therefore, the analysis of UK's foreign policy in this context does not necessarily entail an examination of the complex processes through which policy decision-making takes place, nor does it account for the multifarious factors that might otherwise influence the ideological agenda and political choices of the Foreign Office. The examination of Blair's discourse in relation to the question of Iraq is confined to an analysis of the rationale that underpinned his political views as a Prime Minister, in the general context of British politics. In mundane terms, it is seen as the ultimate offspring of New Labour's new ethical doctrine which prioritized and legitimized liberal interventionist, if not strictly speaking imperialist, tendencies based on claims to a set of ethical values.

On this point Paul D. Williams writes: "Labour's moralism was bolstered by its faith in the universality of its values. At times, this encouraged Blair's government to adopt what Martin Ceadel described as a crusading mentality, especially in relation to the use of force" (2005, p. 31). Essentially, the so-nicknamed ethical foreign policy is the core subject matter of this part of the chapter. The philosophy of humanitarianism has been defined in the previous section; "values" is another equally important word which I intend to shed light on in the remainder of this chapter.

From a qualitative analytical perspective, I seek to map out, in a top-down manner, the structure of the most prevalent thematic categories along with the lexico-semantic patterns in Blair's speeches throughout the period that spans from his election in 1997 up to September 2003. Focus, however, will be drawn particularly to some specific events which left an impact on the conduct of Britain's foreign policy and the development of the Anglo–Iraqi crisis. Further quantitative supplements that consider the whole corpus will also be incorporated by the end of the chapter. As will be explained later on, the quantitative analysis would further illustrate the salience of those thematic categories in the whole speeches, in addition to an array of lexical, syntactic and rhetorical structures. Moreover, the qualitative textual analysis, which is by no means reflexive and interpretive, needs to be contrasted against the quantitative findings.

Since its inception, the ethical dimension of New Labour's foreign policy has been the subject of strident critique by many scholars and political commentators; particular criticism was levelled at the manner in which Blair was promoting the war campaign while proclaiming moral values (Chandler & Heins, 2007; Fairclough, 2000). This new political swing in the party's, both domestic and international, policy was inaugurated by Robin Cook, serving as Foreign Secretary in the Labour government, who ultimately resigned over his dissatisfaction with Blair's hostile stance on Iraq. It is particularly the controversies that arose in Blair's motivation to withdraw Saddam from power that made the humanitarian cause less convincing and somewhat inconsistent.

In order to adequately deconstruct the ideological load in Blair's discourse and comment particularly on his strategies of persuasion, I proceed from the global to the local level in the analysis of some of his early speeches. Hence, the first step to follow is to mark the macrothemes in each of the texts concerned, along with a description of the contextual elements under which these speeches were delivered. This is what was referred to as *macrostructure analysis*. As defined earlier, the concept of "macrostructures" in the socio-cognitive model relates to the global coherence in a given text with reference to its semantic structure. It is worth stressing that macrostructure analysis provides some clues on the cognitive processing of discourse because it identifies the kind of information that is stored in the long-term memory of the listeners about the discourse of a given communicative situation (van Dijk & Kintsch, 1983).

The distribution of the semantic components and their relations could be relatively self-manifest in the case of news articles, which have somehow fixed global schemata (superstructure). Namely, the main themes and topics are more likely to be placed in the headlines and leading sentences, with secondary information and other details to follow in the remainder of the text. Political speeches, however, do not have a standard format or the same narrative structure, and may take different shapes and forms. It follows that, to identify the main themes in heterogeneous genres of text, a summary is needed to bring to the fore the "discourse topic" of the text using the macrorules proposed by the socio-cognitive model (see Chap. 3). It has been noticed that despite the fact that Blair's speeches were delivered in different settings and addressed a wide range of topics and audiences, they do share some high degree of overlap.

The concept of macrostructure as hitherto defined is to be operationalized in the case of the "Doctrine of the International Community" speech, delivered on Thursday, 22 April 1999. The sample text is particularly significant not only in the light of the dramatic events that unfolded in the next few years to come, but because it would precisely identity some of the major *discoursal* traits and arguments of the policy of military interventionism and the way it was framed. Nevertheless, my focus is placed primarily on the topics, arguments and persuasive strategies in relation to the upcoming war against international terror, and subsequently the assault on Iraq. I would argue that though the Iraqi problem was only occasionally mentioned during this early period, as Blair was reluctant to openly discuss the issue, the future decisions about the war were already set forth via what was left unsaid, but often embedded through the implicit assumptions and implications made in this discourse.

Blair and the attendees as participants at the Economic Club in Chicago must have an idea about the circumstances and also the purpose of the event, which are, all in all, relevant contextual properties that make the speech meaningful. Thus, the topics discussed by Blair (that will be squeezed later) sought to justify and defend his ideological stance, and by extension Labour's and British government's foreign policy agenda. Therefore, it becomes clear that the general frame of this speech is UK's rationale in the design and conduct of its foreign policy under New Labour which refocused on ethics in politics and international cooperation. Yet, special consideration of this "ethical policy" has been raised particularly to address the then Kosovo conflict and Iraq problem.

Blair opens his speech by mourning the victims of the school violence incident at the Columbine High School in Littleton, Colorado. As an ordinary British citizen and Prime Minster to speak on behalf of the British people, he expressed his feelings of solidarity and sympathy: "From us in Britain to you here in the United States: we offer you our deepest sympathy, our thoughts and our prayers", stating his privilege as being the first British Prime Minister to visit Chicago. The purpose of this speech was to get the support of the USA to exert more pressure on the Serbian regime to stop ethnic cleansing against the Albanians in Kosovo. However, the speech aimed also, as Blair himself put it, to further help "the cause of internationalism and against isolationism" in dealing with global political, economic and security matters. These preliminary contextual notes on the communicative situation constitute an integral part in the cognitive analysis of the "context models" of the speaker (Blair) and the listeners (conference audience). Moreover, the political speech per se is an act of diplomacy that takes place in a foreign country and a close ally to Britain in the management of political affairs at the international level.

Following van Dijk, to make sense of how the semantic properties of a given text are coherently organized and related to each other, at the global level, it is essential to summarize such a text into a few topical sentences that typically incarnate its hierarchal thematic order and structure, that is, semantic macrostructures (see Chap. 3). This could be done through the transformation of the speech, using the macrorules, into a few propositions that would lead us by the end to specify the "discourse topic" of the speech. Up to this point it is necessary to mention again that by the "discourse topic", what is meant is "a proposition entailed by the joint set of propositions expressed by the sequence" (van Dijk, 1977, p. 136). As previously highlighted, the main topics of the text play a significant cognitive role in the construction and comprehension of discourse.[7]

Accordingly, there is a requisite to delimit the discourse topic of the Chicago speech. Or put in simple words, what is the core subject matter of this political speech? This leads us to undertake a systematic description of the main theme, which is partly expressed in the given title of the speech "Doctrine of the International Community", and also the multiple "atomic parts of the topical proposition" that are subsumed under such title, that is, the various sub-topics discussed, and by extension their "alternatives": Kosovo, global interdependence, globalization, international security and, finally, politics. It is by no means necessary that all these auxiliary elements centre on the *upshot* of text and serve to back up the global coherence of this piece of discourse. A set of the main topics and propositions and their sequences are listed according to their chronological sequence in what follows:

(a) **Kosovo**

The war in Kosovo is a just war which is based on *ethical values*.
The issue of Kosovo cannot be seen in *isolation*.

(b) **Global Interdependence**

Globalization is an economic, political and security phenomenon.
International cooperation is a must, and isolationism is no longer an option.
To be secure, *we must intervene in other countries*.
Other sub-topics and "alternatives" were also addressed, such as the call to reform the system of international financial regulation, free trade promotion, to reconsider the decision-making process of the UN and the UNSC, to boast cooperation between the industrial nations to reduce global warming and, finally, the Third World debt. What matters here is the way in which these issues were bound up under the de facto restraints of globalization. The last underlined sentence refers to the possibility of including Iraq, as it was juxtaposed with the case of Kosovo several times (see example (d)).

(c) **Globalization**

Protectionism is the swiftest road to poverty.
Russia should be integrated in the Western model.

(d) International Security

Both Saddam and Milosevic represent a constant threat to international peace and security.
The spread of "the values of liberty, the rule of law, human rights and an open society" is in our national interests, too. The spread of our values makes us safe.
There are many regimes that are undemocratic and engaged in barbarous acts.

(e) Politics

Under this heading Blair, once again, highlighted the impact of globalization on the conduct of policy-making at the international and local levels. He summarized the procedures of reform implemented by New Labour in economy, education, crime and social exclusion, and thus the decentralization of political power in Britain. The speech closes with a call for the USA to get more engaged in the management of foreign affairs and to drop off what he described as the "doctrine of isolationism".

Taken as a whole, the speech proposed a set of principles that, according to Blair, should govern the international community and introduced some suggestions on how they should be implemented in relation to the mentioned topics. Precisely, it is explicated that Britain's policy on Kosovo was not based on territorial expansion but on a mere ethical perspective. Consider the following extract. Blair declares "I want to speak to you this evening about events in Kosovo. But *I want to put these events in a wider context* – economic, political and security – because I do not believe *Kosovo can be seen in isolation*" (my italics).

Blair's strategy to spin the criticism on his liberal interventionist policy was founded on his appeal to ethical values. In it, he expressed his government readiness to intervene militarily in other countries as well. "We cannot turn our backs on conflicts and the violation of human rights within other countries if we want still to be secure." The "other countries" is an implication that, arguably, incorporated Saddam's regime, which is best hinted at in other excerpts that juxtapose the human rights abuse in Kosovo along with that in Iraq:

> Many of *our* problems have been caused by two dangerous and ruthless men – Saddam Hussein and Slobodan Milosevic. Both have been prepared to wage vicious campaigns against sections of their own community. As a result of these destructive policies both have brought calamity on their own peoples. Instead of enjoying its oil wealth Iraq has been reduced to poverty, with political life stultified through fear. (Blair, 1999)

The "wider context" indirectly hedged to the case of Iraq, which is best illustrated in the analogy he drew between Kosovo and Iraq, Saddam and Milosevic in the above excerpt. From a semantic point of view, a proposition is made via the declaration that Saddam Hussein and Slobodan Milosevic are dangerous and ruthless, whose actions brought misery and destruction to their own people. They are associated with negative imagery such as destructive policies, calamity, poverty and fear. The recipient of this message would induce the connection of the agents, their actions and, ultimately, how they should be dealt with. More importantly, the recipient would be more likely to remember such categorization in future occasions because it is easily retrieved from his episodic memory, as suggested by the accessibility bias theory and the socio-cognitive model. Furthermore, albeit not in straightforward manner, this discourse affirms the positive image of the in-group and their actions (British, American, democrats) and the negative image of the out-group (the other side of the world: Asians, dictators, Saddam, Milosevic and so on).

The next except provides another vivid example of how coherence and persuasion function in Blair's political discourse at the abstract cognitive level. In other words, how specific mental models are invoked through the sequence of the causal relationships established to defend the doctrine of internationalism and military intervention. Indeed, the mental models, as the ones underlined in the excerpt, about jobs (unemployment), drugs and refugees (more immigrants) would activate specific cognitive knowledge, which is both individual and socially shared, about domestic socio-economic issues that would systematically trigger strong feelings of anxiety and frustration:

> Many of our domestic problems are caused on *the other side of the world*. Financial instability in Asia destroys *jobs* in Chicago and in my own

constituency in County Durham. Poverty in the Caribbean means more *drugs* on the streets in Washington and London. Conflict in the Balkans causes more *refugees* in Germany and here in the US. These problems can only be addressed by international co-operation. (Blair, 1999)

What is particularly important about the Chicago speech is the ensemble of implicit assumptions about the policy of New Labour in the management of its *ethical* foreign policy. The latter was expressed in rather holistic ways, appealing to human values which were, for Blair, tied up with national interests in the first place. Blair's morality, as expressed in his speeches, is more likely to be taken in a Kantian sense, though with a more pragmatic touch, which brought national and self-sealed interests with values. It is here, as I argue, where the inconsistency of the ethical dimension lies.

5.2 Tracing the Framing of Terror Narrative in Blair's Discourse

5.2.1 Background Overview on the History and Etymology of "Terrorism"

Although the analysis of the language of terrorism is an auxiliary objective in this research, one may assume that it is still an important element that had a substantial influence on the making of British foreign policy in the last two decades, and particularly Blair's downright hostile discourse on Saddam's Iraq. For this, clarifying the exact meaning of "terrorism" and how it was employed by New Labour is one of the missing pieces in the jigsaw puzzle of the pro-war ideology. Remarkably, this was also bound up with the danger posed by Saddam's alleged WMD, as the war campaigners warned. Jack Holland assumes that "the conflation of WMD and terrorism was central to justifying intervention, helping to integrate Iraq into the logic of the War on Terror" (2013, p. 142).

Further to what has been said about the nature, processes and procedures of PDA, this section of the chapter attempts to operationalize the aforementioned concepts in a systematic qualitative analysis of six selected speeches where the problem of terrorism was mentioned. These speeches were delivered at different occasions during the turbulent time span that extends from the 9/11 up to the declaration of the war on Iraq. In a narrower sense, I seek, in particular, to exhibit the various ways in which the complex issue of terrorism was constructed by Blair, bearing in mind, its link, if any, with Saddam's regime. At first, an account of terrorism, or what might be best termed "New Terrorism" with an uppercase T, from Blair's perspective is described and deconstructed to reveal the backdrop upon which his arguments on Iraq were founded. In the first place, my purpose herein is to question the nature of terrorism as a political phenomenon that is creating much debate and controversy in the academia—more precisely, how it was exploited to advance ideologically charged attitudes and policy preferences, as is the case in Blair's political discourse on the case of Iraq.

In order to elaborate on this point, I cover the following elements: a broad and rather sketchy survey on the etymology of the word "terror", its usage in the context of contemporary British politics, the 9/11 and its repercussions on the Iraqi dossier, and, finally, the conceptualization of terrorism in Blair's speeches throughout the period that preceded Britain's military adventure in Iraq. Stated differently, my concern is to disclose some of the major traits, controversies and the multifarious meanings that revolved around the project of the "War on Terror" *which was enthusiastically embraced by Blair*. By tracing backwards the history of the term and how it was eventually encased with skewed ideologies and political biases that justified state violence, from the early beginning of the century, it would be much easier for the reader to trace the storyline of terror in Blair's pro-war ideology. The latter, it should be noted, cannot be well grasped without a reference to the global and local circumstances under which it was framed.

It will be illustrated in the aggregate quantitative descriptions and categorization of the language items in the CPS that terrorism was among the most salient themes in Blair's discourse, particularly during the pre-war period. Nonetheless, as the output exhibits mere heuristic representations on word co-occurrences and associations between topics, this would necessarily require some further close qualitative analysis at the level of individual texts. Moreover, the language patterns and features used to articulate those silent themes and topics are likewise examined across different texts so as to follow up the metacoherence of this discourse.

At the outset, one might ask once again what does terrorism mean and how has the label of "terror" been used in Britain in the context of the Iraq War? More precisely, it is essential to answer the following question: How did Blair construct the concept of terror in his speeches throughout the period that preceded the Iraq War? Ostensibly, much of the literature on the discourse of terrorism emerged basically after the 9/11 and approached the causes of the incident from a variety of angles and perspectives. Yet, much of the claims made by scholars were lacking some in-depth analysis and were not properly backed up by adequate evidence. Hence, it is argued that the recent debate over the issue of international terrorism, especially within the political circles, is often biased and provides the public with a distorted image of the reality "out there" to serve specific political ideologies. As a corollary, the topic of terrorism might not lend itself easily to a formal scholarly academic research.

Despite the relatively large evolving body of literature that has accumulated recently on terrorism-related studies, the term "terrorism" per se remains, paradoxically, a fuzzy and vague concept.[8] A variety of scholars from different backgrounds, notably academics, lawyers and policy-makers who showed keen interest in terrorism, have attempted to come at a common agreement on the label "terrorist", but ended up with a chorus of interpretations. In retrospect, the term in its literal sense did not change from the time when it was used in Latin to mean "frighten". However, "terrorism" was a frequently used term by the French intellectuals of the Renaissance era, such as Jean Bodin, Thomas Hobbes, Jean-Jacques Rousseau, Montesquieu and many others. It was borrowed into English only by the sixteenth century (Schmid, 2011, p. 41). None dared to label himself terrorist except, perhaps, the State of Terror established by the Grand Jacobin rebels in France. Terror is then becoming the typical synonym of fear, violence, intimidation, brutality and destruction. In all the countries which were hit by terror groups, the word "war" was immediately used to tighten security measures and restrictions on the public. Those special conditions are mostly allowed in the case of war, if we refer to war in its traditional sense.

The American historian and political commentator Walter Laqueur advocates that terrorism "is largely a matter of perception, of historical, social, and cultural traditions, and of political calculus" (1999, p. 36). Based on this kaleidoscopic outlook, one might think of a number of feasible definitions of terrorism that can be generated with reference to international law, theology, ethics and morality, security studies and policy-making, to name but a few. In order to rule out any possible misunderstanding that would emerge from the existing spectrum of definitions, it is to be highlighted that the kind of terrorism addressed in this research work as a whole is associated with the movement that embarked with the attacks on the USA in 2001. The "new terror", as many would call it, is often linked with political violence in the first place and the will of small militias and groups to overthrow established governments or authority through indiscriminate crimes against civilians. Because these groups could not secure legitimacy through democratic means, they tend to resort to coercive means in order to intimidate the established authorities. This is best reflected in the gang-like operations they commit as to draw the attention of the mass media and the public to their cause. In fact, there is a growing body of literature that covers the new terror phenomenon, most of which are, arguably, tailoring different ideological orientations (Randall, 2009).

I strenuously argue that the war on terror, which was crystallized in the subsequent counter-terrorism discourse, has been extremely tied up to the case of Iraq simply because the occupation of Iraq, practically speaking, was declared by the USA three days following the 9/11 attacks.[9] Yet the official decision was delayed for matters that relate to the legal aspect of a unilateral military action and the pressure of the international community. As for Britain, Saddam's alleged relations with terrorist organizations and the threat coming from possible collaboration in nuclear technology were much more insinuated rather than spelled out. This preliminary assumption is to be projected more clearly in the remainder of the chapter. Up to this level, I can claim that there is no universal censuses on what does "terrorism" denote exactly—despite the fact that terror is an ordinary term that could be synonymous with violence and aggression against people, usually defenceless civilians. Thus, it is to be stated, in fairness, that the rising phenomenon of global terrorism was substantively exploited to serve political ideologies and agendas due to its emotionally charged nature and impact on the mass public. After all, there can be no doubt that terror is a very present reality that threatens order and stability worldwide.

It is perhaps the inherent negative connotation of the term, which is well manipulated by politicians, that dashes any hopes of universal consensus. Arguably, the confusion and uncertainty created by the several terror strikes have accelerated Blair's motion to shore up an international support for the invasion of Iraq, or at least aided to quell any serious impediment to the overthrow of Saddam from power.

Since the Iraq War took place around 18 months after the 9/11, the question that strongly suggests itself is the following: Is there any relationship whatsoever between the two events, at least from the point of view of Blair? Indeed, the 9/11 horrendous attack has been the inaugural show for the new, obviously protracted, war of the century, not only for the USA, but also for Britain and many other Western and non-Western countries, as terrorism proved to be a serious international threat that might target any state. As a matter of fact, the discourse of counter-terrorism started to be articulated increasingly in policy-making. Arguably, however, the policy of counter-terrorism that was officially approved in the wake of the terror assault on the USA paved the way for much flexibility in the normalization of state violence against other suspected people, adversary regimes and even the so-called rouge states around the globe. Due to the inherent power of negativity in the term itself, it is exploited by established authorities, pressure groups and some extremist, usually right-wing political parties in the West to get the sway over the public. In the first place, one would ponder how such a dramatic swing affected Britain's policy on the question of Iraq; that is, was Saddam accused of aiding the hijackers and those who planned the attack?

Undeniably, Britain as the closest ally to the White House was thus infected by the repercussions of the incident. Such unexpected terrorist assault which cost the lives of many civilians spread feelings of fear and anxiety all over the world. In the course of the few months that followed, a serious debate unfolded about the future policies to contain the phenomenon and tighten security measures. On the diplomatic level, it seems that the attacks occurred at a time when the Anglo–American relationship was more than just "special", but rather strong and fluid. Within this stringent context, Iraq was by no means the likely target that would not trigger much criticism by US allies and partners. Perhaps this made Blair more enthusiastic than ever about the urge to quell what was labelled as the *failed states*, which were allegedly supporting terrorism and extremism.

As noted earlier, the focus on the ideological aspect of discourse is a cornerstone element in this study and thus the war on terror is seen herein as a sub-discourse of substantial ideological load. Hence, it is essential to follow up the interconnections, if any, between the War on Terror project and the war on Iraq in Blair's political discourse. To rephrase the previous question: How were the problem of terror and the procedures adopted, as part of the counter-terror policy, framed in Blair's speeches? This would lead us to consider the intricate war narratives through the constellation of worldviews, beliefs and assumptions that were advanced to sustain the continuity and legitimacy of the pro-war discourse.

In retrospect, the dawn of the third millennium marked a strengthening in the bond between religious extremism and political radicalism, which is continuously feeding violence and counter-violence in many parts of the world. Remarkably, the 9/11 onslaught, which caused ripples of surprise, was the opening show for a war-like battle against a shapeless enemy called vaguely *Terrorism*. It is needles to add that many subsequent terror attacks targeted also the Continent and Britain, such as the Madrid train bombings in 2014, the 7 July 2005 London attacks, the Paris attacks in November 2015 and, lately, the bombings of Brussels airport. Some scholars advocated that the rapid changing environment of the late twentieth century has halted, at least for a while, the Cold War discourse, which eventually paved the way for an alternative discourse on the issue of high rising levels of organized crime. More alarmingly, perhaps, is the threat of organized terrorism by many heterogeneous groups which endorsed universal utopian ideologies. It seems that after 14 years since the 9/11, Terrorism (with capital T) has proved to be a serious danger to public safety worldwide and remains a complex subject that is triggering much debate in the political spheres and academia alike.

What is relevant in this respect, however, is the language of legitimization, and also manipulation, in the official decision-making discourse. To normalize counter-violence following the assault on the USA was without doubt a tough mission due to the protest of the civil society against the unconditioned and fuzzy decisions that were put forth under the War on Terror agenda. Yet, *l'état d'urgence* of the time that was allowed under special conditions provided the pro-war adherents with much space for the legitimization of another form of violence which was much more organized, destructive and intimidating for the victims of the post-9/11 world. With the aim of deconstructing the ways in which the discourse on terrorism and counter-terrorism was constructed in Blair's language, the CPS is considered again through the lens of PDA, with direct reference to the socio-cognitive model.

In my quest to track the narrative construction of fear from Iraq's assumed threat on Britain, the question of Saddam's ties with the then terrorist organizations, and particularly the symbol of organized terror in the world, Osama Bin Laden, comes as priority. One of the serious scholarly contributions that shed light on the discursive relationship made between Iraq and the 9/11 in the official US discourse was conducted by Adam Hodges. He examined the socio-political reality created by former US president George Bush's administration on the possible collaboration between Iraq and Al-Qaeda in some speeches in what he terms the "Bush War on Terror Narrative". The war on Iraq was seen as part of the war on terror, although the association between the two is often not explicitly spelled out, but rather implied in the rhetoric of Bush's speeches, which emphasize the *adequation* of the two enemies, that is, Iraq and Al-Qaeda, and Saddam with Bin Laden. Hoges notes that both "Iraq's potential for WMD and the issue of international terrorism parallel each other rhetorically to the effect that the issue of terrorism is constructed as a natural concomitant to Iraq's military capabilities (or desires)" (Hodge & Nilep, 2007, p. 72).

As will be discussed in the next sections of this chapter, Blair did not stand apart from the mainstream thrust of, what I might call, neo-imperialist ideology embraced by the other war ideologues in the Bush administration. However, his strategy to make use of the Iraq–terror association was less straightforward and well implicit in his eloquent oratory and manipulative rhetorical strategies.

In this context, I argue that the 9/11 has been an essential turning point in the making up of the pro-war discourse on Iraq. From a cognitive perspective, based on both the qualitative and quantitative readings of the corpora, I postulate that Blair has resorted to the 9/11 script so as to activate the listeners' old knowledge about the threat of possible future attacks on Britain or other countries similar in destruction as the attack of the 9/11. Thus, frequent references were made to the nuclear menace that Saddam would pose or the possibility of handing over mass destructive weaponry to terror groups that had animosities for Britain and the West in general.

5.2.2 Global Semantic Macrostructures and the Terror Narrative

It has been ostensible that the issue of terrorism was framed in a myriad of ways which sometimes served to justify institutional coercion and physical violence against rival political forces. While the Jacobins in France saw nothing wrong with using "institutional" terror to contain the then prevailing disarray, this is becoming no longer acceptable universally as a deterrent by established authorities. Nonetheless, such immoral patterns of behaviour are still adopted by various armed groups and marginal political entities that seek to challenge their own governing elites. One might wonder how this was debated in the context of British politics, particularly after the endorsement of the "War on Terror" project in the wake of the 9/11. Precisely, how *l'etat d'urgence* helped to justify counter-violence against what was nicknamed the "rogue states",[10] with Iraq being included in the top of the list.

In the first place, to trace the narrative structures in Blair's speeches, in which terrorism would reside at the centre, is to account for the global semantic macrostructures in the texts of speeches concerned. As it has been emphasized in the third chapter, macrostructures are one of the cornerstone tools in the socio-cognitive model for the assessment of discourse processing. They are an integral part of the "natural language" and manifest themselves as global semantic structures of language. Hence, the description of the sequence of propositions of the text is a fundamental step in discourse analysis because as, van Dijk advocates, "discourse can not be adequately accounted for at the microlevel alone. Without a level of semantic macrostructures we are unable to account for various properties of 'global meanings' of a discourse" (1983, p. 26). In other words, it helps mark the major discourse topics of the text or talk under examination and the coherence or lack of it in Blair's arguments. Fundamentally, this is important from a cognitive point of view because the discourse topic "defines the linear connection and coherence of the composite sentences and sequences" (van Dijk, 1977, p. viii). Accordingly, this section of the chapter aims to analyse the structure of meaning and coherence in Blair's speeches at the global level, which is carried out with the implementation of aforementioned macrorules (weak and strong deletion, abstraction, generalization and construction).

Based on a conceptual approach developed from the social theory of Jürgen Habermas which takes legitimacy as "an intersubjective sociological phenomenon", James Strong advocates, in a short paper, that Blair himself was responsible for the deficit of the pro-war discourse in Britain in virtue of his inflexibility and excess on being persuasive. The arguments presented by Blair to support his cause for military action proved to be highly exaggerated and unrealistic; he raised more doubts and anxiety rather than conformity within the British public and political elite (Strong, 2015). But the question that remains unresolved here is, why was the decision of war approved and gained majority vote in the Commons? This alludes to my concern about the metadiscourse of legitimization and its workings in the public and political spheres. The question whether the pro-war ideology was partly or fully justified, I argue, would not change the attitudes of the in-group members, who share sympathy with the cause rather than being rationally convinced about the arguments presented.

The controversial parliamentary debate on the 18th of March over the engagement of war on Iraq where Blair called for full support has been the subject of detailed analysis by Teun van Dijk in his monograph *Society and Discourse: How Social Contexts Influence Text and Talk* (2009). In similar fashion, I emulate van Dijk's strategy of analysis to account for the properties and structures of the pro-war ideology in some selected speeches.

In what follows, some of the speeches that date to the pre-war period were taken as a sample for analysis. A good part of the contextual circumstances which shaped Blair's discourse were already discussed in the previous chapters. For example, the Anglo–Iraqi relationship, Saddam's dictatorship and his hostile attitudes towards his neighbours, the 9/11 terrorist attack and the many other elements (legal, political, ideological) which constitute a part of the political knowledge embedded in Blair's ideology. Yet many of these contextual conditions cannot be fully described and analysed. By "context", what is meant is space and time, the attendees, their roles and relationships to each other and so forth. More knowledge about the contextual circumstances, which are various and diversified, would make it easy to comprehended the communicative situation; however, a fully detailed description would take much space. Let us consider the below macrostructures of two speeches arranged in accordance with their temporal chronology:

(a) **Speech to the Global Ethics Foundation, Tübingen University, Germany 2000**

1. The nature of global change

- There is no place for "narrow and exclusive traditions" in today's world.
- The global change is driving us towards more interdependence.
- The challenge of globalization is not economic only but relates to security.
- The values of "community" are both local and global.

2. Community within a nation

- Values of community at the local level stands for opportunity, equality and responsibility.
- Government action must be tough on crime and violence to establish law and order.

3. The doctrine of international community

- Issues of modern world cannot be faced by nations in isolation (e.g. nuclear proliferation).
- Values of the "international community" stand for law and order, cooperation, collective security, freedom and human rights.

- There is a serious threat of nuclear weapons proliferation that must be eliminated.

4. The role of religious faith and understanding

- We have to bridge the gap between the religious faiths to promote peace and mutual understanding.
- Divisions in religions can be reduced through a commitment to shared values of international community.
- The idea of community revolves around the "acknowledgement of our own interdependence".

(b) **"Faith in Politics", London 2001**

- Faith traditions are deeply intertwined with political allegiances and support the values New Labour is calling for.
- Values and politics: equal wealth, respect, responsibility, mutual obligations within the "national community".
- The New Labour government supports faith institutions and their engagement in the community.

(c) **Leader's speech, Brighton 2001**

- The 9/11 is an act of "evil" and a "turning point in history".
- Osama Bin Laden and the Taliban regime are among the chief organizers of the 9/11 atrocity.
- Afghanistan is a big exporter of drugs, fanaticism and terror, and military action must be taken to destroy the terrorist network of Bin Laden.
- *"Those that finance terror, those who launder their money, those that cover their tracks are every bit as guilty as the fanatic who commits the final act".*
- The challenges of security must be faced with the power of "community".
- Inter-independence is a defining character of today's world and there is no room for isolationism.

The previous squeezed propositions were made through the use of macrorules, which recursively reduced the texts into a few topical sentences deemed to be representative of the gist of each text in isolation. Attention, however, is given to some specific sequences of propositions and their macropropositions that best defined the ethical dimension in Labour's politics. The ones ignored were not directly related to the making of foreign policy, for example, the reform of the British education system, which has been one of the recurrent themes in most of his speeches (see the empirical results at the end of the chapter).

The propositions listed in (a) expound New Labour's ideology and, particularly, the logic underpinning its foreign policy that is, as Blair deliberately advocates, not "self-interested" but grounded on human values and the, somehow vague, idea of "community". On the whole, the text covers numerous topics, such as the accelerating motion of change in the modern world and the impact of globalization, and the idea of international community, in addition to the role of religious faiths in the promotion of peace. The same topics were in fact reverberating in his speeches at the George Bush Senior Presidential Library (Crawford, 2002), Trades Union Congress (TUC) conference (Blackpool, 2002) and the Leader's speech (Blackpool, 2002), yet with varying degrees of clarity and precision. Nonetheless, what seems interesting in this discourse is, rather, Blair's attempt to coalesce all these themes together under the umbrella of globalization to justify New Labour's Third Way stance, most specifically its disputed appeal for active diplomatic, economic and military interventionism as a model for international politics. The increasing inter-independence posed by the motion of globalization, as Blair put it, is not restricted to economy but also to many other issues, such as poverty, health, education and, most importantly, the security challenge posed by the rise of international terror and the proliferation of WMD. The association between terrorism and WMD has been very frequent in the aforementioned texts to justify the war on Iraq. It is ostensible that the question of terrorism in this context is not taken up as a separate topic, but one of the major repercussions of the shift of power that is facing the new world order set up under the restraints of globalization.

Another distinctive persuasive strategy is Blair's insistence on the use of paradoxical expressions and binary relationships between many opposing entities. This language of dialectics places Labour's political ideology in the centre rather than at the extreme. It is safe to argue that Blair's discourse has always been spinning around a paradox resulting from the conflict between the traditional and the modernizer, old and new, past and present, faith and reason, good and evil, individual and community, moral values and political pragmatism, left and right, to name but a few. In this sense, the Third Way and the idea of "international community" with shared values compromise these dichotomies and, as Blair put it, "resolv[e] the paradox of the modern world" (Blair, 2000).

But what remains paradoxical is the shift from the local to the global. The British national values were also valid, according to Blair, to the international community, which should consider states and nations as individuals with shared responsibility and obligations towards each other. In this respect, international organizations, the UN in particular, play the role of the established authority that ensures the implementation of the "ethical doctrine".

It is to reiterate that Blair's discourse prioritized collective responsibility, which is put into stark relief vis-à-vis issues of poverty, health, education, environment and, most significantly, the security challenge by the spread of drugs, organized crime and the proliferation of WMD. The tapestry of this discourse put special emphasis on the threat of international terrorism and the complicity of the "rogue states" with the networks of terror. Blair's idea of "community" was the quintessence of Labour's ideology and the driving force of its active diplomacy and interventions abroad, which has also been reverberating in the pro-war stance on Iraq. The Leader's speech of 2001 was made to justify the next military strike against the Taliban regime in Afghanistan. In this case, the justification of military intervention was founded on Labour's commitment to the rule of law and recommendations of international institutions. This case was contrasted with previous British interventions in Kosovo, Congo and Rwanda to halt ethnic cleansing against minorities. Though Iraq was not clearly mentioned, the next move against Saddam's regime was implicated by Blair in the aforementioned speeches.

5.2.3 Microstructures: Local Coherence

By the microanalysis of the CPS, what is meant is the examination of the various lexico-semantic fragments of discourse, and particularly those small chunks and components of language that are hardly discernible at a macro level. In other words, the bottom-up analysis, which is conventional by virtue of its means and underlying theories, would allow us to bring together the pieces of the aggregate picture of Blair's discourse that was constructing itself across an extended period of time and in different communicative situations. Much of these linguistic chunks form the cement that strengthens the meaningfulness and coherence of discourse by relating the text to its immediate context, and also to previous real experiences or imaginary future situations—but most of which might not be remembered by the audiences because they are mere examples, comparisons, presuppositions, metaphorical expressions, implications and the like. Indeed, the macropropositions squeezed from the sample texts in the previous section are largely dependent upon the kind of micropropositions and argumentative strategies employed in the text.

The assessment of discourse coherence at a micro level is approached through the examination of the structure of knowledge which is loaded in the sequences and the causal relationships between the previously listed propositions, lexical choice, self- and other representation and the use of evidentials, including many other rhetorical and manipulative strategies that contribute to making sense of Blair's point of view and attitudes on Saddam Iraq. Decoding these traits in the texts would unravel the embedded meaning that is guided and controlled by the speaker (Blair) as to persuade the listeners about the righteousness of his claims (about Iraq, terrorism, WMD, 9/11, etc.). Van Dijk writes, "Both referential (model-based) as well as intensional (meaning-based) coherence of sequences of propositions show how knowledge is organized, for instance by causal structures, thus providing insight into the ways authors manage the explanation of social and political events" (Hart, 2011, p. 37).

One of the reverberating rhetorical features in the selected corpus is the ideologically based polarization drawn between the self "We" and the other "They", albeit the imaginary boundaries are subtly created and enhanced in many different ways and at different levels of abstraction. This complex inclusion–exclusion process, which can be compared to the shape of a few zones of proximity, is perhaps best ostensible in the George Bush Senior Presidential Library speech (Crawford, 2002). By declaring that "the world works better when the US and the EU stand together", Blair positions the USA and the European Union (EU) at the centre of this zone, as they do share mutual socio-political and cultural values, while at the same time denouncing the anti-Americanism spirit in Europe. He moves a bit further to reduce the ideological chasm with Russia as the inheritor of the former Soviet socialist legacy. And then including China and India in the third zone, he redresses, "whom the only question is not whether they will be huge powers in the world, but how huge, and how that power will be used".

Other close in-group members incorporated Japan and South America. Remarkably, the out-group members in this categorization referred to Syria, Iran and North Korea, with whom negotiation and diplomacy is, as Blair proceeds to postulate, still possible on some pending issues, such as the abuse of human rights, nuclear ambitions, and the anti-Western stance of these countries. What is relevant here, however, is the fact that Afghanistan (Taliban) and Saddam's Iraq as out-group members were placed in the enemy circle, with the emphasis on the impossibility of mutual understanding or "meeting of minds". Likewise, international terrorism and WMD were placed in the same category of threat:

> We must be prepared to act where terrorism or Weapons of Mass Destruction threaten us. The fight against international terrorism is right. We should pursue it vigorously. *Not just in Afghanistan but elsewhere*. Not just by military means but by disrupting the finances of terrorism, getting at the middle men, the bankrollers of the trade in terror and WMD. Since September 11 the action has been considerable, in many countries. But there should be no let up. (Crawford, 2002)

Additionally, the ways in which the in-group and out-group members are described in the texts of the corpora is another powerful element and constitutes what van Dijk's dubbed "the ideological square". From a cognitive perspective, this is important because part of the knowledge that circulates in our everyday conversations and public discourses substantially shapes our views and evaluation of ourselves against other people. In most cases, but not always, politicians do avoid using direct prejudiced, xenophobic or stereotypical expressions in their formal speeches or conferences. Typically, a comparison between in-group and out-group descriptions and categorization in the CPS would clearly reveal how the positive-self image and negative-other image are discursively enhanced in the memory of the audiences. Consider the following random excerpts taken from the aforementioned speeches:

1. This is a battle with only one outcome: *our victory not theirs*.
2. *Our way of life* is a great deal stronger and will last a great deal longer than the actions of *fanatics, small in number* and now facing a unified world against them.
3. But the fundamentals of the *US, British and European* economies are strong.
4. In Afghanistan are scores of *training camps for the export of terror*. Chief amongst the sponsors and organizers is *Osama Bin Laden*.
    Any action taken will be against the terrorist network of Bin Laden.
5. Those that finance terror, those who launder their money, those that cover their tracks are every bit as guilty as the *fanatic* who commits the final act.
6. The *values we believe in* should shine through what we do in Afghanistan.

Arguably, the boundary is created between the in-group and out-group in a very broad and rather vague manner. In the Leader's speech of 2001 Blair draws the line between the "creative power of the free citizen" and the "the violence and savagery of the fanatic", with the first being a quality of Western liberal societies, as "free citizenry" is one of the ideal values that are avowed, safeguarded and defended in those societies—with delicate differences from one country to another. The second description, based on the other references that follow in the text, refers to the terror network that orchestrated the 9/11 calamity, Bin Laden, Taliban regime and terrorists. In fact, this description is fully justified based on the huge damage which was caused by the terror and violence of the Al-Qaeda, which was, the least to say, an act of aggression and intimidation. Whilst there has been no explicit mentioning of Iraq, some implicit associations with similar cases were already presented. For example, excerpt (5) includes an implicit reference to the regime of Iraq, which is equally put in the out-group circle in the other speeches. The dictatorship of Milosevic and the subsequent British intervention are brought to the fore to establish an analogy with the issue of terrorism and the case of Iraq. A few other parallel analogies had also been made at many different occasions:

> If necessary the action should be military and again, if necessary and justified, it should involve regime change. I have been involved as British Prime Minister in three conflicts involving regime change. Milosevic. The Taliban. And Sierra Leone, where a country of six million people was saved from a murderous group of gangsters who had hijacked the democratically elected government. (Crawford, 2002)

Amongst the goals of a political speech is to provide the background for new decisions, information and opinions on a variety of matters. Partly, the new knowledge introduced, especially on decisive maters, is built upon previous concrete experiences and knowledge. In my case study, Blair as a speaker knows to which "system of belief" his listeners belong to, and based on this, and other contextual elements, he tends to invoke special memory retrieval of similar events by the suggestions of new information. For example, the failure of the policy of appeasement followed by former British Prime Minister Neville Chamberlain to stop Hitler's territorial ambitions is compared against the inaction to thwart Saddam Hussein. Blair declares, "There's a lot of it about but remember when and where this alliance was forged: here in Europe, in World War II when Britain and America and every decent citizen in Europe joined forces to liberate Europe from the Nazi evil" (Blackpool, 2002).

Another major theoretical aspect in the socio-cognitive model is the notion of *shared knowledge* in a given epistemic community. As has been hitherto discussed, the socio-cultural knowledge is only implicitly and unconsciously communicated amongst the in-group members. Therefore, to have some clues on the shared stock of knowledge on particular events, people, actions, collective values, identity and the like, one might simply need to decipher the various entailments and presuppositions encoded in the structure of language. Several presuppositions and implications were made to enhance the likelihood of relating the Iraq problem with the rising threat of international terrorism. Although Blair's polarization is not surprising, since he is explicitly biased in his views on the question of military intervention in Iraq, it is evident, for example, that part of his manipulative strategies to legitimize the pro-war cause is to implicitly associate Saddam with the international network of terror. On his speech to the TUC, Blair announces:

> Suppose I had come last year on the same day as this year – September 10. Suppose I had said to you: there is a terrorist network called al-Qaida. It operates out of Afghanistan. It has carried out several attacks and we believe it is planning more. It has been condemned by the UN in the strongest terms. Unless it is stopped, the threat will grow. And so I want to take action to prevent that. (Blackpool, 2002)

Likewise, discourse and knowledge are manifest in the use of evidentials in language. They do function as strong argumentative strategy to make speculations and assumptions sound more rigid and convincing. Blair made numerous references to recognized experts in the field of nuclear science and intelligence agencies to prove the allegations about Saddam's links, on the one hand, with terror groups, and his active programme to produce mass destructive bombs, on the other. However, all these claims turned out to be untrue and highly exaggerated.

There are quite a good number of rhetorical devices that make Blair's discourse very persuasive and manipulative. Consider the following except of the speech which best exemplifies the emotive and passionate tone used at the very beginning of his speech:

> *Just two weeks ago, in New York, after the church service I met some of the families of the British victims. It was in many ways a very British occasion. Tea and biscuits. It was raining outside. Around the edge of the room, strangers making small talk, trying to be normal people in an abnormal situation. And as you crossed the room, you felt the longing and sadness;*

hands clutching photos of sons and daughters, wives and husbands; imploring you to believe them when they said there was still an outside chance of their loved ones being found alive, when you knew in truth that all hope was gone. And then a middle-aged mother looks you in the eyes and tells you her only son has died, and asks you: why? I tell you: you do not feel like the most powerful person in the country at times like that. Because there is no answer. There is no justification for their pain. Their son did nothing wrong. The woman, seven months pregnant, whose child will never know its father, did nothing wrong. (Brighton, 2001)

This story-like narrative has a special rhetorical function, which is, I argue, to detach the listener from the *status quo* to a previous past experience as to have their sympathy for subsequent future decisions. Blair continues in the same speech:

The action we take will be proportionate … Listen to the calls of those passengers on the planes. Think of the children on them, told they were going to die. Think of the cruelty beyond our comprehension as amongst the screams and the anguish of the innocent, those hijackers drove at full throttle planes laden with fuel into buildings where tens of thousands worked. (Brighton, 2001)

The seemingly passionate tone of Blair in addressing the 9/11 and other related terror events is justified based on the pain and horror inflicted on the people, who were mostly civilians and innocent. Yet the boundary is once again drawn between the positive-self and the negative-other. The former is quite obvious in references to the values of "Our" nation, way of life, actions and political decisions, ideologies and so on. While the *Others* "slaughter the innocent", "*WE* will do all we humanly can to avoid civilian casualties". The stereotypical prejudices are also strong and manifest in many other speeches.

Both contemporary and traditional critical methods of language attribute much attention to the expression of ideology through the analysis of wording and lexical choice. Van Dijk claims that "shared sociocultural meanings, for example as codified in the lexicon, are used in the construction of meanings of specific situated meanings of particular discourses" (1995, p. 257). The use of vocabulary does not only unravel the ideology of the agent, but would tremendously influence the way the target audience interprets the text or talk. In the case of the Iraq war, plenty of words are worthy of consideration due their charged meanings and references. The so-called *jihad* in Islamic tradition has been taken out of its original context, which dates back hundreds of years, to falsely justify the barbarism of pseudo Islamic groups.

The messianic dimension is rarely invoked by Blair in his political discourse, except when it comes to some specific issues, most plainly perhaps when tackling the problem of terrorism, religion and politics, Islam and the West, and other related themes. His personal moral endorsements were sometimes explicitly expressed to reflect his evangelical stance. The fight against terror and the other out-group members is represented as a struggle against evil. He declared several times that Britain must stand against the act of evil, such as the 9/11 and Saddam's dictatorship:

> I believe their memorial can and should be greater than simply the punishment of the guilty. It is that out of *the shadow of this evil*, should emerge lasting good (Brighton, 2001).
> In the end, it is not our power alone that will *defeat this evil*. Our ultimate weapon is not our guns, but *our beliefs* (Washington, 2003).

5.2.4 Quantitative Highlights on Blair's Political Discourse (1996–2007)

As a sequel to the previous qualitative analysis of the CPS, which is hardly satisfactory alone, a quantitative strategy is also implemented in this closing part of the chapter—and likewise in the exploration of similar thematic categories and local coherence structures, in addition to many other semantic relations and linguistic patterns of the news corpora in the chapter to follow. It is worth noting that this content analysis–based approach is not considered in isolation, but set against the theoretical framework, which is crucially based on linking text with its context.

One has to bear in mind that the quantitative analysis of the textual data is only an empirical explanation and holistic reading of the ways in which the pro-war ideology was constructed and justified, with a close focus on the structures of the language components in the text corpus (phraseology, lexis, syntax and the like). Nevertheless, the interpretation which I propose here with reference to the quantitative outputs does not rule out, inter alia, the historical, political and (social) cognitive structures and processes which were discussed in the previous chapters. Putting all these elements together would showcase some aspects of the "unconscious" mechanics of legitimization in discourse.

This quantitative strategy is carried out through the application of a blend of statistical operations using sophisticated computer programmes: Lexico3 and IRaMuTeQ, which best sort out and categorize the various lexico-semantic features of the corpora in a variety of ways (see Lebart, Salem, & Berry, 1998). In so doing, the quantifying tools of lexicometrics assist us to identify what Max Reinert (1993, 2003) calls the "lexical worlds" that were constructed in Blair's political speeches and the content of the press in relation to the then political crisis over Iraq. The software produced meticulous and multivariate statistical textual descriptions that describe a variety of discourse characteristics that might not be discernible at the level of individual speech texts.

Basically, the various figures and visualizations of this chapter and the following one, some of which are put in the Appendix, exhibit the concordances, frequency counts and co-occurrences analyses of keywords such as Iraq, Saddam, weapons of mass destruction, terrorism and other related vocabulary. In this respect, the main "discourse topics", which were discussed in the previous sections, are equally examined across different texts in the aggregate corpus. This is done to redraw the picture, or at least a fragment of it, that is likely to remain stored in the memory of the target audiences about the dossier of Iraq in general.

The CPS incorporates 30 essential texts. Those speeches were delivered by Blair at a number of occasions, most of which are typical epideictic pieces of oratory, starting with the Leader's speech in Blackpool, 1996. The texts were retrieved from the British Political Speech, an online reference that contains speeches of Britain's party leaders dating back to 1895.[11] Because the data concerned is homogenous in type (formal political speeches only) and coming from a single source (Blair), it was annotated only by tags that indicate the title and date of each of these texts (in

Lexico3). The coding of the CPS in this simple way yielded a variety of descriptive representations and thus allowed comparative analysis to be undertaken across time. Noise data was manually removed, such as some of the spoken markers (laughter, applause and pause) that were appended to the written form of the speeches in the source archives.[12] As for IRaMuTeQ, the corpus was taken as a single text without any partitions in order to produce tables of word classes.

In essence, the corpus was examined through different quantitative operations in order to categorize the various linguistic and semantic items of the selected texts. Because the software is a customizable and multi-function tool, its output could be displayed in a myriad of representations that exhibit a range of lexico-semantic aspects of discourse. The output text–based representations do not only enable us to reassess the validity of the qualitative interpretive assumptions made earlier, but also to discern some further textual features when considering Blair's speeches as a whole, and thus as discrete parts. Both Lexico3 and IRaMuTeQ produced the multivariate figures shown in this part of the chapter.

I shall highlight once again the cognitive background endorsed in the interpretation of the infographics resulted—as it has been described in the socio-cognitive model, whose logic of analysis is drawn from cognitive psychology and social cognition. In mundane terms, my premise is based on the belief that the prominence of specific topics in discourse during a particular period of time not only mirrors the writer's or speaker's worldviews and beliefs about a particular issue, but also has a crucial cognitive role to play. In this context, I argue that priming the then question of Iraq along with terrorism and WMD, among many other things, would substantially influence the audience's evaluation and judgements. In the sense that the large public that is exposed to this discourse is more likely to associate the aforementioned topics together because they are easy to retrieve from the long-term memory, but they may not remember all the details and circumstances, which are also germane to understanding the state of affairs in general. Robert Wyer and Thomas Srull advocate that there is only a small portion of knowledge that is actually retrieved from people's memory in order to judge and evaluate a particular situation. Thus, they would believe that such knowledge is representative of all that they have learned about such a situation or similar ones (2014, p. 82). However, what is of importance in this regard is to go beyond the level of topic priming and association and produce a detailed description of the co-text of each of these terms so as to be able to scrutinize the framing processes and persuasive strategies featured in Blair's discourse.

Figure 5.1 is a relative frequency distribution generated by Lexico3 of "Iraq" along with "terrorism" and "weapons", which were considered previously as main "discourse topics". It should be mentioned in passing that the ubiquitous acronym WMD was replaced by the phrase "weapons of mass destruction" in the whole original texts of the corpus in order to consider all the occurrences of the topic of Iraq's WMD which were made through other words and phrases, such as nuclear weapons, biological and chemical weapons, anthrax, sarin and mustard gas weapons, including other related vocabulary. As is shown in the concordance figure of the word "weapons", the latter was used exclusively when referring to the question of Iraq, except once when Blair addressed the peace process in Northern Ireland. This means that the word "weapons" is a reliable replacement of the phrase "weapons of mass destruction" in this context.

It is not surprising, as the graph indicates, that these were amongst the salient topics in Blair's speeches, notably in the wake of the 9/11, when Blair ramped up his attack on the Iraqi regime. The frequency ratio of each of these items is different, but they do shift up and down in similar ways. Clearly, the representation shows the importance attributed to the three topics during the period, which extends particularly from September 2001 up to March 2005, as the incidence reference is relatively high. Thus, "Iraq" and "WMD" are high-frequency words which correlate, to some extent, particularly between March 2003 and March 2005. While the former is still present in the aftermath, the latter seems to decline in frequency. Comparatively, the topic of terrorism remains salient, but with a lower frequency rate throughout the whole period.

Despite its high frequency between 2002 and 2004, "Iraq" does not seem to be a central theme in some other texts and is only rarely or accidentally mentioned. This figure does not solely count the frequency of the term in each text, but also points out the kind of associations, implications and references made to the question of Iraq during the delimited time frame, which is of particular importance to the argument

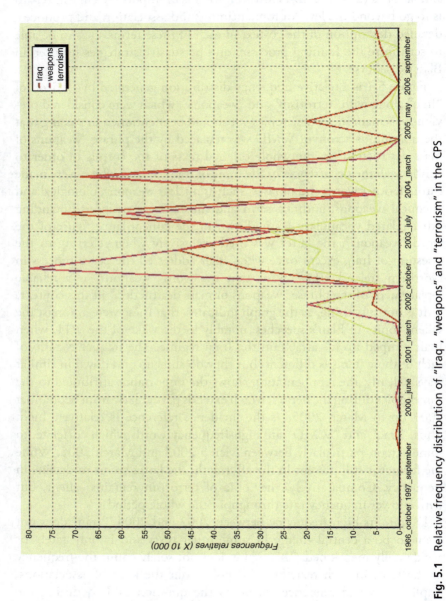

Fig. 5.1 Relative frequency distribution of "Iraq", "weapons" and "terrorism" in the CPS

I pursue. The relative frequencies of these key words will also be compared against their relative frequencies in the news corpora which are much larger in size.

The occurrence of those essential query words was also examined through concordance analysis. The latter helps us discover the relationships between different grammatical, lexical and semantic patterns in sample texts separately and as a whole (see Sinclair, 1991). One aspect of ideology in language, as postulated earlier, relates to the manner in which the speaker (Blair) used the aforementioned query terms, the kind of word forms that occur in close proximity to them and the type of associations made. It is a truism that the analysis of vocabulary is, in many respects, the analysis of the knowledge loaded in words, which can be uncovered based on both their co-text and context. Such knowledge, as previously postulated, is subjective and mirrors, by the end, the ideology of the writer or speaker.

Based on the same software tool I generated concordances of each of these essential words in the whole corpus. The lines of concordances taken in this section show the immediate contextual environment (co-text) of the following: "Iraq", "WMD" and "terrorism" across the 30 speeches.[13] Consider first "Iraq" and its co-text in the following excerpts (Fig. 5.2).

The concordance lists provide numerous examples of pathos (in italics) and logos in Blair's discourse, where he deliberately mingled emotions with evidence. Remarkably, emphasis is put on the oppressive nature of the Iraqi regime, particularly its persecution of the Shi'a sect and the Kurds. Indeed, this ethically based argument has been a defining character

```
les . Instead of enjoying its oil wealth Iraq has been reduced to poverty, with political
ed , sensible but firm way . But leaving Iraq to develop weapons of mass destruction ,
truction to be developed by a state like Iraq without let or hindrance would be grossly
the weapons inspectors were evicted from Iraq in 1998 there were still enough chemical
estruction of the marshlands in Southern Iraq , around 200 , 000 people were forcibly removed
cause of Iraqi intransigence . Meanwhile Iraq ' s people are oppressed and kept in poverty
sm . It ' s both . I know the worry over Iraq . People accept Saddam is bad . But they
llars trying to perfect a nuclear bomb . Iraq , under Saddam became the first country
children born in the centre and south of Iraq have chronic malnutrition . Where 60 percent
over 150 , 000 Shia Moslems in Southern Iraq and Moslem Kurds in Northern Iraq have been
uthern Iraq and Moslem Kurds in Northern Iraq have been butchered ; with up to four million
will be hard pressed to find a family in Iraq who have not had a son , father , brother
cs for the next generation . But first , Iraq and its weapons of mass destruction . In
pectors probed . Finally in March 1992 , Iraq admitted it had previously undeclared weapons
s used weapons of mass destruction , and Iraq has done so in the past - and we get sucked
oss the Atlantic.If we retreat now, hand Iraq over to alqaida and.., we won't be safer; we
will be committing
```

Fig. 5.2 Concordance of "Iraq" in the CPS

of Blair's foreign policy discourse ever since its early days in power. Obviously, the semantic profile of the above selected word is overwhelmingly loaded with negative imagery and connotations. Iraq, when it co-occurs with Saddam or his regime, is often associated with negative events, organizations or phenomena, such as poverty, threat, weapons of mass destruction, Taliban, Al-Qaeda, terrorism, dictatorship and the like, which certainly invoke negative emotional responses. Thus, these latter collocations of the word frame the Iraqi problem in security terms, with an alarming tone on the threat that it puts on peace with its WMD arsenal.

Thus, the boundary that is created between the in-group and the out-group, or to borrow van Dijk's terminology, the "ideological square", is self-evident. There is no question that Saddam was a brutal dictator, but his demonization as the most "ruthless dictator in the world" was highly exaggerated, as other totalitarian regimes with a heinous record in abusing human rights also existed at that time, such as North Korea. Consider the following concordance of "Saddam", which displays vivid examples of the negative representation attributed to Saddam (Fig. 5.3).

Regardless of the validity of Blair's allegations, the knowledge that has been constructed in his discourse over the controversial issue of Saddam's Iraq is a fundamental part of the knowledge that is shared and communicated in the British community and elsewhere. This shared knowledge, which incorporated a lot of prejudices, stereotypes and negative attitudes, as illustrated in the semantic prosodies of the concordances, would have a paramount impact on people's judgement and perception. This is especially

```
used by two dangerous and ruthless men - Saddam Hussein and Slobodan Milosevic . Both have
perly , is not an option . The regime of    Saddam is detestable . Brutal , repressive ,
political
scription . So let me tell you why I say    Saddam Hussein is a threat that has to be dealt
hension of most decent people . Uniquely    Saddam has used these weapons against his own people
en the weapons inspectors were in Iraq ,    Saddam lied , concealed , obstructed and harassed
ept in poverty . With the Taliban gone ,    Saddam is unrivalled as the world ' s worst regime
know the worry over Iraq . People accept    Saddam is bad . But they fear it ' s being done
is neighbours , against Israel perhaps ?    Saddam the man who killed a million people in an
ill blind to the bigger truths in Iraq .    Saddam has murdered more than a million Iraqis
low him to kill another million Iraqis ?    Saddam rules Iraq using fear - he regularly imprisons
tortured and / or " disappeared " due to    Saddam ' s regime . Why it is now that you deem
inal report is a withering indictment of    Saddam ' s lies , deception and obstruction , with
course of action share my detestation of    Saddam . Who could not ? Iraq is a wealthy country
ope of liberation lies in the removal of    Saddam , for them , the darkness will close back
n supported alqaida . We know Iraq under    Saddam gave haven to and supported terrorists .
September 11th did not create the threat    Saddam posed . But it altered crucially the balance
mercy of religious fanatics or relics of    Saddam , but to stand up for their right to decide
```

Fig. 5.3 Concordance of "Saddam" in the CPS

so if such knowledge was reproduced through other means of interaction and information channels, such as the press, TV and social media.

Perhaps the most evident paradox in this discourse is Blair's constant appeal to authority (UNSC, UNMOVIC, intelligence, international community, scientists and the like) to justify his ideological stance, which he breached by his engagement in a unilateral military action that was not authorized by international organizations.

Some further illustrative clustering and distribution infographs were generated using IRaMuTeQ. In this case the corpus was taken as a whole without any specific partitions. After the lemmatization of the text, the various lexical components of the input were distributed into six heterogeneous clusters, as shown in Fig. 5.4, in the form of a tree graph. The goal of using hierarchical clustering is to exhibit the relationships between the different lexical items in Blair's discourse, which incorporates all of his speeches from 1996 to 2007. However, only the elements related to foreign policy and Iraq are put under scrutiny.

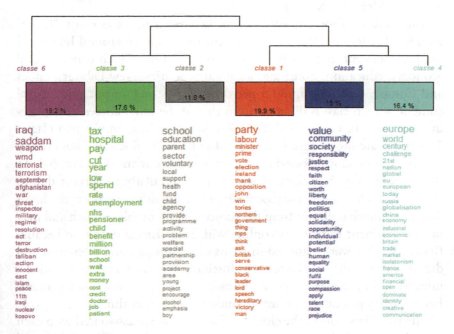

Fig. 5.4 Dendrogram of DHC

In broad terms, the cluster tree (or dendrogram) is a result of a hierarchical clustering analysis of the linguistic components of the text corpus according to their co-text and semantic relatedness. As shown in the figure, it constitutes several clusters, where each of these has a single or compound chunk and, in turn, each of these chunks lists the words of the corpus in a top-down manner based on their frequency and closeness. Thus, the visitations show how much of the text in the corpus of data is represented by the resulting chunks (the percentage at the top of each class). That is to say, the linguistic items are distributed into different word classes according to their correlation and the co-text—in the sense that the closely correlated language components are the ones clustered into the same chunk (class). Thus, the correlation between the classes read in a bottom-up manner, that is, classes which correlate strongly are near to each other under the same clade. At the higher level, the classes under the same ancestor clade are more similar to each other than other classes under another clade and so on (for further details and explanations, see McEnery & Wilson, 2001).

The next dendrogram exhibits six heterogeneous classes or "lexical worlds". The lexemes that often co-occur in the speech around Iraq stand for 19.2 per cent in proportion to the other classes, which concern local economy, education, home and local party politics, New Labour's values and Europe, representing 80.8 per cent of the total output. The lexical content of each class is different from that of the other classes, with varying degrees of proximity and dissimilarity. Note, for example, that classes 1, 4 and 5 are more close to one another than the *simplicifolious* class 6. Clearly, the semantic boundaries are much more marked in Fig. 5.4. In the DHC in Fig. 5.5, classes 5 and 6 are particularly important due to their direct relevance to the case study, while the other wordlists in classes 1–4 are somewhat distant from the subject matter of this research and may not be pertinent to Britain's conflict with Iraq. This is simply so because Blair's speeches were manifold in terms of their topics and references and did not tackle solely the conduct of foreign policy on Iraq, but included a number of home issues such as education, local economic management, Labour party politics and Europe, among many other things.

The wordlists exhibit the clusters of words that are associated with each other based on their co-occurrence and usage in the text. The grouping of

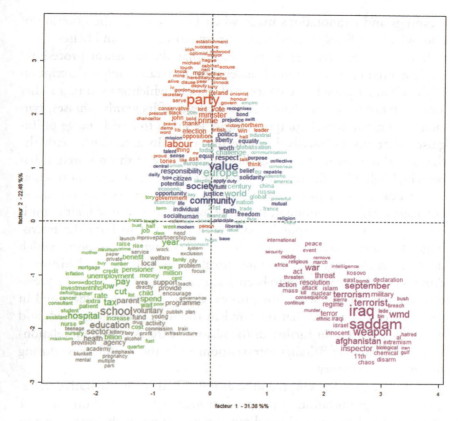

Fig. 5.5 Descending hierarchic classification of the CPS vocabulary co-occurrences

words in this sequence and order mirrors the "linguistic repertoire" in Blair's speeches, which could be relatively difficult to discern through mere qualitative consideration. From a cognitive perspective, these clusters of words, which are centred around a specific theme (the first word on the top of each list), are, indeed, "frames" or "mental scripts" that construct specific meanings and associations about each of these themes. Clearly, class 5 shows the shades of meanings associated with the word "values" in New Labour's policy, which lay emphasis on a hybrid of social democratic and neoliberal values. Class 6 brings to the fore the various meanings and connotations made when Blair refers to the question of Iraq, which are firmly loaded with negative correlations and biases.

It must be emphasized at this stage that the statistical procedures implemented in this section of the chapter generated only a description of the CPS. At issue is the concept of *context*, which is used in a rather loose manner to refer to language at the level of its words, phrases, syntactic and grammatical composition, in addition to a wide range of linguistic patterns as inscribed in the text only. In accordance with the theoretical framework that underlies the rationale of this research, it has been highlighted earlier that the critical study of discourse, as most scholars advocate, ought to consider language in its context that is beyond language itself. My comment, therefore, on the structure of Blair's political language in this corpus is made with reference to both the microlinguistic components and the wider, non-linguistic, aspects which moulded such language structure, notably the political and historical dimensions that have hitherto been discussed—albeit briefly in the previous chapters. In this sense, the pro-war discourse is only understood in the light of the events that occurred in the time frame identified, and might hark back a bit further in the history of the Anglo–Iraqi relationships, and likewise Britain's interventionism in the Middle East during the twentieth century.

In this chapter, I attempted to re-examine Blair's argumentative strategies in the legitimization of the pro-war ideology as spelled out in some of his political speeches throughout the period when the war plan was being designed. The qualitative analysis targeted very specific components and properties of language at the macro- and microsemantic levels in order to bring to the fore the mechanisms of persuasion in Blair's discourse. The latter was considered as a personal as well as an interpersonal political behaviour. It has already been established that political messages, whether embedded or explicitly stated, are not only personal convictions but rather social in character. Van Dijk postulates that "talk expresses cognitive representations of knowledge, beliefs, and attitudes, as well as the mental operations or strategies that are applied in their retrieval, storage, and usage in discourse production" (1987, p. 22). This is done without downplaying the cultural and social aspect of knowledge production and comprehension in the context of this case study.

What is strikingly remarkable about Blair's discourse is his frequent reference to the economic, security and geopolitical restraints and challenges put on Britain by the accelerating motion of globalization and how to safeguard and protect Britain's interests abroad. Nonetheless, the concept of "international community" is not a totally new invention, but a reproduction of an old imperialist tendency to maintain Britain's positions as an elite state and a leading power in today's world. In the postmodern era the physical geographical territories have been replaced by another imaginary boundary that is created based on who joins the motion of internationalization governed by the rules set out by the elite nations and those who remain at the margins.

Thus, through many rhetoric devices, stylistic variations and presuppositions, the case of Saddam's Iraq has been framed under the "War on Terror" agenda, which vehemently influenced the public opinion, as tested against the opinion polls. Terrorism and WMD have been one of most efficient means of persuasion that have been reverberating in the British political debates during the last few years. Yet, the concept of terrorism was strongly linked with "radical" or "extremist" religious movements that were trying to challenge the order of power through organized terror and violence. There is a call here to redefine the concept of New Terrorism, which remains highly contested and linked with Islam, which is mistakenly described by some media outlets as a religion of intolerance and xenophobia. In brief, the elements discussed here point out the ways in which elite and public consensus on an aggressive political ideology, which was by no means unnecessary and destructive, took place in Britain.

Notes

1. It is to be mentioned that the Prime Minister in Britain, as part of the so-called Royal Prerogatives, has the power to declare war without the need to consult the parliament.
2. The vote over the Iraq War caused what was seen as the largest "backbench revolt" by members of any political party in the modern history of Britain. Many New Labour members of Parliament (MPs) opposed the

action of war, such as Tam Dalyell, Alan Simpson and former ministers Glenda Jackson, Peter Kilfoyle and Mark Fisher.
3. The use of force against sovereign states is firmly prohibited by the constitutional law of the UN Charter. As stated in the UN Charter Article 2(4), there are only two exceptions for the authorization of the use of force: either a full authorization by the UNSC or in the case of self-defence against an aggression.
4. The just war theory, which is usually identified with Saint Augustine and Thomas Aquinas, has been the first endeavour that sought to put the war into an ethical and legal framework.
5. Under New Labour, Britain intervened militarily in Kosovo (1999); Indonesia, East Timor, and Sierra Leone (2000); Macedonia (2001); Afghanistan (2001) and Iraq (2003).
6. It is important to note that New Labour's foreign policy was not a totally new drift in British politics; many inspiration from the past were still endorsed by Blair and his cabinet. Take, for example, Labour's support for the prohibition of arm sales to countries accused of abusing human rights, particularly during the 1970s. The influence of the subsequent Secretaries in the making of the party's foreign policy must also be taken into account; see, for example, Theakston (2004).
7. The thematic and cognitive structures (topicalization) and other auxiliary linguistic features of the speeches are best illustrated in the quantitative analysis of Blair's discourse, which will show much overlap with the qualitative interpretation.
8. For an extensive list of bibliographical references on the issues of terrorism as discussed in a variety of disciplines, see Tinnes (2013).
9. "The Authorisation for Use of Military Force", a document issued by the White House on 14 September 2001 to empower the president declaring the war on Iraq.
10. The phrase "rogue states" was widely used in the USA, but less in Britain, to refer to a few countries that showed explicit hostility to West. Many scholars advocated that though such an informal label had no legal perspective, it was widely used by US senior officials. For the case of Iraq, see, for example, Litwak (2000), pp. 123–157.
11. For a full list, see the Appendix. The texts of the speeches were taken from the following website; britishpoliticalspeech.org bar Blair's speech on Iraq in the House of Commons, see *The Guardian*, 18 March 2003.

12. For a thorough analysis, it is important to include some markers of the speech which cannot be found in the written script unless transcribed, such as the verbal features: intonation, pauses, laughter, changes in rhythm and timbre, and the like.
13. Due to space limit, only a few lines from each partition were exhibited.

References

Barnett, M. (2011). *Empire of humanity: A history of humanitarianism*. New York: Cornell University Press.

Carlton, F. T. (1906). Humanitarianism, past and present. *The International Journal of Ethics, 17*(1), 48–55.

Chandler, D., & Heins, V. (Eds.). (2007). *Rethinking ethical foreign policy: Pitfalls, possibilities and paradoxes*. London/New York: Routledge.

Chilton, P. (2004). *Analysing political discourse. Theory and practice*. London: Routledge.

Chilton, P., & Schäffner, C. (Eds.). (2002). *Politics as text and talk: Analytic approaches to political discourse*. Amsterdam/Philadelphia: John Benjamins.

Comte, A. (1853). *The positive philosophy of Auguste Comte* (trans: Martineau, H.). London: J. Chapman.

Cook, R. (1997, May 12). Robin Cook's speech on the government's ethical foreign policy. *The Guardian*. Retrieved from https://www.theguardian.com/world/1997/may/12/indonesia.ethicalforeignpolicy

Fairclough, N. (2000). *New Labour, new language?* London: Routledge.

Hammond, P. (2007). The humanitarian spectacle. In P. Hammond (Ed.), *Media, war and postmodernity* (pp. 37–58). London/New York: Routledge.

Hart, C. (Ed.). (2011). *Critical discourse studies in context and cognition*. Amsterdam: John Benjamins Publishing Company.

Heinze, E. (2009). *Waging humanitarian war: The ethics, law, and politics of humanitarian intervention*. Albany, NY: SUNY Press.

Hodge, A., & Nilep, C. (Eds.). (2007). *Discourse, war and terrorism: Discourse approaches to politics, society and culture*. Amsterdam/Philadelphia: John Benjamins Publishing Company.

Holland, J. (2013). *Selling the war on terror: Foreign policy discourses after 9/11*. London: Routledge.

Jenks, E. (1900). *A history of politics*. New York: Macmillan.

Laqueur, W. (1999). *The new terrorism: Fanaticism and the arms of mass destruction*. London/New York: Oxford University Press.
Lebart, L., Salem, A., & Berry, L. (1998). *Exploring textual data*. Dordrecht, The Netherlands: Kluwer.
Litwak, R. (2000). *Rogue states and US foreign policy: Containment after the Cold War*. Washington, DC: Johns Hopkins University Press.
McEnery, T., & Wilson, A. (2001). *Corpus linguistics: An introduction*. Edinburgh, UK: Edinburgh University Press.
Randall, D. (2009). *Terrorism: A history*. Cambridge, UK: Polity Press.
Reinert, M. (1993). Les "mondes lexicaux" et leur "logique" à travers l'analyse statistique d'un corpus de récits de cauchemars. *Langage et Societe, 66*, 5–39.
Reinert, M. (2003). Le rôle de la répétition dans la représentation du sens et son approche statistique dans la méthode Alceste. *Semiotica, 147*(1–4), 389–420.
Schmid, A. P. (Ed.). (2011). *The Routledge handbook of terrorism research*. Abingdon, OX: Routledge.
Simms, B., & Trim, D. J. B. (2011). *Humanitarian intervention: A history*. Cambridge, UK: Cambridge University Press.
Sinclair, J. (1991). *Corpus, concordance, collocation*. Oxford: Oxford University Press.
Strong, J. (2015, October 17–18). *Blair's failure to legitimize the Iraq War*. Presented at the Failure and Denial in World Politics conference, London. Retrieved from https://drjamesstrong.files.wordpress.com/2015/09/strong-jr-_understanding-tony-blairs-failure-to-legitimize-the-iraq-war_-2015-millennium-conference.pdf
Tannen, D., Schiffrin, D., & Hamilton, H. E. (Eds.). (2001). *The handbook of discourse analysis*. Malden, MA/Oxford, UK: Blackwell Publishing.
Tester, K. (2010). *Humanitarianism and modern culture*. University Park, PA: The Pennsylvania State University Press.
Theakston, K. (Ed.). (2004). *British foreign secretaries since 1974*. London: Routledge.
Tinnes, J. (2013). Terrorism and the media (including the Internet): An extensive bibliography. *Perspectives on Terrorism, 7*(1), 145–147.
Towle, P. (2009). *Going to war: British debates from Wilberforce to Blair*. Basingstoke, UK: Palgrave.
Van Dijk, T. (1997). What is political discourse analysis. In J. Blommaert & C. Bulcaen (Eds.), *Political linguistics* (pp. 11–52). Amsterdam: Benjamins.
Van Dijk, T. A. (1977). *Text and context: Explorations in the semantics and pragmatics of discourse*. London: Longman.

Van Dijk, T. A. (1987). *Communicating racism: Ethnic prejudice in thought and talk*. Newbury Park, CA: Sage.

Van Dijk, T. A. (1995). Ideological discourse analysis. *The New Courant, 4*, 135–161.

Van Dijk, T. A. (2009). *Society and discourse: How social contexts influence text and talk*. Cambridge, UK: Cambridge University Press.

Van Dijk, T. A., & Kintsch, W. (1983). *Strategies of discourse comprehension*. New York: Academic Press.

Williams, P. (2005). *British foreign policy under New Labour, 1997–2005*. New York: Palgrave Macmillan.

Wyer, R. S., & Srull, T. K. (2014). *Memory and cognition in its social context*. New York: Psychology Press.

6

The Discursive Construction of the Iraq War in the British "Quality" Press

6.1 The Mainstream Ideology and the Fourth Estate in Britain

6.1.1 The Evolution of the News Culture in Britain

Comparatively speaking, bias is often less orchestrated in the broadsheets than in the tabloids, which are more informal in their editorial practices, as they often tend to espouse traditional techniques of propaganda, such as the use of excessive sarcasm and pictures. The former is more serious in tone, with less political satire and moderate partisanship. Though the quality press is not always impartial, its distortions in reporting the day-to-day events, particularly conflicting issues, as is the case in this research, are less visible and well encoded in the structure of language. It goes without saying, after all, that the "manufacturing of consent" by the established authority is also enacted by the other media outlets in their ongoing flow of information, which is by no means heavily imbued with much skewed interpretations and judgement than with facts.

Therefore, a systematic analysis of the news texts selected would vividly illustrate the inherent power of language in the promulgation of political ideologies and normalization of illegitimate coercion and violence. In a narrow and rather technical sense, this chapter seeks to decode the various framing patterns and values that are embedded in the coverage of the Iraqi dossier in three of the best-selling British national dailies: *The Daily Telegraph* (commonly referred to as *The Telegraph*), *The Guardian* and *The Independent*, starting from the early 2000s up to the end of major military operations on 1 May 2003. Post-war coverage, however, has not been given a priority in this research, as it has been less poignant on the pace of events.

Before doing so, it is requisite to succinctly survey the overall circumstances and practices that moulded the media industry in Britain, which, it should be highlighted, has a long-dated tradition that goes back to the early days of English Renaissance. In *The History of British Journalism* (1859), the press chronicler Alexander Andrews depicted the main stages in the British newspaper's development, with a focus on its enduring struggle with the successive royal authorities and other social and economic conditions in its early beginnings. In the below quotation, he draws a broad picture about the major trammels that stunted the growth and evolution of the English press in its infancy. He writes:

> Dependent as it was on the progress of public enlightenment, of government liberality, of general liberty and knowledge; checked by the indifference of a people or the caprices of a party; suppressed by a king, persecuted by a parliament, harassed by a licenser, burnt by a hangman, and trampled by a mob, the newspaper has been slow in climbing to its present high. (p. 1)

Despite this miserable start, however, the press became both a formal instrument of state propaganda and a tool for the enlightenment and education of an increasing literate audience. More significantly, thanks to the high profitability in the then flourishing information business, the press proprietors made the newspaper a legitimate political partner just to emerge as an independent "Fourth Estate" by the turn of the nineteenth century. From the early amateurish endeavours of the English and Dutch traders working in the shores of Amsterdam and zealous religious reformers who strived to challenge Catholic hegemony in the British Isles, to the contemporary sophisticated press enterprise with its skilled labour force, the British newspaper underwent a matrix of transformations in its arduous evolution. Furthermore, the practice of journalism was mostly unprofessional and a highly risky business that took the lives of many adventurers. The very few approved pamphlets and newsbooks by the respective royal authorities were put under strict regulation, as publication necessitated legalization and their content was checked routinely (Temple, 2008, pp. 3–20). Such firm state control of the whole information and publishing industry continued to shape the destiny of the press till the beginnings of the Victorian period, where the last stamp act was lifted up, ushering for a new era characterized by economic rivalry, diversity and more political engagement.

Broadly speaking, the Victorian era was a period of huge socio-political transition and economic growth in Britain that shored up the progress of the press. Ostensibly, the impact of the Industrial Revolution was profound and permanent, which brought with it deep changes in the life of the Britons. The manifestation of this socio-economic transformation, as many historians point out, was crystallized more perfectly at the turn of the century. As far as the press is concerned, the thriving economy, accelerating demographic growth rates/the population boom and the rise of large cities created more audiences and generated more sales. In addition to traditional industries, such as textiles, steel and coal, the publishing business as a whole started to boom and attract increasing numbers of readers and investors. This is often considered the golden age of British journalism, when the London papers were printed regularly, some of which sold on a daily basis, creating therefore a culture of news reading that incorporated a large segment of the middle class. Nonetheless, the centralized form of political authority that imposed many forms of censorship and legislation was a serious impediment to the freedom of speech and the free circulation of the papers, at least in the first half of the century.

It has been clear that there were a plethora of socio-political, and significantly economic, factors that had enormously facilitated the evolution of the newspaper to become eventually labelled as the Fourth Estate.

As just mentioned, in their abiding struggle against the dominating forces, newsmakers and journalists faced intense pressure and persecution, yet such a situation was reversed around the mid of the nineteenth century as the tide of protest reached its highest point. One of these was the widespread commercialization of the newspaper, thanks to the high revenues of advertising, which attracted the attention of ambitious burghers and businessmen, many of whom were parliamentarians and party leaders. The increasing demand for information, which was by then a product to be sold on regular basis, made the press one of the most profitable investments. One has to remark here that the convergence between politics and news industry generated an asymmetric relationship between two inherently opposing forces and, therefore, created a new space for the struggle over power and domination.

During the first half of the nineteenth century, a campaign was already in motion, led by some progressive MPs, civil society and the bourgeoisie in order to break the seals of state restrictions, and particularly to relieve the press from the burden of the stamp acts, known then as "taxes on knowledge" (Curran & Seaton, 2003, pp. 5–22). It was also noticed that during this sensitive period, journalists started to distance themselves from the political elite, playing instead the role of a watchdog and the defender of the mass public against the frequent abuses by people of power. At first sight it would appear that the papers gained a full emancipation from the restraints of the government, but this was indeed a swing to another phase of auto-censorship, which was, the least to say, more complex and replete with ideological biases and political partisanship. Arguably, such conditions continued to shape the destiny of the press up to current times.

It is true that there has been a sharp decline in print readership during the last few years, which brought with it a huge loss in revenue. Such an unfortunate situation is likely to continue, as audiences and advertisers are moving towards the open Web, which provides more sophisticated information services. Conversely, however, the technological leap in communication created more virtual audiences for the papers in the vast digital space. Latest estimates from the British National Readership Survey (NRS) and the Audit Bureau of Circulation (ABC) show an increase in the virtual readers of the national dailies, with a record of millions of unique browsers.[1] In fact, the technological advent might not reduce the influence of the press, as it is still responding positively to the challenges posed by technology. It is fairly reasonable to advocate that the papers are still having a good share in the information industry and playing their traditional role in setting the public agenda and the making of politics in Britain.

In Western liberal democracies the press has always been considered the "watchdog" that guards against the abuse of power by the elites, most particularly the Establishment. In reality, the British newspaper, as is the case for the other mass media outlets, was always in clash with the major political forces and pressure groups by virtue of its function as a medium and a gatekeeper of information. It is also required from the news producers to adhere to a code of practice that idealizes freedom of speech, neutrality in reporting and plurality of voices. Such a de facto power struggle is usually quite manifest between the various contesting ideologues from across the political and civic spectrum. In parallel to the preceding chapter, which dealt with Blair's political discourse with reference to his official speeches, the present one accounts for "news" as another distinct genre of communication and interaction which is tremendously charged with ideological preferences and inextricably interwoven with politics.

Nonetheless, the media are only one of the tools of hegemony which, above all things, has its roots and logic in the fabric of society per se. This means, among many different things, its history, political traditions, social conventions and cultural norms. Hence, it is perhaps intriguing to look more closely into how these existing cultural codes, social relations, values and customs that are still vividly manifest in the postmodern British society continue to feed, and assist to (re)produce, the dominant ideology. Indeed, I tackled this aspect in the case of Iraq War rather incidentally through reference to the so-called cultural membership and its impact on the representation of the *Other* in language use. Blair, for example, would resort to the use of specific language strategies, style and rhetoric that aim to trigger a positive reaction from British audience, but this would not receive the same reaction from an Iraqi audience. This is simply so because of the cultural gap between the two social groups, which have little shared knowledge and distinct worldviews. Similarly, Saddam Hussein's political speeches to the people of Iraq, some of which were routinely published by the British papers, when compared with Blair's, are distinguishably different in terms of their linguistic categories, references and style.

In this context, mainstream ideology means the dominant political trends, economic models, social practices and attitudes, and the major cultural traits that distinguish the identity of the "British". As has been discussed, albeit briefly, in Chap. 2, the culture–ideology complex has been abundantly studied by the neo-Marxists, in particular, who argued that consensus arises from the "subaltern" social groups and peripheral forces in endorsing the ideology of their elites (see the notion of "cultural superstructure" in Gramsci's works). Such claim, perhaps, though still, to some extent, theoretically valid, may need some further update in the light of the current socio-political and economic changes, first and foremost, the advancement in communication technology and the dissolution of the Left ideologies, in addition to the flow of migration and demographic changes.

Accordingly, it has been advocated by CDS scholars that culture is very much germane to the notion of ideology and social cognition—though this point is not fully explored in this research. In essence, the mainstream ideology in a given society is the product of social conformity, which grows out of a web of factors interweaving in the course of history, yet moments of dissonance and marginal counter-ideologies do still exist. The dominating social norms, values and patterns are routinely promoted, in a positive and affirmative way, through what Gramsci calls "articulatory practices" in social institutions, and notably sustained via the various channels of interaction and communication. In the context of today's world, the mass media outlets are perhaps the most prominent and effective tool in the maintenance of hegemony and supremacy at the local and international levels.

Of special theoretical significance here is the cognitive aspect of ideology, which is, as postulated by the thitherto cited works, monitored by the use of language in the first place. Within the conceptual framework of this research, it was advocated that just like individuals, society has its own cognition and mannerism, which in turn affect the cognition of all its individual members. This view has seminal implications in relation to the theory of discourse analysis. Ideology is, in many different respects, shaped and guided by the ideas, beliefs and worldviews that are embedded in the collective mind of the public through the various social institutions and channels of information. It is becoming widely accepted, particularly within communication studies, that oriented media coverage has a substantial influence on the unconscious mind of the mass public—this assumption is fundamental in the socio-cognitive model.

Undeniably, the newspaper left a peculiar imprint on the British culture, as it was the only instrument for information and knowledge sharing in the public and political domains for quite a long period of time. At its early beginning in the form of amateurish *Mercurries* and "flimsy" newssheets, it served no more purpose than the entertainment of the minority literate bourgeoisie. Shortly thereafter, however, it turned out to be a colossal brainwashing machine that made its presence strongly felt in the political landscape. But still, the English papers were most of the time exploited by authority, starting with the monarchs of the sixteenth century up to the modern political parties and corporate. By the mid of the nineteenth century, the press campaign freed the whole information business from the patronage of the government. Henceforth, the practice of journalism became more professional, diverse and innovative. It was perhaps the high-profit revenues of the newspaper industry and its potential to mould the public opinion and influence the political choices of the elite which explain the persistence of the freedom of speech campaigners in the face of state restrictions and censorship. After all, although it is now relegated to a relatively inferior position due to the technological transformations of the day, it is still one of the vehicles of propaganda that contributes, to some measure, in framing the complex socio-political realities of postmodern Britain.

Notwithstanding that there is no regulation whatsoever on the newspaper bar its own code of ethics, self-censorship, partisanship and explicit ideological bias are still present as distinctive features of the British press. With reference to complaints from the left-wingers, I would argue that the hostility of the newspapers to the socialist doctrines, which was quite obvious throughout much of the twentieth century, was an outcome of the economic structure of the media industry. In the following section, it will be shown how the bulk of British newspapers complied only with the mainstream ideology and echoed, in essence, a pro-capitalist and conservative tone. As just mentioned, what lies beneath such ideological reasoning cannot be considered in isolation from the culture of the British society as a whole, which was accumulated over an extended period of time. It is obvious that the press, which progressively attracted large audiences, made a huge contribution in the education and enlightenment of the public, which became politically conscious of its own conditions and simultaneously engaged in the practice of politics.

6.1.2 The Economic Structure and Political Bias

Throughout its long history, the newspaper industry in Britain has always been in confrontation with a range of socio-political, economic and technical labyrinths that slowed down its natural progress. An in-depth look at its political history, during the last 300 years or so, would show that it had undergone a fierce battle for its emancipation, notably against state censorship and repression. Yet, this campaign started to show success only during the second half of the nineteenth century when some ambitious businessmen, such as Alfred Harmsworth, militant MPs and professional journalists brought the press to another phase characterized by commercialization, artistic creativity and more political engagement.

Despite the fact that print readership is sliding backwards, the newspaper maintains a fairly strong position in the market and is still a crucial apparatus for political and social change. Nonetheless, the argument I want to advance at this stage does not overlook the impact of the other means of communication on the pace of politics and public mood. In liberal democracies the exercise of power is highly intricate and decentralized, as there are various patterns of political authority where the media are vehemently exploited in the pursuit of, so to speak, ideological dominance—in the sense that neither the prime minister alone, nor key politicians and senior officials can fully take a decision in isolation from the other players in the civil society and rival political forces. One of these players is the media owners and news community as a whole that continuously put pressure on decision-makers. In Britain, it is assumed that the laissez-faire economic policy would preserve the autonomy of the press so as to promote the interests of the general public. From the traditional Marxist standpoint, the role of the press, including the other information channels, is believed to maintain the economic interests and political supremacy of the minority bourgeoisie, who control the industry as a whole.

High levels of concentration in the British press were particularly remarkable at the dawn of the twentieth century, which was a period of exceptional opportunity for investment in the information industry. It was at this turning point that newspapers were becoming tightly interlocked with business and politics. The then barons and entrepreneurs, such as Lord Northcliffe,[2] his brothers, Lord Rotheremere and Sir Lester Harmsworth, were among the proprietors who held a monopoly over the national British press for decades and were driving this market towards an increasing concentration. The same concentrated structure existed for the regional press, which was dominated by the Berry brothers, Lords Kamrose and Kemsley. The relationship between politicians and journalists, the specialist in political journalism Mick Temple explains, "went beyond the payment of bribes: then, as now, there was a symbiotic relationship, especially as politicians began to understand the importance of the press as a conduit to the ever-fickle public" (2008, p. 12).

Northcliffe's mass-market *The Daily Mail*, established in 1896, "sold well over 200,000 copies daily in its first years and reached half-a-million sales after three years" (Negrine, 1989, p. 58). He was an ambitious journalist driven, in the first place, by commercial motivation, which enabled him to build the "Amalgamated Press", which was seen then as the largest periodical publishing empire in the world. Media commentator Brian McNair clarifies, "[B]y 1910, Lords Pearson, Cadbury and Northcliffe between them controlled 67 per cent of national daily circulation, establishing a trend of concentration of ownership that has persisted in the British newspaper industry ever since" (2009, p. 87). From another angle, Alfred's brother Rothermere and the majority of the barons were firmly anti-socialist and continued to exploit their newspapers to promote anti-communist and anti-socialist ideology. Overall, the communist credo was represented as an "alien culture" and a threat to the political order and stability in the traditionally conservative and pro-capitalist British society.

Many structural changes, however, occurred in the aftermath of the Second World War, for the press sales dropped dramatically, as measured by the percentage of circulation. Some unprofitable titles, mostly the Left ones, closed down due to the steady decline of readership, lack of funding, the harsh competition and, importantly, the technological advancement that led to the emergence of television and radio, which rendered the press to a secondary position as a source of news.

There emerged new proprietors, while others maintained their presence in the market for more than a century, as is the case for the Rothermeres. For example, Rupert Murdoch's News International is one of most influential media players that supported the campaign for the Iraq War, as Murdoch was ideologically committed and involved in politics and very well known for his support for New Labour. British journalist and writer Anthony Sampson noticed that "in 2003 nearly all his 175 editors across the world echoed his support for the war" (2004, p. 234). Traditionally, Murdoch's press followed a right-wing political stance, starting with its back up for Margaret Thatcher in 1979 and John Major in 1992. His newspapers were accused of tailoring their content to curry favour with Tony Blair's government in 1997, 2001 and 2005 general elections. However, the group's reputation has been severely damaged by allegations of telephone hacking scandals during the 2000s.

It is important to stress the fact that the press was largely growing out of the bowels of politics, and therefore wielded immense political power, as it was the only available means of communication in ancient eras. The early British press barons of the twentieth century had a lasting impact on the press business. Thus, there has been a long tradition of mutual influence between these barons, journalists and politicians. In the course of the time, the newspaper secured a position at the heart of politics, as some of its owners were appointed to high-level political leadership positions. Alfred Harmsworth, for example, was appointed Director for Propaganda in Lloyd George Liberal government during the First World War, and Beaverbrook joined the wartime cabinet as Minister of Information in 1918, and later Minister of Supply during the Second World War. Ralph Negrine stated that "there were six or fewer newspaper proprietors in the House of Commons. By 1880 that figure more than doubled to 14 and continued to rise. From 1892 to 1910, there were between 20 and 30 newspaper proprietors in the Commons" (1989, pp. 43–44). Therefore, some British politicians such as Lloyd George and his supporters seemed keenly interested in having the press on their side. They managed to win the support of *The Daily Mail* and also purchased *The Daily Chronicle* in 1918.

It has been clear that the increased concentration of ownership into the hands of a few proprietors is a distinctive feature in the development of the British newspapers, at least for the last two centuries. The same holds true for the other outlets. Similar levels of concentration do exist in the magazine and periodical market, the broadcasting systems and also in network services. Then as now, the ensemble of media tools in Britain is dominated by a few transnational firms and corporations. Thus, with the convergence of these companies, which are increasingly fusing their mutual interests within the media industry and other business activities, the owners are having substantial political weight that is apparently beyond control.

Additionally, partisanship is another ethical issue where objectivity was twisted to suit political ends, though this is becoming less rigid these days. There are ample examples of such political bias either to the right-wing ideology, which was in fact the general tendency, or to the left and centre-left ideology traditionally associated with Labour Party. Partisanship in news reporting was becoming remarkable, starting from the nineteenth century. This was the time where newspapers were free to make their alliance with political parties, especially when politicians began to be fully aware of the potential of the papers to receive a favourable coverage. Mick Temple again claimed that "at the start of the nineteenth century, journalists mostly reported news in a biased and openly partisan way: papers generally supported a political party and tailored news to suit the party line" (2008, p. 26). Radical sentiment then was enhanced by a number of relatively successful working class newspapers, such as *The Political Register*, *The Republican* and *The Poor Man's Guardian*, which achieved relatively small circulation.

In brief, the overall situation of British journalism nowadays is much more sophisticated with the increase in audiences and the emergence of new tools of information, which created other public spheres for political interaction and communication. However, the barons' financial interests intermingled with their political motivation, which set the ground for an everlasting economic monopoly in the press sector. Indeed, a number of ethical issues are still debated in Britain, notably the threat of the current economic structure of the media on the plurality of voices and freedom of speech. This line of argument has also been endorsed by Edward

Herman and Noam Chomsky (2008) in their "propaganda model", providing a critical account of corporate ownership of the media as one of the crucial structural factors that reproduces the ideology of the elites. Central to this thesis is the fact that mass media control content in order to serve the ends of the dominant elite. Effective censorship according to their propaganda model occurs through the ownership concentration. In short, media ownership is viewed as an effective propaganda filter that determines the output of the press.

To further elaborate on the hitherto sketched argument, it should be emphasized that the view held in this research work about the press and its function is congruent with that of Richard C. Stanton, who called for a reassessment of the Habermassian, somehow idealist view of the, particularly Western, media. Stanton notes that "the press, or in its more widely accepted form, the media, are not in fact an institution but agents working on behalf of stakeholders" (2007, p. 193). Regardless of the commercial and political considerations that constitute a firmly established character of the newspaper, the latter is also supposed to have a positive social contribution and responsibility towards the civil society and the government alike. It is true that the liberal approach in Western liberal democracies idealizes the freedom of speech, which would best spur the provision of a more professional journalism. But it is still problematic whether the news community adheres to its ethical code of practice, and this is especially so when it comes to controversial and conflicting issues such as Britain's military intervention in Iraq.

As a new practice in political communication and agenda setting, press secretaries, widely labelled nowadays as "spin doctors", are often appointed by political leaders in order to eschew the pressure of the media and influence news reporting in ways supportive of the official stance. For example, as part of its strategy in communication, New Labour founded the Strategic Communications Unit, headed by Blair's chief spin doctor Alastair Campbell. The latter, including a few other journalists and media experts, made the party able to not only communicate effectively with the large public, but also respond immediately to the criticism of the conservatives.[3]

6.1.3 News Discourse Analysis

It is fairly reasonable to advocate that the production of news in the media is a discursive process that is substantially moulded by the social, political and economic circumstances at a given period of time. It goes without saying that political parties, pressure groups and people of power are always in need to forge a symbiotic relationship with journalists and news producers as part of their communication strategy to get an adequate coverage. Though the press market is dying out, the discourse of the Fourth Estate is, in many different ways, interlocked with decision-making and political processes in Westminster. To date, politicians are still obsessed with the media, which Blair, by the end of his career as Prime Minister, described as a *feral beast*. Thus, businessmen protect and promote their economic interests through advertising and appropriate communication strategy to preserve their presence in the market, which cannot be fulfilled without real engagement with the media community. Likewise, the various social and pressure groups, ostracized minorities and those who are at the margins of society would need visibility in the media to voice their own concerns and interests.

Arguably, even in a democracy such as Britain, the media have never been neutral reporters but typical gatekeepers of information which produce versions of the reality "out there" that advance their own interpretation and ideological preferences. This is exactly what makes the media one of the most effective centres of power and political pressure. They do not only shape the public mind but also can stir up division within the public and political parties, monitor the pace of politics and set the agenda. Moreover, as part of routine journalistic practices, decision-making about the events to be reported undergoes further bureaucratic processes before being made available for public consumption. Yet the institutional practices and their impact on the content of the papers are not considered in this research.

Bearing these elements in mind, news discourse analysis in this respect entails the possibility of studying a web of variables, among which the language practices in the representation of events and the construction of reality is only one part. In this research, the critical study of language and its components, both the linguistic and non-linguistic, will patently illustrate how the (official) ideology is articulated in the coverage of the press. Nonetheless, there are many other variables that could jointly affect this process, some of which were previously discussed, such as the concentration of press ownership, political partisanship, routine bureaucratic practices and so on.

Although there are other alternative definitions of news, it is after all, as Gerald J. Baldasty put it, "a malleable compound, a synthesis of interests. It is defined through the relationship of the press and society, through the economic forces that shape newspapers as businesses, and through the structure and day-to-day operation of the press itself" (1992, p. 144). Roger Fowler (1991) adds that the making of news is not a mere reflection of the real world and its happenings, but a product of, inter alia, the press industry, economy and the existing bureaucratic and political relations. Placed within this general framework, the analysis of news discourse in this chapter would further elaborate on the ideological aspect of warfare politics in Blair's Britain, yet with a narrow focus on language rather than on the internal professional practices or external forces of pressure.

I have previously alluded to some basic discrepancies between the news discourse and the discourse of politicians, at least from a stylistic point of view. This will, henceforth, be referred to with the phrase "schematic superstructure" of the text. Overall, the news text is distinguishably different in terms of its strategies, schemata, components and aims. To wit, the structure of language, the semantics and lexical components of a formal political speech and of a news article are quite heterogeneous. Unlike the arbitrary nature of formal political speeches, which could follow numerous modes of narration and styles, news articles are usually, but not always, structured in a regular fashion. A news article is preceded by a summary in the headline, which provides the *upshot* of the text; further information is to be found in the leading sentence and, finally, other related details in the subsequent paragraphs about the circumstances of a specific event in terms of its timing, place, participants and the like. It is worth noting that the most important information about the reported event of the article is to be placed at the very beginning. This might not be the case for editorials and opinion articles, which have no specific layout and are mostly explicit in their views and ideological trappings.

Another major difference between the political discourse and the news discourse, at least in relation to the corpora of this research, is that the former is originally an utterance that has been transcribed into a written form, while the latter is a text. Those contextual nuances are important in the analysis of discourse. Many of the circumstances that occur in a political event, such as delivering a speech by Blair to an audience in a parliamentary session or a conference, are quite different from writing a news article, by a journalist, directed to the mass public. From a contextual point of view, the first is a real-time communicative situation where there is a direct interaction between the agents, which is not the case for the second. Van Dijk comments that "the writer, the text, and the reader are less closely participating in one spatiotemporally identifiable situation. Yet, even in this case, it may be appropriate to account for texts in the more dynamic terminology of discourse use in production, understanding, and action" (1988b, p. 9). As a matter of fact, the analysis of these two types of discourse would require slightly different strategies and procedures.

Based on theoretical and analytical insights taken from the socio-cognitive model, which can also be found in other classic approaches, a suggested explanation of the process of legitimization is carried out by bringing together the social, linguistic and cognitive perspectives. There are, indeed, a number of language properties that are worthy of detailed analysis. Nonetheless, as I did with Blair's speeches in the preceding chapter and for the sake of methodological consistency, I shall proceed with the macrosemantic description and analysis of the structures of the news texts as a strategy to decipher the ideological inclination that is implicit in the sequences of the sentences and chunks of the texts as a whole. The same macrorules applied on the political discourse are also valid for the news discourse, or any other type of text, because the purpose is to delineate the *discourse topics* out of the propositions made by the writer (journalist) in the news article.

Further to what has been suggested about the elements that establish coherence in the text, the schematic superstructure should also require some attention because the form of the text is related to its semantics. Patently, the news article is more formalized compared with a political speech, which is more arbitrary in its overall schematic, and also thematic, structure. This structure is firmly related to what has been conceptualized earlier as the global semantic structure of the text, that is, its macrostructure. In simple words, the upshot of the text is addressed in the headline, or the lead, which is best recalled by readers and would be used for future evaluations and judgements. Other details and less important information and circumstances are often placed in the bottom of the text and are not likely to be remembered by most readers. This is important, as, van Dijk advocates, "an analysis of produced relevance distribution in news reports also enables us to study the cognitive, social, and ideological production conditions of such reports, as well as their processing, and hence their memorization and uses by readers" (1988b, p. 16).

Some of the elements in the socio-cognitive model are not taken into account, such as morphology and the formal superstructure (schemata) in the language of the news. One has to also bear in mind that news discourse analysis cannot be adequately performed at the level of the text only. The overall contextual variables should also be incorporated along with the examination of mere linguistic structures in the text. The current economic concentration of the news industry, the limits of self-regulation, the convergence of media with other business, interests of political elite and pressure groups, and thus the bureaucratic practices in the media enterprise itself are just a few factors that shape the output of the newspapers (see the first section of this chapter). I have illustrated the de facto interplay between the media and politics, and precisely the amount of pressure coming from the owners, which was abundantly noticeable during the twentieth century with the early press barons. Arguably, similar tendency does still exist, though it is becoming a more intricate and complex practice in the media community due to the huge expansion of this industry. The sudden swift of the traditionally right-wing papers of Rupert Murdoch, for example, to support the New Labour government is an indication of the influence of the ideological preferences of the owners themselves on the political orientation of their papers.

In addition to these elements, the unconscious impact of the shared social cognition on people's worldviews, beliefs and judgements is another major perspective in the theory of context. Part of this cognitive aspect in the analysis of discourse can be found in van Dijk's theory, and particularly his emphasis on the "cognitive interface" in the analysis of the relationships between the social structure and the structure of language (see Chap. 3). The socio-cognitive model postulates that knowledge is structured in the mind in the form of "frames" or "scripts", which are shared among the members of a society or community. Those scripts help individuals to understand the various communication situations and events in their social world. Because most of what is meant is left implicit, through memory retrieval of information from these nodes, people are able to make sense of language. A script about migration, for example, in the nowadays context of Britain would mean, in the first place, political asylum seekers, war refugees coming from disturbed regions such as Syria and other related information that is associated with the script of migration. Based on this simple explanation of how cognition affects the perception of social reality, it is important to identify the kind of associations, collocations and word co-occurrences in the news texts which might reflect the ideological skew of the newspapers in their day-to-day coverage of the Iraqi dossier.

Therefore, the goal of this chapter is to further examine the interplay between language and ideology at the level of the news texts. This is carried out with reference to the socio-cognitive model in the analysis of the structure of news and the accompanying manifestations of ideology, along with the use of lexicometrics in the statistical treatment of the corpora. By using this mixed methodology, I wish to transcend from the mere systematic analysis of chunks of language to expose the impact of the shared cognition on the consciousness of the in-group members that belong to a specific "epistemic community". This point has, in fact, been emphasized throughout the whole work.

6.2 The Metanarratives of the Iraq War in the British Press

6.2.1 Macrosemantics

Under the CDS framework, there is certainly a rich toolbox of analytical procedures and strategies that could be practically useful to explore the ideology–language dichotomy through a close reading of the thematic and semantic structures of text and talk in a variety of communicative situations and settings. In this section of the chapter, I shall concentrate on this aspect of language and proceed with an analysis of the overall topics and their structures in some selected articles taken from the news corpora (CNA). Once again, this is carried out with reference to the macrostructure theory. The purpose of this preliminary stage of global macrosemantic analysis is not only to describe the main themes of Iraq-related news reports, but also "to establish their conditional (linear) hierarchical relationships and their semantic specification in the text" (van Dijk, 1988b, p. 73). Therefore, to particularly exhibit how the pro-war ideology was reproduced *semantically* in the press coverage, headlines are given special priority, as they best express the highest macropropositions (upshot) of the news reports. Ideology, as explained earlier, is loaded in the content, form, style and grammar, and in the representation of outgroup members in the headlines. This is equally important from a cognitive point of view because headlines are easier to remember, as most readers may not recall the other details about the reported event.

On the whole, the British press was robustly criticized for its soft reaction to Blair's unconditioned support of the US neoconservative agenda that sought to overthrow Saddam's government, even without a UN resolution—which eventually turned out to be the case. Many critics claimed that the press was submissive and less critical of the war propaganda, as it served to promote a distorted picture about the then problem of Iraq. Ex-Walton MP Peter Kilfoyle complains that "the whole thrust of British policy on Iraq post 9/11 was to portray it as a threat to Britain, and to the West generally [...] Fear was to be the emotion shared by government propaganda, aided and abetted by a complaint and complicit press" (2007, p. 97). Though the reproduction of the official ideology in the press was sometimes self-evident, notably during the war period, there is still some reticence about this holistic interpretation and critique. In this chapter, I opted for qualitative and empirical analyses that arise out of a close examination of the language of the press, simply because the quality press covered the Iraqi dossier in a welter of articles. Hence, it would be methodologically erroneous to draw general conclusions based solely on a scrutiny of the broadsheets selected in this research—these are top national dailies with high rates of circulation though.

Undoubtedly, the official pro-war discourse was not wholeheartedly welcomed and caused much frustration in the public and political society, and even within Labour itself. As for the press, a multifaceted analysis of its content is necessary to better approach how its ideological stance was codified in its language, which, it should be emphasized, oscillated between pro and contra. Worth noting in passing that like any qualitative analysis, there is still a minor methodological weakness which is germane to the representativeness of the sample texts considered for qualitative textual analysis. To overcome this hindrance, only news articles were selected for analysis because they do not show quite straightforwardly their point of view, which is only subtly drawn and embedded within the structure and linguistic items of the text. For this reason, opinion articles and editorials cannot be taken as samples for analysis.

Moreover, one has also to bear in mind that journalists, editors and media producers, in general, have different backgrounds and ideological affiliations, and range from political pundits, academics, economists and social theorists to ordinary journalists, whose points of views, judgements and commentary on the events and circumstances of the Iraqi crisis were varied and diverse. In the light of these general considerations, it would be perhaps more reasonable to talk about a cluster of metanarratives produced by an amalgam of ideologues that altogether created a mosaic picture about the Iraqi scene. This is not to neglect, however, the impact of the media owners on the editorial practices of their papers. In this respect, the implementation of the socio-cognitive model is deemed to overcome intuitive criticism and generate a more comprehensive understanding of the processes involved in the (re)production of elite ideology, bias and propaganda in the language of journalism when responding to war-related topics. I would like to note here that despite the major role of Blair's government and British media in the conflict of Iraq, the US press received relatively more scholarly attention and much ink has been invested in the study of the language practices that were courting affinity with the interventionist policies of the Bush's administration.

In essence, Blair led Britain to intervene militarily in Iraq on the basis that Saddam Hussein had developed mass-destruction weaponry that represented a constant threat to UK national security and its strategic interests abroad. Indeed, this line of argument was present in Blair's discourse ever since the days of the containment policy, but proved to be groundless in the aftermath. Other charges were also added to Saddam's profile in the wake of the 9/11 terror attacks. Furthermore, it is important to note that there has been a blatant inconsistency in the arguments provided by war campaigners. While the Bush administration was explicitly calling for regime change, Blair "begged" the motion for a military strike due, chiefly, to his fears of Saddam's ability to launch biological and chemical strikes against neighbouring countries, and possibly Britain. Obviously, the US call for regime change overlooked the necessity to go through the UN, which has been a subject of much political controversy and debate. Thus, Blair's claim proved to be highly exaggerated in the light of the mounting evidence. In his speech to the Commons, Blair deliberately accused the Iraqi regime of possessing an arsenal of lethal weapons prohibited by the UN. Blair declared:

> Saddam had used the weapons against Iran, against his own people, causing thousands of deaths. He had had plans to use them against allied forces. It became clear after the Gulf war that the WMD ambitions of Iraq were far more extensive than hitherto thought. This issue was identified by the UN as one for urgent remedy. Unscom, the weapons inspection team, was set up. They were expected to complete their task following the declaration at the end of April 1991. (March, 2003)

What made the issue more inadequate is the lack of such evidence as the war came to an end. The military, who were in charge of searching weapons, declared only some remaining stockpiles of chemical warheads, shells and aviation bombs, which were abandoned from the time of the Iran–Iraq war. An active nuclear programme as such did not exist in Iraq.

With the release of the report of the Chilcot Inquiry in July 2016, further witnesses from the British Secret Intelligence Service made new revelations about how Blair, with his press advisors and spokesmen, attempted to spin the information delivered by UN inspectors and intelligence services. Despite warnings from the 700 inspectors working across the military sites in Iraq and the assertion of the chief weapons inspector Hans Blix about the absence of concrete evidence of an active WMD programme, Blair relied on the memos of the US intelligence and fake data to justify the intervention. Most intelligence information about Iraq's WMD activities was drafted in the two dossiers published in September 2002 and February 2003, known collectively as the Iraq Dossier.[4] *The Daily Telegraph* published the Prime Minister's foreword to the Iraq Dossier and some edited parts of the report which reviewed Iraq's activities since 1998, intelligence reports, and a separate section for biological, chemical, nuclear capabilities and their delivery systems.

In retrospect, Iraq resumed its negotiation with the international community in 2002 where the UN inspection teams were allowed to return back to the country. The Iraq Dossier contained much fabricated and misleading information about the nuclear capabilities of Iraq, most noticeably the highly disputed note in its foreword which claimed that Iraq's WMD *could be activated at 45 minutes' notice*. The dossier demonstrated Downing Street's anxiety about Saddam and its determination to hasten the war plan. Consider the below headlines about the dossier from the broadsheets:

(1)	"Saddam has to be stopped"	*The Daily Telegraph* 24 Sep 2002
(2)	Iraq's "nuclear countdown"	
(3)	Blair outlines Iraqi threat	
(4)	British intelligence provided main source for dossier	25 Sep 2002
(5)	"Saddam has had 10 years of second chances. It is time to act"	
(6)	Why Saddam must be stopped	
(7)	Iraq has the expertise, Saddam has the desire	*The Independent* 24 Feb 2002
(8)	Iraq takes journalists on tour to expose Blair "lies"	
(9)	Left-wingers rebel as MPs tell Blair not to bypass UN	
(10)	US claims proof of Iraq terror link	25 Feb 2002
(11)	British dossier is scorned as "propaganda"	
(12)	Kennedy takes US to task over Iraq strategy	*The Guardian* 24 Sep 2002

From the few excerpts shown on the question of WMD, one of the inferences that could be drawn from these headlines is that Saddam represents a "threat" to UK national security and interests. Thus, it is to be argued here that the lexicon utilized in *The Telegraph* and *The Guardian* tacitly reinforces the official slant, which amplified, through a hard line tone, the danger of Iraq's assumed "nuclear" arsenal. *The Independent* however expressed some reticence about the allegations declared by the dossier. At this stage, analysis is concerned with the global semantic structure of the news text which would reflect how the views of the elite, Blair's views in particular, about war-related topics permeate through the news discourse. It is important to draw attention to the relations between mere textual structures and the respective mental processes involved in comprehension, perception and manipulation, albeit at a very global abstract level in the semantics of discourse. In a news article, the headline and leading sentences or paragraphs adequately express the macroproposition of the text, but they could sometimes be incomplete or equivocal though. This is cognitively relevant because the information that is communicated first is more likely to be stored in the long-term memory and would be easily retrieved in future occasions as part of the personal and collective experience by the respective readers about the news event covered in the press (Dijk, 1988a, 1988b, 1991).

The main theme in the sample article (3) (see previous page) from *The Telegraph* is expressed in the headline "Blair outlines Iraqi threat". The sentence clearly highlights the imminent danger of Iraq in its commentary on the weapons dossier. In order to describe the hierarchical macrostructure of the "threat" presupposition as expressed in the article, the latter is summarized in the below few sentences, which represent its main topics, though at a lower level. The purpose of this bottom-up semantic processing of the text is to showcase how the Iraqi threat is constructed by the journalist through the semantic propositions and implications made after the publication of the dodgy dossier. It should be mentioned once again that such a summary is recursive:

(a) Government published a dossier stating that Saddam's WMD programme is "up and running".
(b) Policy of containment failed.
(c) Iraq could have a nuclear weapon in two years.
(d) Saddam can activate WMD within 45 minutes.

There are a number of remarks to highlight. From a cognitive perspective, the comprehension of the news report requires extensive information, which is already stored in the memory of the audience; that is, readers would need much knowledge about Iraq, WMD and other related topics in order to be able to assign meaning to the text in hand. Thus, the less they know, the more they are likely to be manipulated. For example, it is fundamental to know about Saddam himself and his relationships with Britain, the first Gulf War, the requirements of the containment policy, the meaning of WMD, the UN inspection investigations and the like. The sample articles provide a new piece of knowledge about Iraq's WMD and will be, of course, part of the knowledge, which will be used for judgements in future occasions when the problem of weapons is once more discussed. The use of the word "nuclear" in heading (2) is quite misleading, as there were no nuclear weapons and the inspection team was primarily concerned with other less destructive biological and chemical weapons.

I would assume that the justification of the military action is strengthened with the implicit suggestion about the failure of diplomacy and the international economic blockade, which lasted for around a decade (1990–2003). The declaration in (b) does patently suggest what comes next. It suggests that all peaceful means were exhausted to topple Saddam and military option was the last resort. By the use of the model verb "has to" in *The Telegraph*'s headline (1), which is in fact a direct quote from Blair's foreword to the Iraqi dossier, it is implied that the paper shares the view that Saddam is a constant threat that requires urgent reaction. Word choice, particularly in headlines, is poignant and indicative of the writer's standpoint. Because words and phrasing matter, the next section of the chapter will focus more closely on this aspect of language.

From another perspective, many scholars alluded to the reproduction of ideologies in the news through the incorporation of institutional sources and references (Van Dijk, 1991, pp. 151–175; Herman & Chomsky, 2008). Ample examples were, in fact, found for the case of the British dossier on Iraq's WMD, some of which are signalled in the aforementioned headlines with quotation marks, such as the reference to British intelligence and Blair himself. The sample article (3) is entirely a paraphrase of Blair's address to the commission and the government's report. There was no reference whatsoever to the Iraqi sources or the anti-war campaigners.

There has recently been an ongoing debate about the dangerous security repercussions of the Iraq War and the misguided Western policies in the Middle East. Many complain that Western interventionism in the region has created more political disarray than stability and alarmingly led to the rise of terrorism, notably the so-called Islamic State of Iraq and Syria (ISIS), which launched terror attacks against European countries, such as the lately Belgium airport bombings. The link between Saddam's regime and terrorism, under the heading of Al-Qaeda, which was examined in the political discourse of Blair, needs also to be reassessed again. Throughout the stringent period that preceded the military action, the press made frequent references to the ongoing government reports and briefings about the allegation around the Iraqi–Al-Qaeda cooperation, notably in *The Telegraph*. Some pertinent examples that illustrate the reproduction of this major official trait in the news discourse are shown in what follows:

		The Daily Telegraph 13 Dec 2002
(13)	Al-Qa'eda has VX nerve agent from Iraq, claims report	
(14)	Bush rallies support by linking Iraq to Sept 11	09 Oct 2002
(15)	Blair's Iraq dossier will show how Saddam trained al-Qa'eda fighters	15 Sep 2002
(16)	First strike "may trigger Saddam's terror weapons"	10 Oct 2002
(17)	Saddam "giving al-Qa'eda agents shelter"	30 Jan 2003

Previously, *The Telegraph* has ruled out the Iraq–terror assumed relationship following the September attacks, yet this came to the surface once again as further government reports and documents were released. Similar associations were headlined in *The Guardian* and *The Independent*:

		The Guardian 23 August 2003
(18)	Militant Kurds training Al-Qaeda fighters	
(19)	Mountain camps extremists suspected of testing chemical weapons and links to Iraq	
(20)	Straw warns Iraq on terror threat	
		The Independent 26 April 2003
(21)	"Bin Laden envoy met Saddam's officials"	
(22)	"Intelligence papers" found in Baghdad point to regime's links with Bin Laden	27 April 2003

The Independent's headline (10) "US claims proof of Iraq terror link" sounds neutral, but, in fact, it enhances the Saddam–terror proposition in the memory of its audiences. Though this is a mere claim, as the headline indicates, it is still cognitively relevant because it influences the judgements of the audience, who are more likely to believe in such an association. The word "terror" evokes negative feelings and emotions in readers, who unconsciously recall such moment of anxiety along with Iraq. This was much more voiced in the US media, which assisted significantly to shape the public mind, as many American citizens believed that "Bin Laden and Saddam are the same man".

6.2.2 Microstructures: Grammar and Ideology

At the outset, it should be highlighted that I follow, in this section of the chapter, a slightly different strategy of analysis from the one applied on Blair's discourse. This is so because the "schematic superstructure" of a political speech is quite distinct from the somehow standard layout of a news article, and thus the peculiar thematic structure and pragmatic contextual characteristics of these two types of text. Nonetheless, in both cases, attention is still drawn solely to the minute parts of language that may express subjective knowledge or are loaded with ideological biases because microanalysis entails the analysis of a text at a very local level.

In this respect, the language–ideology relationship is seen only fragmentarily through the grammar structure and lexical choices made by newsmakers when reporting major war-related events. Therefore, unlike the previous macrosemantic analysis, which accounted for meaning as expressed by the various chunks of language seen as a single piece of an integrated whole, microanalysis considers, in particular, the smallest fragments and units of language in isolation from one another. Basically, reference is made to individual lexemes, phrases, sentences, grammatical structures in headlines, the use of model verbs and so on.

As sketched in the second chapter, the theoretical assumptions about the incarnation of ideology in the linguistic components of language find its starting point in the pioneering structuralist traditions that questioned the form–content dichotomy. Much care was paid to the connections between the linguistic surface structures and the meanings that they convey, which many linguists and social theorists believed to be ideologically charged, as postulated, for example, by Roger Fowler, Bob Hodge, Gunther Kress and some others (1979). This analytical procedure, though little reference is made to context as defined in the socio-cognitive model, would reinforce the premise made about the tacit reproduction of the ideologically skewed discourse of the establishment in the structure of the news language. For example, the choice of specific linguistic forms rather than others, notably in headlines and leading sentences, as it has been advocated earlier, does not report reality objectively, but echoes the journalist's views and opinions about the reported event. This analytical strategy is often nicknamed transitivity, which, as Paul Simpson writes, "refers generally to how meaning is represented in the clause. It shows how speakers encode in language their mental picture of reality and how they account for their experience of the world around them" (1993, p. 82). A plethora of approaches of discourse analysis, particularly those under the CDS framework, employ this technique, such as stylistics, Critical Linguistics and other sister models and methods of inquiry.

A salient journalistic practice is the standard schematic superstructure adopted in the writing of news whose narrative structure is often, but not always, congruous with the type of the article. In other words, a news article, for example, is different from editorials, feature and opinion articles in its schemata and thereby the structure of its semantic components. As for the former, the prominence of information is distributed in a top-down manner, from the most to the least important, with the gist in the headline, circumstances in the leading paragraph and the other details and possible brief comments to follow in the remainder of the text. It follows that word choice, syntactic structure of sentences, agency and the grammar used specifically in headlines would best mirror the ideological standpoint of the writer and also guide, or at least partially manipulate, the interpretation of the text (see, e.g., Fowler, 1991). In similar fashion to these earlier studies, in this section, I should analyse the grammatical patterns and forms in the corpus with the aim of identifying their ideological function. This mode of analysis is perhaps less convenient to the study of editorials, where the point of view of the paper, or a specific commentator, just like a political speech, is explicitly expressed and clearly embraced by the author or speaker.

The collective works of Zellig Harris and other traditional grammarians, which are still widely referenced, gave birth to a bunch of theories and terminology in the field of discourse analysis. The term "transformations", though conceptualized in slightly different manners, has been borrowed by subsequent CDS scholars to point out the tacit meanings that are embedded in syntax and word order. This questioned seriously another crucial aspect of language, where it has been suggested that grammar is not neutral and its structure actually does reflect the worldviews and ideologies embraced by the writer. The early scholarly endeavours sought to fathom the function of language through its grammatical structure and yielded insights into how ideology is implied in word choice and the rules of grammar.

It is a common practice that journalists use impersonal passive constructions, particularly in headlines, which make the information being addressed in somewhat inchoate fashion, and might therefore lead to a misinterpretation of the information. The concealment of the participants of an action, its circumstances and consequences is believed to have an ideological nature. This could also be made through the use of other similar grammatical structures that mask part of the contextual elements, such as the use of noun phrases and intransitive verbs. According to CDA scholars, the passive form is one of the grammatical devices that could unveil ideology and bias in a given text or talk. This is nicknamed *passivization,* which is "the rendering of verbs in the passive form – also involves the deletion of actors and focuses the attention of the hearer or reader on certain themes at the expense of others" (Thompson, 1984, p. 120).

Conversely, the active form is more likely to appear in headlines to highlight blame or de-humanize the Other. In one of the street battles between the Iraqi *Fedayeen* and British troops in the south-east of Basra, Martin Bentham reports how these armed Iraqis held kids as human shield: *Iraqi paramilitaries "used children as human shields"* (01 April 2003, *The Independent*). Unlike the passive form and noun phrases which may obscure the agents, the active form places them at the onset of the sentence to make them more visible to the reader. While this is not necessarily about bias, it indicates the kind of preferred evaluation attributed by the journalist to the reported event. The placement of civilians to shield military objectives from attack during armed conflicts is an immoral act that is considered to be a war crime, as stated in the additional *protocols* to the Geneva Convention.

In fact, there are many ways to express positive-self image along with negative-other image. Condemnable actions were most often attributed to Iraqi agents, while the responsibility of the in-group was rendered more invisible. Consider the following headline from *The Independent*:

(1) <u>Iraqi missile may have caused</u> Baghdad market horror, says US general	27 Mar 2003
(2) UK bomb experts were executed <u>by Iraqis</u>, Blair insists	28 Mar 2003
(3) <u>Iraqi troops</u> fire on <u>families</u> fleeing Basra	29 Mar 2003

Whatever the real circumstances of the events mentioned above, the problem, as so often, is that journalists are more likely to make visible the agents of such negative incidents whenever found related to the "Other" to demonize the Other out-group agents.

Nominalization is also another strategy that is often used, whereby the agency of the in-group members is deliberately omitted in order to hide their responsibility. The US–British forces were usually not mentioned to conceal their misconduct during military operations and clash with civilians, yet their upright behaviour was often highlighted and brought to the fore. Thompson once again explains that "[n]ominalizations occur when sentences or parts of sentences, descriptions of action and the participants involved in them, are turned into nouns; the effect is to attenuate the feeling of activity, to eliminate agency, modality and tense, to transform processes into objects" (1984, p. 120). Following the attack by the Allied military forces on the city of Basra, *The Independent* reported the following on 24th March: "*Fighting on the streets of Iraq's second city leaves 77 civilians dead.*" The noun phrase "fighting" has a similar ideological function to *passivization*, whereby many of the circumstances are left unspecified, notably the agents, who were obviously responsible for the death of 77 civilians. Let us consider the following headlines:

(4) Day 13: Deadly firefights in Iraq, political skirmishes in London – And the bombs keep falling on Baghdad	*The Independent* 1 Apr 2003

Just like *passivization*, the participants of the event are deliberately not mentioned, leaving no room for negotiation and, most importantly, this contributes to the normalization of violence. The invisibility of participants would make it difficult for readers to pass tough judgement and criticism. Numerous similar cases can be found with regard to the way in which the agency of actions was handled. It has been observed that negative attributions to the coalition forces were undermined by the use of noun phrases and passive constructions. On 23 March 2003, after the bombardment of the southern city of Basra, which resulted in the death of about 50 Iraqi civilians, journalist Severin Carrell from *The Independent* headlined the story as "*50 civilians dead, says Arab TV*". In this sentence, both the act of killing and its circumstances are not made clear, which leaves the agency of the action unspecified, while the source clearly charges the coalition forces of the massacre.

Equally important to this line of argument is the reference to inanimate objects or abstract nouns instead of direct reference to humans, as in the below-listed headlines. Indeed, this could divert the attention of the reader towards the readings and interpretations preferred by the journalist[5]:

(5)	Shock and awe air assault blasts Baghdad	21 Mar 2003
(6)	The longest day: From surgical attack to full scale attack on land and by air	

One of the narratives that filled up the front pages of the press particularly during the war period was the shift to reporting the day-to-day military skirmishes and street fights between the allied forces and the Iraqis in general. See some of the examples in the following headlines:

(7)	In the Cotswold's sunshine, B-52 s load deadly cargo	21 Mar 2003
(8)	Minute after minute the missile came with devastating shrieks	22 Mar 2003
(9)	Laden with death and with destruction the B-52 take off in front of peace demonstrators	
(10)	14 dead as missile hit Baghdad market	26 Mar 2003

The regular reference to inanimate objects when reporting, for example, about the violence occurring during the war, such as causing or bringing about the indiscriminate mass killings of civilians, to devastate, bomb, blast, destroy and the like, instead of their real human agents, would have a strong impact on the reader's perception, unconsciously though. The previously mentioned headlines tend to create a sort of machine war–like atmosphere, which undermines the human presence in a brutal war taking lives and resulting in considerable damage and suffering. It is obvious to readers that the damage, devastation and death brought to the streets of Baghdad are attributed to military equipments and hardware, which are considered the actual actors (B-52, tanks, missiles and so on) rather than American or British soldiers, who are commanding them and performing the action. The imperative to using these kinds of constructions is not made at random because it has a valuable unconscious effect. As in the case of passive constructions, agency could also be vaguely expressed through other forms and constructions, such as the reference to Allied forces, coalition of the willing, the UN and similar organizations.

Another important framing technique is the use of modal verbs. This falls under the rubric of the ideational function of language, which can be defined, as Fowler puts it, as a "comment or attitude, obviously by definition ascribable to the source of the text, and explicit or implicit in the linguistic stance taken by the speaker/writer" (1991, p. 85). Modality allows for the expression of subjective, yet implicit expression of the writer's opinions and evaluations. The use of modality markers expresses different degrees of probability and certainty that would have a significant impact on meaning and interpretation.

In brief, the broadsheets were more inclined to assign agency to the Others when they are, or assumed to be, involved in violence and, conversely, opt to hide the agency of the in-group when they are accountable for similar acts of aggression and violence. It was abundantly remarked that this was carried out through various grammar structures and transformations. Some of these are briefly summed up in what follows: First, the use of passive forms and *nominalization*, which made the participants invisible by drawing the attention to the act per se rather than to the actors. Second, the frequent reference to inanimate agents also served to create a virtual world where acts of killing and falling down bombs are performed by inanimate objects rather than by humans, which, after all, intended to avoid blaming the real human doers. This strategy mirrors the ways in which the boundary between "They" and "We" is drawn by journalists, whereby positive-self image is often highlighted along with negative-other presentation. With reference to the numerous cases found in the news corpora, some of which are taken as illustrations in this part of the chapter, I advocate, with little hesitation, that the "ideological square" has provided important clues about the reproduction of the mainstream ideology in the news discourse.

The "ideological square" could also be noticed at the level of personal pronouns. The pronoun "We" is often used by editors and columnists instead of "I", where they could include the addresses and invite them to share their viewpoints. This displays, Kress and Fowler write, "the added complexity that the source claims to speak of and for himself and on behalf of someone other than himself" (1979, p. 201). The three papers extensively used these interpersonal pronouns in their articles and editorials to bridge the gap between the voice of the press and the opinion of their target audience. Though this could have limited influence on readers, it always reminds them about the necessity to stand together and support "our boys", "our soldiers", "our government", "our civilization" and so on.

Based on these notes on how ideology is embedded in the surface structure of the news language, it is suggested in this case that the omission of agency and other contextual conditions in the passive form, the use of noun phrases instead of verbs and, thus, the numerous references made to inanimate subjects, notably international institutions, helped to omit reproach and de-emphasized the role of human agents. Those news frames were potently driving the attention of readers in ways that aim to put blame on the "Other", and undermine the agency of in-group members in any negative situation. This tends to normalize and legitimate the actions of the in-group, which is, in a way or another, a very subjective portrayal of the reality out there and contributes only in providing a partial and biased view. Further remarks and commentary will be made through the subsequent empirical account provided on the news corpus.

Grammar and wording have both crucial ideological functions to play. In this case, I argue that the vocabulary baggage in the news corpus reveals a great deal of skew and implicit endorsement of the in-group pro-war ideology. The word *West* is one of the key terms that has been exploited to strengthen the "Us versus Them" fissure. It was quite often used as a synonym to the Anglo–American alliance, which was quite misleading—or at least unrepresentative. It is well known that the unilateral engagement in Iraq has been rejected by the majority of Western countries, notably the two major powers: France and Germany. Only a few countries backed up, albeit symbolically, the military invasion, such as Spain, Italy and the Netherlands. Moreover, the large public, even in Britain and relatively less in the USA, voiced their denunciation of the military strike based on the large and active public protest movement throughout Western Europe. Consider the following random excerpts from *The Telegraph* and *The Guardian* where the word "West" appeared in headlines:

(11) Saddam's agents launch bloodbath against <u>West's allies</u>	*The Daily Telegraph*
(12) Time for <u>the west</u> to stop being Saddam's scapegoat	*The Guardian*
(13) Iraqi <u>nerve</u> gas "could paralyse <u>western</u> cities"	
(14) Most <u>western</u> bombs missed Iraqi targets	
(15) Saddam <u>chokes</u> off oil to put pressure on <u>west</u>	
(16) <u>West's failure</u> to donate humanitarian aid threatens catastrophe for millions	
(17) All is <u>ominously</u> quiet on the <u>western front</u>	

Thus, the West is frequently juxtaposed against Saddam, Muslims, and Arabs, which created two blocks in confrontation. Equally important is the use of ethnic and religious vocabulary, such as Arab, Islamist, and Jihad, which have also been misused in the context of the Iraq War. This encased the Anglo–Iraqi conflict with a religious touch, though both governments were secular and far away from being theocratic. Moreover, the word "jihad" in the context of Iraq could simply be used to mean the defence against a foreign aggression, which is void of any religious connotations. A few other examples would illustrate the religious aspect that has been attributed to the struggle with Saddam. On 14 December 2002 David Blair from *The Telegraph* reported how "Saddam has Koran written in his blood", which alludes to his religious commitment.

On the whole, what has been discussed so far is not discrete from the previous assumptions made about the dyadic link between ideology and language, but it served, in particular, to operationalize van Dijk's concept of the "ideological square" in relation to the use of grammar and vocabulary. It was ostensible that the de-humanization of the out-group and positive-self presentation constitute a recurrent feature of the press discourse. Bias in favour of the in-group, as has been illustrated with ample examples, was materialized via the selection of particular vocabulary and syntactic structures which were loaded with negative images about the "Others". "They" (basically Saddam, top Iraqi officials and army) are inhuman, tyrants, brutal, violent and religious fanatics, while "We" (Western, British, American) are civilized, human, democratic and liberty fighters.

In the light of these remarks, it is fairly reasonable to claim that the British quality press provided a non-balanced coverage that tailored its tone, in many cases, with the campaign launched by the Prime Minister, who was determined to topple Saddam Hussein even by unauthorized use of military force. The process of legitimizing this unequivocally illegal and aggressive policy in the news was articulated in the various language practices which had been successfully played out in the British anti-Saddam propaganda. However, this ideologically based discourse was fluctuating in its judgements and evaluations from one period to another, driven by the immediate political conditions, which were often highly volatile. It is clear, throughout what has hitherto been discussed, that what I meant by "news analysis" is the examination of a myriad of narratives coming out of the stories told, and the ways they are told, by newsmakers. However, part of this relates also to what has not been said or downgraded, which might well be equally newsworthy at a particular point in time.

6.2.3 The Quantification of the British Press Discourse (January 2000–May 2003)

This last part of the chapter accounts quantitatively for the lexico-semantic structure of the news corpora (*The Daily Telegraph*, *The Guardian* and *The Independent*). A scrupulous quantitative analysis would help us to assess more adequately the theoretical assumptions and the validity of the interpretations made throughout the previous parts of this study; therefore, the content of the news corpora is equally explored using the same quantitative tools implemented in the analysis of Blair's discourse (Lexico3 and IRaMuTeQ).

A myriad of tables, charts and graphical representations were generated by the automatic clustering and classification of the language components of the CNA. The resulting empirical findings, such as the relative/absolute frequencies of selected key vocabulary, term co-occurrences, and other pertinent statistical distributions and collocations substantiate the hitherto made qualitative analyses, which considered only fragments of the news corpora. Indeed, the quantification of the latter provides a holistic view about the structure of press discourse, as it metamorphosed during the delimited time span, with reference to the major linguistic and syntactic features prevailing in the language of the broadsheets. Thus, it allows also for close qualitative readings of different parts of the corpora at particular point in time. Furthermore, such a multifaceted quantitative analysis enables comparisons between the narratives of the newspapers along with that of Blair on the question of Iraq.

Unlike the previous corpus (CPS), the CNA is larger in size and composed of heterogeneous news items, but mostly news articles. More precisely, it contains 3000 manually collected and labelled texts from the official online archives of *The Telegraph*, *The Guardian* and *The Independent* (from 2000 to 2003). The corpus of each paper was treated separately to allow for multidimensional assessments and comparisons and also as a whole at a later stage. The "noise data" was removed for a proper function of the segmentation processes.[6] Indeed, the software packages offer the possibility to perform various statistical tasks, but only a few were considered. The corpora were partitioned with reference to the source of the texts (*The Independent*, *The Guardian* or *The Daily Telegraph*) and the date of publication only, that is, 2000, 2001, 2002 and 2003. The purpose behind this simple coding of the news text input is to demarcate the salient semantic and linguistic features across the content of the three papers and to bring to the fore their newsworthy topics and top stories at different periods in time.

First, in order to describe and analyse the patterns and relationships of similarity and dissimilarity among the linguistic forms of the news corpus, I used once again IRaMuTeQ, which generated the visual representations displayed in the next two pages (Figs. 6.1, 6.2, and 6.3). Each of these figures refers to the corpus of a single newspaper, *The Independent*, *The Daily Telegraph* and *The Guardian*, respectively.

As shown in the figures, the three dendrograms constitute two major clades, with five classes in *The Independent* and *The Guardian* and six in *The Daily Telegraph*. This shows a great deal of affinity in the coverage of the broadsheets—notably that the wordlists stand more or less for similar topics with slight differences. Nonetheless, *The Telegraph*'s dendrogram generated six classes, which indicate its rich and diverse content in proportion to the other papers. It was noted that *The Telegraph*'s articles were lengthier than those of *The Guardian* and *The Independent*, and varied in terms of the topics they tackled under the umbrella of the Iraq dossier.

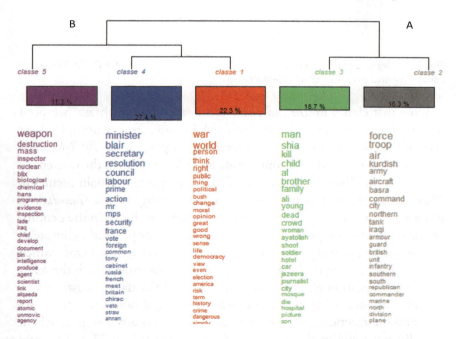

Fig. 6.1 Dendrogram of classes drawn from the corpus of *The Independent* using descending hierarchical classification

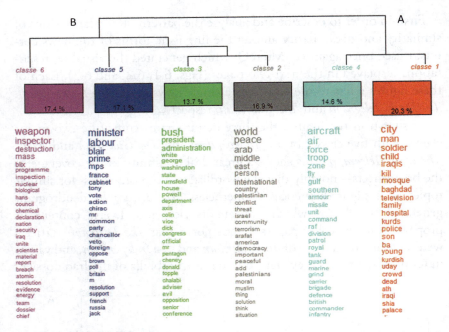

Fig. 6.2 Dendrogram of classes drawn from the corpus of *The Daily Telegraph* using descending hierarchical classification

Note that class 5 in *The Independent* is headed by the phrase "weapons of mass destruction", which is by itself a major topic, representing 15.3 per cent of the corpus. Similarly, it represents 17.4 per cent of *The Telegraph*'s text, as exhibited in class 6, but significantly less visible in the content of *The Guardian*. Though the issue of WMD was one of the main themes in Blair's discourse, it does not seem to be newsworthy in *The Guardian* in proportion to *The Independent* and *The Telegraph*, as shown in the dendrogram. From another perspective, the vocabulary lists provide a glimpse of the lexical world and word associations made under this theme, which strongly refer to Iraq in the first place, but more alarmingly with the reference to the question of terrorism (Bin Laden, Al-Qaeda, terrorist).

New Labour's political debates and wrangling about Blair's policy on Iraq and the reaction of major international powers are also quite salient as a distinct topic in the news, which is represented by 27.4, 17.1 and 16.8 per cent in *The Independent* (class 4), *The Telegraph* (class 5) and *The*

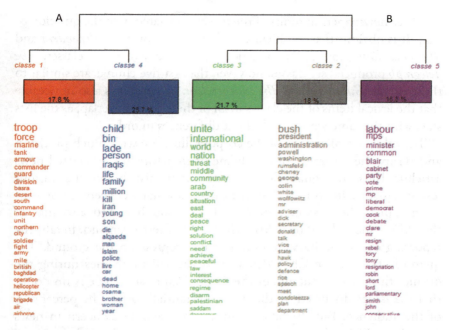

Fig. 6.3 Dendrogram of classes drawn from the corpus of *The Guardian* using descending hierarchical classification

Guardian (class 5), respectively. The US politics is another major theme that is heavily covered by *The Telegraph* (class 3) and *The Guardian* (class 2), but is quite absent in the coverage of *The Independent*. Thus, the military operations and day-to-day clash with resistance during the war period constitute another topic in the threes papers. It could also be noted that clade A in the three broadsheets denotes the coverage of the war period, as it contains much war-related vocabulary, such as military equipment and acts of war (infantry, armour, troops, tank, marine, shoot, fight and the like). This was also coupled with names of specific local regions and settings in Iraq (Basra, city, Baghdad, northern, southern). The remaining classes belong to clade B and relate to international relations and party politics.

A few interesting remarks can be made from the descending hierarchical clustering of the corpora through a comparison between the word listings of the visualizations. First, there is a great degree of overlap between the three newspapers in terms of the topics associated with the question of Iraq. It is obvious that the hierarchical clustering of *The Independent* and *The Guardian* produced two major clades and five word classes. *The Telegraph* produced six classes; however, the first five chunks are similar to those of *The Guardian* and *The Independent*. Second, it is also noticeable that the lexical items of the classes in all of these papers overlap, as the lists start with the same words, with slight differences in order.

The other visualizations of the corpora illustrate with much precision and clarity the centrality of the theme of *Iraq War* in the selected news articles. Thus, the quantification operations distributed the various lexico-semantic items into different categories that were centred on four main topics: the discourse of New Labour on Iraq and also that of the USA, issues related to WMD, the threat of terrorism and, finally, the reporting of the military motion and its progress on the ground. The quantification of the CNA demarcated the salient themes during the 40-month period in the life of the Anglo-Iraq crisis. There is no doubt that the issues discussed by the press substantially affect the perception of the audience. But this alludes to another seminal concern in news reporting which relates not only to what was reported and how it was reported, but on the unsaid which was equally newsworthy. I believe that the discourse of the press undermined many other pertinent aspects of the Anglo-American military intervention, notably the legal aspect and also the damage done to the Iraqi people, whose tragic repercussions are still unfolding. These distortions undercut the role of the press as an apparatus of social critique and public enlightenment against the abuses of the elite.

The representation of the Other also matters in the news, such as the kind of individual or collective stereotypes, prejudices and other language patterns that are used to denote the out-groups. Some of these are displayed in the concordances (Fig. 6.4) produced by Lexico3 to further comment on the representation of Iraq in the news. The concordances point out how Saddam was demonized through the frequently made association between the Iraqi leader and international terrorism.

Put succinctly, it is important to highlight that the assumptions made in this study are based on one possible way of looking at wartime reporting. In fact, the press reported thousands of stories and events in a language

```
             Partie : Guardian, Nombre de contextes : 175
t only was Saddam a suspected sponsor of terrorism , he was also likely to be a willing
Clearly , they do have their own form of terrorism , and they still have Saddam Hussein .
tion over the second phase in the war on terrorism when he insisted that Saddam Hussein
ians have argued that a campaign against terrorism which excluded Saddam Hussein would
tween President Saddam and international terrorism cannot be ignored . Few observers expect
after Saddam at some time if the war on terrorism was to be taken seriously ' . Secretary
re probably is a link between Saddam and terrorism . I would be in favour of an attack ,
 cking President Saddam - regime change , terrorism or weapons of mass destruction . But the
            Partie : Independent, Nombre de contextes : 172
port extending the campaign to eliminate terrorism to Saddam Hussein ' s regime during a
und linking Saddam Hussein ' s regime to terrorism , the alliance ' s secretary general
w Saddam Hussein . States that sponsored terrorism were seeking weapons of mass destruction
lso demanded that Saddam stop supporting terrorism , persecuting minorities , trading oil
nt Saddam would be tantamount to " state terrorism " . Cautious EU backs second resolution
 from President Saddam and international terrorism were " two halves of the same coin " .
 in and again Mr Bush played the Saddam / terrorism / alqaeda card . Americans , polls show
 s a victory for Saddam and international terrorism . The same thing was said about Pan Am ,
            Partie : Telegraph, Nombre de contextes : 237
 Clearly , they have their own form of terrorism , and they still have Saddam Hussein .
ent Bush that the only way to crush Arab terrorism is to topple Saddam . That case received
rely on its closest ally in the war on terrorism . What to do about Saddam Hussein ' s
ad shown no willingness to oppose global terrorism and that while Saddam " is keeping his
depose Saddam as part of its war against terrorism . He admitted that the " direct ,
to proceed in the wider campaign against terrorism . " There is a threat from Saddam
will be the next target of the war on terrorism and it worries him . " We can beat Saddam
 who was trained by Saddam ' s regime in terrorism techniques against the Kurds in northern
 threat posed by Saddam Hussein to global terrorism . However , the Prime Minister said that
ill struggle to link Saddam with alqaeda terrorism . British and American intelligence
tually guarantee an explosion of Islamic terrorism if it attacked Saddam Hussein without
```

Fig. 6.4 Concordance of terrorism in the news corpora

rich in imagery and metaphors that provided a colourful picture about the crisis of Iraq with the (Western) global powers. I have already advocated that the press purports to concern itself with objectivity and neutrality, which is, in fact, a myth, as the problem relates to the complexity of representation, ideology and what it is referred to collectively as *discourse*. At a narrow level, I argued that the reproduction of the ideology of the pro-war campaign was becoming more salient with Blair's active diplomatic campaign after the 2002 Crawford Summit. Starting from this juncture, Iraq became a newsworthy topic. Language was often abused for the sake of normalizing violence against its leadership.

The macropropositions discussed so far were amongst the most sensitive Iraq-related themes in the pre-war period. Post-war Iraq and reconstruction, the role of the UN and military technology were the topics covered most often in news during and after the war. As just mentioned, this would lead us to another seminal aspect about language and manipulation; it is simply what was left unsaid. It is incongruous to assume that language alone would shape the interpretation of the audience, but the choice of what to include and exclude in news-making is also a poignant factor in the orientation of our understanding and perception of reality.

After all, although there is plenty of evidence which identifies a great portion of distortion and bias in reporting, it amounts several times to the level of mere propaganda. I advocated earlier that the endorsement of a particular worldview is not always rational, and that there is a great deal of complex emotional and unconscious elements, some of which are still ambiguous, that have their own ways of influence on people's thought and behaviour.

Notes

1. See estimates and other relevant data about press readership and its audiences on the website of the National Readership Survey: nrs.org
2. Lord Northcliffe was one of the most influential figures in British politics who used his newspapers, *The Daily Mail* and *The Times* to put pressure on the government. These newspapers, as many political commentators noted, were behind the downfall of the Asquith's coalition government in December 1916.
3. See Jones (2001) for further details on the techniques used by Blair's spin doctors to manipulate the media and the public as well.
4. The report "Iraq – Its Infrastructure of Concealment, Deception and Intimidation" was said to be plagiarized by civil servants working under Blair's Director of Communications and Strategy, Alastair Campbell. The report was presented at the UN Security Council on 5 February 2003.
5. On the use of Critical Linguistics in the analysis of US press coverage of the Iraq War, see, for example, David Weiss' "'New Mexico's Been Always Patriotic and Loyal to the Country': Uncritical Journalistic Patriotism in Wartime", Haridakis, Hugenberg, & Wearden, 2009, pp. 183–204.
6. Some symbols such as the dollar sign ($), the asterisk (*), and the underscore (_) have specific function to play in the software and should be omitted to avoid possible errors.

References

Andrews, A. (1859). *The history of British journalism: From the foundation of the newspaper press in England, to the repeal of the Stamp Act in 1855: With sketches of press celebrities*. London: Richard Bentley.

Baldasty, G. J. (1992). *The commercialization of news in the nineteenth century*. Madison, WI: University of Wisconsin Press.

Curran, J., & Seaton, J. (2003). *Power without responsibility*. London: Routledge.

Fowler, R. (1991). *Language in the news: Discourse and ideology in the press*. Abingdon, UK: Routledge.

Fowler, R., Hodge, R., Kress, G., & Trew, T. (1979). *Language and control*. London: Routledge & Kegan Paul.

Herman, E. S., & Chomsky, N. (2008). *Manufacturing consent: The political economy of mass media*. New York: Pantheon Books.

Jones, N. (2001). *The control freaks: how new labour gets its own way*. London: Politico's.

Kilfoyle, P. (2007). *Lies, damned lies and Iraq: An in-depth analysis into the case for war and how it was misrepresented*. London: Harriman House.

McNair, B. (2009). *News and journalism in the UK*. London: Routledge.

Negrine, R. (1989). *Politics and the mass media in Britain*. London: Routledge.

Sampson, A. (2004). *Who runs this place? The anatomy of Britain in the 21st century*. London: John Murray.

Simpson, P. (1993). *Language, ideology and point of view*. London/New York: Routledge.

Stanton, R. C. (2007). *All news is local: The failure of the media to reflect world events in a globalized age*. Jefferson, NC/London: McFarland & Company.

Temple, M. (2008). *The British press*. Maidenhead, UK: Open University Press.

Thompson, J. B. (1984). *Studies in the theory of ideology*. Berkeley, CA: University of California Press.

Van Dijk, T. A. (1988a). *News as discourse*. Hillsdale, NJ: Erlbaum.

Van Dijk, T. A. (1988b). *News analysis: Case studies of international and national news in the Press*. Hillsdale, NJ: Lawrence Erlbaum.

Van Dijk, T. A. (1991). *Racism and the press*. London/New York: Routledge.

Weiss, D. (2009). "New Mexico's been always patriotic and loyal to the country": Uncritical journalistic patriotism in wartime. In P. M. Haridakis, B. S. Hugenberg, & S. T. Wearden (Eds.), *War and the media: Essays on news reporting, propaganda and popular culture* (pp. 183–204). Jefferson, NC: McFarland & Company.
www.independent.co.uk/archive
www.telegraph.co.uk/archive/
www.theguardian.com/uk

7

Conclusion

In sum, it has been demonstrated how Blair's political discourse sought to normalize institutional violence against the state of Iraq, particularly after the 9/11 attacks. The latter period was, the least to say, an era of wide public hysteria and much political anxiety, which, as I argued, gave a boost to Blair's interventionist policy. The pro-war ideology was also assessed in the discourse of British quality press, which, in its enduring struggle against the pressure of determined political elite, partly resisted but entirely reproduced the dominant official stance. The purpose of analysing the news discourse was to critically comment on how the reality of war was represented and, more particularly, how the official story was reproduced and legitimized in the eyes of a large sceptical public.

Apart from the socio-cognitive model which advocates a systematic and detailed analysis of discourse, I also intended to situate this research work within the general CDS framework. Hence, the language-based critique that is advanced here relied upon other empirical approaches and also drew some insights from similar methods of language analysis, which, all in all, provided more theoretical flexibility and pictured many facets of the research problem. Thus, the controversies of the case study have shown with clarity the multiple articulations of ideology in the structure of language at the linguistic and non-linguistic levels. Part of the complex link between language and ideology has been assessed in the ways in which Blair attempted to prop up his warfare ideological stance. Three major arguments were put under scrutiny: Blair's controversial plea for ethics as a means for military intervention, Iraq's nuclear capability and the rising threat of terrorism. Whatever their inconsistencies and limitations, Blair's allegations were eventually approved by the British parliament, though this was a mere symbolic support, and transformed into a destructive rather than a pre-emptive political behaviour whose repercussions are still unfolding in the Middle East. Ideological bias in favour of the government was less manifest in the reluctant and sceptical tone of the broadsheets, which incorporated various narratives, yet with the start of the military strike, they toyed with doing the same.

I shall recast some of the core concepts of the applied methodology and shed light on the existing lacunae in the analysis of the corpora. Indeed, I have already signalled in the third chapter some of the inherent limitations and shortcomings in the broad theory of discourse analysis, notably the difficulty to operationalize those approaches that draw heavily on cognition to interpret the various communicative situations and discourses. This is certainly the case for the socio-cognitive model as applied in this case study research. Whilst the quest in this direction sounds tempting and rewarding, there are still a handful of theoretical and practical labyrinths in the way towards a comprehensive theory of discourse that is wholly anchored on a cognitive paradigm.

As for the socio-cognitive model, the validity of its theoretical domain assumptions is less disputed than its strategy and tools of analysis. One of the pragmatic difficulties relates, in particular, to the cognitively-based concept of "macrostructure". In very mundane terms, this was defined as the global semantic structures in a specific discourse (van Dijk, 1980). The operationalization of this basic notion means literally the reduction of a huge amount of complex information into a few sentences that best represent the *upshot* of a given discourse. To achieve this, the model suggests the aforementioned macro rules which make visible the underlying coherence relations in discourse. Though this technique is relatively easy to handle in the case of short pieces of text and talk, such as a conversation, this would be much more complex in longer discourses, as van Dijk himself acknowledges, which is typically the case vis-à-vis the corpora of this study.

Thus, the recursive nature of this process (i.e. macrostructure analysis) makes it difficult to arrive at a single "representative" abstract or a summary of a given text by two or more analysts. This means also that readers of a news article and the attendees of Blair's meetings may not attribute the same meaning to what they have read or heard. Whether the proposed cognitive interface to explain the mechanistic processes involved in discourse production and comprehension, with reference to the functions of the memory, storage and retrieval of information, sufficiently expounds the order and processing of discourse remains perhaps a concern for further empirical investigation and research. This does not, however, impinge on the validity of the process-oriented logic of the socio-cognitive model as much as it begs the question of whether the cognitive processes of language and meaning are fully explored and known.

Basic concepts in the theory of language and ideology were discussed in the second chapter. It has been suggested, based on the domain assumptions that underlie the adopted methodology, that ideology, as hitherto defined, is a constant feature of any written or oral discourse. Hence, the coverage of British newspapers is by no means ideologically driven. Plainly, as a fundamental concept that has been reverberating along with discourse, ideology has been given a neutral meaning as it was first employed by the early French idealists in Post-revolutionary France. This is so because the purpose of this research is to mediate on unconscious and tacit processes of legitimization and reproduction of ideology as a *belief system* in society, which is projected through Britain's conflict with Iraq. The brief historical sketch made in the second chapter sought to draw the boundaries between discourse and ideology as distinct concepts, yet mutually dependent processes. Nevertheless, the applied methodology does not require discourse and ideology to be clearly demarcated from one another. The former is taken as language in use, while the latter denotes the ensemble of values, opinions, beliefs and worldviews that are naturally imbued in discourse.

The impact of the mass media on the public mind has also been explicated, with particular focus on the unconscious and cognitive aspects of such influence. Most significantly, this was linked with the assumptions made about the workings of memory and the role of *knowledge* that is shared amongst the members of a given epistemic community. A brief reference was also made to the agenda-setting theory.

In order to put the reader into context, it was important to look at the Anglo–Iraqi relationship from a historical perspective. The survey provided in the fourth chapter has highlighted some of the aspects of this relationship, reflecting the deeply rooted involvement of Downing Street in moulding the politics of Iraq since the First World War. Indeed, the whole Middle East was a strategic sphere of influence that the successive British imperialists struggled to maintain under their control at a time when Britain started to lose its supremacy as a political and military power on the world stage. Nonetheless, British control over Iraq, which started officially with the League of Nations mandate in 1921, was becoming less formal and disguised in many forms in the following years to come.

As mentioned at the onset, the causes of the war were not set as a primary goal in this research, but were sparsely hinted at in the fourth chapter. To find a feasible answer on why Britain stood shoulder to shoulder with the USA, and particularly Blair's impulses to rally support for war, would definitely be a research problem in its own right that exceeds the frame of this essentially language-oriented study. However, a little comment on this controversial point is needed as part of the general context of the case study.

Apart from its geostrategic and economic significance, Iraq was used to deter neighbouring Iran, which turned to be a radical theocratic state with the fall of the Shah in the 1979 revolution. Shortly thereafter, Saddam became a close ally to Britain and the USA. The British press used to represent him as the new "rebuilder of Babylon", but in the wake of the First Gulf War, he was often represented as a "ruthless dictator", a "tyrant", and his regime, as Blair declared, the "world's worst regime: brutal, dictatorial, with a wretched human rights record" (Blair, 2002).

Blair is criticized for attempting to draw too simple a link between Saddam's regime and international terrorism through his frequent presuppositions and allegations about the clandestine meetings of Iraqi agents with terrorist groups. It is enough to note that the secular and anti-theocratic ideology of the Ba'ath party during Saddam's rule, and even earlier, is sufficient to discourage any such pretensions. In my understanding, the hysteria created by the random terror atrocities around the globe since the 9/11 was exploited by war campaigners to procure sympathy for the "pre-emptive" military strikes in Iraq and elsewhere.

Due to its importance, Iraq's arsenal of mass-destruction arms was also encompassed in the fourth chapter. As postulated and illustrated in the generated infographics from the corpora, this was a topic in Blair's speeches that addressed the question of Iraq and was equally primed in the press. The phrase "weapons of mass destruction", though plain in its common-sense usage, remained quite vague in the more technical meaning it holds, at least for the large uninformed public. This was already a pending issue in the legislation that sought to contain the spread of mass-destruction weaponry, as the diversity of these weapons made it difficult to come up with a unified definition. Therefore, the reference to this topic was rather ambiguous and served to exaggerate the danger posed by Saddam's regime and his infringement of international accords.

New Labour's foreign policy was briefly discussed in the fifth chapter in order to adequately analyse the legitimization of the war ideology in Blair's political speeches, which is tackled in the broader context of the then British politics. The aim was, of course, to comprehend the rationale of Blair's pro-interventionist policy abroad and how it was justified.

I argued that Blair's political rhetoric echoed in many different respects the discourse of the orthodox British imperialists in previous epochs of history that legitimized the British imperial rule overseas based on "evangelical" values of philanthropy and humanitarianism. The word "values" was quite salient in the selected texts, as the empirical findings showed, but such a basic concept was expressed vaguely and rather inconsistently. The attempt to move from the very local to the global was perhaps a major setback in the rhetoric of New Labour, which endorsed putatively universal human values, but yet from a British standpoint. This is so because the word "values" collocated with British, Western, democratic and capitalist in the first place. I would assume that Blair's discourse, which resorted to recurrent appeals to humanitarianism, ethics and the rule of law in the management of international affairs, yielded a repulsive and aggressive foreign policy that was based on non-cogent arguments, and this is especially so in the case study of this research.

The other aspect of the warfare ideology was assessed in Britain's top national dailies through qualitative and quantitative modes of inquiry. Under these two approaches, a variety of techniques were implemented to glean light on the ways in which the official pro-war ideology permeated in the language structure of the news discourse.

The historical sketch in the first part of Chap. 6 provided a bird's-eye view on the political, economic and regulatory practices that substantially exercise a pressure on decision-making in the production of news. It depicted the enduring struggle of the British press against the constraints imposed on it, some of which are still shaping the news discourse. As is the case in all liberal democracies, the British media in general are supposed to be a counterpoise against the abuse of authority by people of power, including the government. I have emphasized that this idealist vision of the Fourth Estate is no more than a utopia because power struggle is an integral part of the media discourse. Arguably, even in a democracy such as Britain, the media have never been neutral reporters but typical gatekeepers of information, manufacturing versions of the reality "out there" that promote their own interpretation and ideological preferences. Besides, throughout much of its history, the British press was pro-capitalist and conservative in tone, showing deliberate hostility to the Left ideology. Nonetheless, New Labour was an exception, as the party managed to win the papers over to its side, yet it did not always escape its criticism.

In relation to the sample data, van Dijk's socio-cognitive model was once again applied in the analysis of an extended corpus of news items selected over a 40-month time period. The samples treated were carefully selected to critically assess the performance of the press and to provide an accurate image about its representation of the Anglo-Iraqi conflict, which ended up with the declaration of war. This was undertaken through the use of a range of analytical devices and procedures that scrutinized the semantic and lexical components of language and its structure. Overall, three strategies of analysis were taken into account to examine the reproduction of the pro-war ideology in the discourse of the quality papers.

First, the systematic description of the thematic structure of the news samples—with a focus on headlines—has identified some of the framing techniques used at the level of "discourse topics". The ensemble of macro-propositions was filled with numerous implications and presuppositions that reproduced the point of the view of the war proponents rather than critiquing them. It was also advocated that the stories and events presented to the public provided a soft critique to the official propaganda, and aided, in many cases, in normalizing the use of force against Iraq.

Ostensibly, there has been a tendency to include more references to government and military sources and rarely to the Iraqi ones, though Saddam's emotionally charged speeches were routinely published. Direct quoting and rephrasing, and excessive references to official sources prevailed in the news texts. As has been advocated, the overuse of references to the "in-group" was not made at random. Rather, it performed an ideological function, since it framed the whole situation to suit the storyline of the government.

Second, grammar has also been given some priority, as this could potentially be loaded with ideological biases. It was shown through a number of examples how the taken-for-granted syntactic constructions, such as the passive form, the use of nouns instead of verbs and the frequent usage of inanimate subjects, could divert the attention of the audience and shape their interpretations of the reported events. Along with these grammar structures, the lexical choice was also indicative of positive-self and negative-other representations.

Third, with the lexicometric analysis of the corpora, further empirical results were drawn which plainly backed up the intuitive qualitative generalizations made through the close reading of individual texts. The visualizations show with great clarity the similarity in reporting in the three papers in terms of topic selection and focus, prevalent vocabulary and grammar patterns such as key term frequency, co-occurrences and collocation.

At a global thematic level, it has been evident that the themes of terrorism, WMD and Britain's ethical responsibility towards the people of Iraq came to appear at the very centre of discussion. Relatively, recurrent references to the threat of terrorism were systematically attributed to Saddam Hussein, as illustrated in the headlines. The press coverage was, in fact, imbued with false interpretations of the state of affairs, which was by no means a major weakness.

Taken as a whole, a high degree of overlap was identified between Blair's language and that of the press in terms of the de-humanization of the "Other" enemy and the glorification of the in-group. This was demonstrated with reference to three broad lexico-semantic aspects of discourse. It was noted that the press was framing the struggle with Iraq as a security problem for Britain, where Iraq was represented as a constant threat to the stability of world peace—the same claim raised by Blair, who recurrently mentioned the danger of Saddam's nuclear weapons. Furthermore, there has been a noticeable tendency to negatively portray the East in general and the Iraqis in particular. Thousands of articles reported the violence and terror caused by Saddam's regime throughout the period he was the head of the state. The persecution of minorities, notably Kurds, Christians and the various Shi'a sects, was a recurrent theme. Thus, the depiction of the deteriorating situation of Iraq due to the economic siege under the containment policy helped to charge Saddam with full responsibility, while the role of Westminster in the problem was relatively overlooked.

During the pre-war period, both *The Independent* and *The Guardian* deliberately denounced Blair's plans over a military strike on Iraq, which he heralded during his early meetings with George Bush in the Texas Summit of 2002. The conservative *Telegraph* was however ostensibly less critical and, most of the time, sustained the government's line. In fact, the ideology of the political elite and the press coverage were welded together as the war became a reality by the 19th of March. The launch of the "shock and awe" attack and the advance of the allied military machine to the borders of Iraq marked a sharp shift in the press coverage. The threat of Iraq's assumed WMD came to dominate the coverage of the papers, though with slight difference in tone and style. Thus, it was remarked that the moral cause of the war, which was largely ignored for a while, came to the fore again as the only legitimate cause of the war, as *The Independent* suggested.

Imagery of prejudice and stereotyping, with reference to ethnicity and religion, was subtly expressed, which often implicitly linked Arabs and Muslims with violence, religious intolerance and extremism, but more alarmingly, with terrorism. I demonstrated how the case of Iraq was associated with previous events that left a negative surge on the collective memories of people. One of the language strategies to invoke such associations with these negative experiences was made through metonymy, comparisons and contrasts between Saddam and Adolf Hitler, Saddam and Milosevic and, finally, Saddam and Osama Bin Laden.

The representation of the in-group members was, however, positively drawn—such as the professionalism of the British army in the conduct of the war, the huge technological gap and military advancement of the allies in proportion to the traditionally equipped Iraqi army and so on. This was also demonstrated with ample evidence at the level of grammar, where more attribution to agency has been noticed when the *Other* is involved in violation of human rights or any criminal behaviour. Conversely, agency is deliberately hidden for the case of in-group members. After all, the war ideology has not been constructed in Blair's speeches and the few selected papers only, the bulk of information and accumulated knowledge about the Iraqi case in general was derived from many other channels of information and public spheres that were created by the advent of information technology.

In closing, it is worthwhile noting that the ideological leaning of the news discourse towards the official stance, as has been seen in the corpus and also the matrix of historical, legal and socio-political circumstances discussed throughout this study, is, to a substantial degree, an outcome of a subliminal impact of the knowledge manufactured by information centres and consumed by in-group members during a long period of time. The latter definitely exceeds Blair's premiership. It is this shared subjective knowledge about the state of affairs in general that pictured the invasion of Iraq as a liberation mission. The emotional and unconscious influence of language remains, however, beyond the reach of any procedures of verification and measurability.

In sum, the debate over the Iraq War has reached its end with the release of the Chilcot report on 6 July 2016, which charged Blair and his team with full responsibility in misleading the British public about the question of Iraq. In a two-hour conference, Blair responded to the verdict with an apology to the victims of the war, but paradoxically insisted that he made the right decision. It was surprising that the press, notably the Murdoch papers, which supported Blair during the build-up to the war, responded rather harshly on him recently. After 13 years, it is evident that the Blair–Bush assault on Iraq was a foolhardy venture that did not bring democracy to the Middle East, nor did it make the world safer, as the whole region is now more fragile and vulnerable than ever, notably with the rise of terrorism, sectarianism and ethnic antagonism.

Appendix: List of Speeches by Former Prime Minister Anthony C.L. Blair (CPS)

Leader's speech, 1996. Location: Blackpool.
General election victory speech, 1997. Location: 10 Downing Street.
Leader's speech, 1997. Location: Brighton.
"Bringing Britain Together", 1997. Location: London.
Leader's speech, 1998. Location: Blackpool.
"Doctrine of the International Community", 1999. Location: Chicago, Illinois.
Leader's speech, 1999. Location: Bournemouth.
Speech to the Global Ethics Foundation, Tubingen University, 2000. Location: Germany.
Leader's speech, 2000. Location: Brighton.
"Faith in Politics", 2001. Location: Westminster Central Hall, London.
General election victory speech, 2001. Location: 10 Downing Street.
Leader's speech, 2001. Location: Brighton.
Speech at the George Bush Senior Presidential Library, 2002. Location: Crawford, Texas.
Speech to Trades Union Congress conference, 2002. Location: Blackpool.
Leader's speech, 2002. Location: Blackpool.
Speech at Labour's local government, women's and youth conferences, 2003. Location: Glasgow.

Speech to the House of Commons, 2003. Location: London.
Speech to the US Congress, 2003. Location: Washington, DC.
Leader's speech, 2003. Location: Bournemouth.
"Prime Minister warns of continuing global terror threat", 2004. Location: Sedgefield.
Leader's speech, 2004. Location: Brighton.
"Speech to Faithworks", 2005. Location: London.
General election victory speech, 2005. Location: 10 Downing Street.
"Speech on improving parenting", 2005. Location: Watford.
Leader's speech, 2005. Location: Brighton.
"Respect Agenda" speech, 2006. Location: London.
"Our Nation's Future – Social Exclusion", 2006. Location: York.
Leader's speech, 2006. Location: Manchester.
Resignation speech, 2007. Location: Sedgefield.
Speech to the "Islam and Muslims in the World Today" conference, 2007. Location: London.

Index[1]

NUMBERS AND SYMBOLS
9/11, 93, 126–133, 135, 138, 140, 143, 144, 147, 178, 180, 203, 207

A
Afghanistan, 135, 137, 139, 140, 142, 156n5
Agenda-setting theory, 47, 48, 206
Al-Qaida, 142
Althusser, L., 24, 33, 34
Andrews, A., 162
Anglo-Persian Oil Company (APOC), 85
Articulatory practices, 29–34, 166
Artificial intelligence, 40, 72
Asia, 84, 115, 124
Asquith, 200n2
Audit Bureau of Circulation (ABC), 15n7, 164
Augustine, Saint, 114, 156n4
Austin, J. L., 57
Axis of Evil, 99

B
Ba'ath, 87–91, 206
Baghdad, 47, 84, 93, 184, 188–190, 197
Bakhtin, M., 59
Basra, 84, 187–189, 197
Beaverbrook, 170
Blair, T., 1, 4–7, 9, 12–14, 18, 36, 41, 43, 44, 58, 71, 78, 82, 91–93, 105–155, 165, 170,

---

[1]Note: Page numbers followed by 'n' refer to notes.

Index

172–175, 178–185, 188, 194, 196, 199, 200n3, 200n4, 203–207, 209–211
Blix, H., 180
Bonaparte, N., 23
Bourdieu, P., 62
Britain, 4, 5, 9, 10, 12–14, 18, 27, 31, 35, 38, 42, 71, 81–89, 91, 93, 95, 98, 100, 105–108, 115, 117–119, 121, 123, 126–133, 141, 144, 145, 152, 154, 155, 155n1, 155n2, 156n5, 156n10, 161–180, 183, 192, 205, 206, 208–210
Bush, G., 91–94, 99, 131, 136, 139, 179, 180, 184, 210

C

Cairo Conference 1921, 88
Chilcot Inquiry, 82, 180
Chilton, Paul, 2, 43, 58, 110
Cognition, 6, 8, 9, 13, 22, 27, 38, 40, 41, 67, 69, 70, 73, 74, 77, 146, 166, 176, 177, 204
Cognitive
 Interface, 10, 57, 65, 71, 177, 205
 Linguistics, 71
 psychology, 8, 15n4, 48, 65, 72, 79n2, 146
Coherence, 44, 73, 75–78, 119, 122, 124, 133, 138–144, 175, 204
Commons, 7, 9, 25, 34, 36, 44, 60, 64, 73, 92, 95, 127, 170, 180, 187
Communism, 109
Communist Manifesto, 24
Concordances, 145, 147, 149, 150, 198, 199

Consciousness, 24, 25, 27, 28, 30, 35, 47, 63, 66, 77, 78, 177
Context, 5, 7, 8, 11, 18, 19, 21–24, 29, 30, 34, 36–40, 42–44, 49, 50n1, 57, 58, 60, 62–65, 68–72, 74, 76, 77, 79n1, 89, 96, 106–108, 111, 113, 118, 126, 127, 130–132, 134, 136, 138, 144, 146, 147, 149, 154, 166, 176, 177, 186, 192, 206, 207
Context models, 68, 72, 121
Co-occurrences, 11, 126, 145, 152, 153, 177, 194, 209
Corpus, 10–12, 14, 44, 77, 91, 108, 119, 138, 145–147, 149, 151, 152, 154, 186, 191, 194–197, 208, 211
Crawford, 136, 139, 141, 199
Critical Discourse Analysis (CDA), 2, 3, 9, 10, 14n1, 19, 29, 37, 56–62, 64, 187
Critical Discourse Studies (CDS), 2, 3, 7–10, 13, 15n4, 19, 34, 39, 42, 55–62, 67–70, 72, 166, 177, 186, 187, 203
Critical linguistics, 19, 56, 58, 186, 200n5
Culture, 14, 23–25, 27, 161–168

D

Daily Mail, 169, 170, 200n2
Daily Telegraph, 4, 12, 162, 181, 184, 192–196
Damascus, 89
De Tracy, A. D., 22, 23, 50n2
Democracy, 4, 38, 44, 110, 165, 168, 172, 173, 208, 211

Index

Dendrogram, 151, 152, 195–197
Descending Hierarchical Classification (DHC), 12, 151–153, 195–197
Dialectical–Relational Approach (DRA), 59
Discourse, 17–50, 55–78, 94, 105–155, 173–177, 203
Discourse analysis, 2, 3, 10, 12, 13, 15n3, 17–50, 56–59, 62–65, 70–74, 76, 78, 132, 166, 173–177, 186, 187, 204
Discourse Historical Approach (DHA), 59
Discourse studies, 2, 8, 55–78, 108
Discursive, 1, 3, 5, 10, 17, 20, 27, 29, 31, 34–36, 40, 62, 105, 109, 110, 131, 161–200
Dominance, 19, 30, 38, 60, 84, 87, 92, 109, 168
Domination, 24, 25, 30, 31, 57, 62, 91, 109, 164
Downing Street, 82, 89, 106, 181, 206

E

East Anglia, 28, 60
Engels, 25
Enlightenment, 22, 28, 162, 168, 198
Episodic memory, 73, 124
Epistemic, 5, 70–74, 77, 78
Epistemic community, 7, 18, 74, 141, 177, 206
Epistemic discourse analysis, 78
Epistemological anarchism, 20
Ethics, 14, 95, 106, 107, 114, 117, 120, 128, 134, 167, 204, 207
Europe, 12, 18, 22–24, 28, 31, 89, 115, 139, 141, 152, 192

F

Fairclough, N., 2, 19, 30, 37, 41, 56, 59, 60, 62, 65, 72, 110, 119
First World War, 81, 83, 85, 86, 100, 170, 206
Foucault, Michel, 29, 36, 59, 62
Fourth Estate, 46, 161–177, 208
Fowler, R., 19, 27, 28, 58, 174, 186, 190, 191
France, 22, 23, 86, 101n3, 127, 132, 192, 205
Frankfurt School, 60
French Revolution, 23

G

Geneva Convention, 188
Geneva Protocol, 96
Global coherence, 119, 122
Globalization, 122, 123, 134, 136, 155
Grammar, 4, 20, 28, 37, 39, 43, 56, 59, 68, 78, 185–193, 209, 211
Gramsci, A., 24, 27, 29–34, 62, 166
Guardian, 4, 13, 101n6, 156n11, 162, 171, 181, 184, 192–198, 210
Gulf War, 15n2, 47, 82, 180, 183, 206

H

Habermas, J., 62, 133
Halliday, M., 40, 59, 69, 70
Harmsworth, A., 168, 170
Harmsworth, Sir Lester, 169
Harris, Zellig, 51n3, 187
Hart, Christopher, 3, 69, 138
Hegemony, 19, 20, 29–34, 38, 39, 60, 84, 87, 109, 163, 165, 166

Hiroshima, 96
Hitler, A., 141, 210
Human rights, 92, 106, 112, 116, 117, 123, 134, 139, 150, 156n6, 206, 211
Humanitarian militarism, 107, 112–117
Humanitarianism, 105–125, 207
Hussein, Saddam, 1, 5, 6, 13, 48, 81, 89–95, 98, 100, 107, 119, 123–126, 128, 129, 131–133, 137–139, 141, 142, 144, 145, 150, 155, 165, 178–185, 192, 193, 198, 206, 207, 209, 210
Hymes, D., 56

I

Ideological square, 48, 139, 150, 191, 193
Idéologie, 17–23
Ideology, 1, 4–9, 13, 14, 17–50, 50n2, 57–60, 63, 67, 73, 77, 78, 89–91, 94, 97, 98, 105, 106, 110, 111, 117, 125–127, 129–131, 133, 134, 136, 137, 143–145, 149, 154, 155, 161–179, 183, 185–193, 199, 203–208, 210, 211
Imperialism, 14, 82, 84, 87–91, 118, 155, 206, 207
Independent, 4, 13, 19, 26, 43, 83, 86–88, 135, 162, 182, 184, 185, 187–189, 193–198, 210
Industrial Revolution, 163
Iramuteq, 14, 15n5, 145, 146, 151, 194, 195
Iran, 84, 85, 90–92, 95, 97, 98, 139, 180, 206

Iraq, 1, 18, 46, 58, 81–91, 105–155, 161–200, 203, 206
Iraq Dossier, 181, 184, 195
Iraq War, 1, 4–6, 8, 10, 13, 14n2, 43, 81, 91–94, 106, 115, 127, 129, 144, 155n2, 161–200, 200n5, 211
Iraqi Petroleum Company (IPC), 85
Istanbul, 86

J

Jacobin, 127, 132
Jus ad Bellum, 112–117

K

King Faisal I, 83, 88
Knowledge, 3, 7–10, 15n3, 21, 26, 27, 29, 35–37, 40, 41, 48, 49, 57, 63, 67, 69, 73, 74, 76–78, 124, 132, 134, 138, 140–142, 146, 149–151, 154, 162, 164, 165, 167, 177, 183, 185, 206, 211
Kosovo, 107, 114, 120–124, 137, 156n5
Kuhn, T., 20
Kuwait, 93, 97, 98, 101n8

L

Labour, 44, 93, 105–107, 111, 115, 117–125, 135–137, 152, 153, 155n2, 156n5, 156n6, 163, 170–172, 176, 179, 196, 198, 207, 208
League of Nations, 83, 87, 100, 101n4, 206

Legitimization, 1, 4, 7–9, 41, 43, 46, 68, 71, 75, 82, 106, 130, 131, 133, 145, 154, 175, 205, 207
Lexico3, 14, 15n5, 145–147, 194, 198
Lexicometric, 11, 12, 14, 145, 177, 209
Liberal, 13, 24, 26, 31, 32, 97, 110, 113, 118, 123, 140, 165, 168, 170, 172, 208
Linguistics, 2, 3, 5, 11, 12, 18, 19, 23, 28, 29, 34, 36, 37, 39, 40, 44, 55–58, 61, 62, 64, 68–72, 74, 75, 79n1, 138, 144, 146, 152–154, 156n7, 165, 174–176, 179, 185, 186, 190, 194, 195, 200n5, 204
Literary criticism, 4, 12
Local coherence, 75, 78, 138–144
London, 47, 84, 91, 93, 108, 125, 130, 135, 163, 188

M

Macrorules, 77, 120, 121, 133, 136, 175
Macrostructure, 8, 75–78, 119–121, 132–137, 176, 182, 204, 205
Marx, K., 25
Marxism, 17, 23–29, 31–33, 166
Media, 2, 14n2, 31, 33, 41, 45–49, 59, 82, 92–94, 114–116, 128, 151, 155, 161, 162, 165–173, 176, 179, 185, 200n3, 205, 208
Mental Models, 8, 9, 15n3, 72, 73, 124
Mesopotamian Campaign, 91

Middle East, 1, 6, 81–91, 101n3, 105, 108, 154, 183, 204, 206, 211
Milosevic, 123, 124, 141, 210
Morality, 23, 106, 107, 112, 117, 125, 128
Murdoch, R., 170, 176, 211

N

Nagasaki, 96
National Readership Survey (NRS), 164, 200n1
Neoconservative, 9, 92, 93, 178
Neuroscience, 72, 79n2
News discourse, 6, 10, 14, 21, 28, 38–50, 58, 66, 173–177, 182, 184, 191, 203, 208, 211
Nominalization, 59, 188
Non-Proliferation Treaty (NPT), 97
North Atlantic Treaty Organization (NATO), 114
Northcliffe, Lord, 169, 200n2
North Korea, 26, 139, 150

O

Oil, 81–91, 93, 98, 124, 192
Organization of the Petroleum Exporting Countries (OPEC), 93
Ottoman, 83–86, 88, 89, 101n2

P

Paris Peace Conference, 101n4
Passivization, 59, 187–189

Index

Persuasion, 3, 32, 40, 110, 111, 119, 124, 154, 155
Political discourse, 4, 5, 9, 14, 18, 28, 40, 42–44, 46, 49–50, 59, 66, 95, 108–111, 118, 124, 126, 130, 144–155, 165, 175, 184, 203
Political discourse analysis (PDA), 44, 105–112
Popper, K., 20
Power, 4–7, 9, 14, 18, 19, 21, 24–33, 35–39, 41, 43–45, 57, 58, 60–63, 67, 73, 84–86, 88–90, 92, 94, 96–98, 100, 101n4, 108–110, 112, 116, 117, 119, 123, 129, 135, 136, 139, 140, 144, 150, 155, 162, 164, 165, 168, 170, 173, 192, 196, 199, 206, 208
Pragmatics, 9, 33, 39, 40, 55, 77, 78, 84, 87, 101n3, 125, 185, 204
Press, 1, 18, 78, 145, 161–200, 203
Propaganda, 42, 161, 162, 167, 170, 172, 178, 179, 181, 193, 200, 209

Q

Quality press, 1, 18, 78, 161–200, 203

R

Racism, 59, 60, 62, 66
Renaissance, 89, 113, 127, 162
Resolution 687, 101n9
Resolution 1441, 99
Rhetoric, 2, 4, 5, 14, 15n2, 26, 44, 46, 106, 110, 131, 155, 165, 207
Ritter, S., 99
Russia, 30, 84, 114, 122, 139

S

San Remo Conference, 86, 101n4
Schematic superstructure, 174, 175, 185, 186
Semantic macrostructures, 75–78, 121, 132–137
Semiosis, 59
Shah, 98, 206
Social cognition, 40, 146, 166, 176
Social knowledge, 35, 74
Socio-cognitive, 1, 4, 8, 10, 11, 13, 17, 22, 27, 37, 40, 41, 50n1, 58, 59, 66–78, 119, 120, 124, 131, 132, 141, 146, 167, 176, 177, 179, 186, 203–205, 208
Soviet Union, 20, 96, 97
Structure, 1, 4–6, 10, 11, 14, 17, 19, 22, 24, 27–29, 31, 33, 34, 36–42, 44–46, 50n1, 60, 64, 65, 67, 68, 72–75, 77, 78, 107, 110, 118–121, 132, 133, 138, 142, 144, 145, 154, 156n7, 161, 167–172, 174–179, 182, 185–187, 190, 191, 193, 194, 204, 208, 209
Subaltern, 32, 166
Superstructure, 57, 68, 119, 176
Sykes-Picot Agreement, 101n3
Systemic Functional Linguistics (SFL), 69, 70, 79n1

T

Terror, 6, 14, 90, 92, 107, 120, 125–155, 180, 181, 184, 185, 207, 210
Terrorism, 1, 14, 107, 125–132, 136–139, 141, 142, 144–150, 155, 184, 196, 198, 204, 206, 209–211
Text, 8, 10–13, 19, 25, 29, 36, 42, 44, 48, 58, 60–66, 69, 71, 72, 75–77, 111, 119–122, 126, 127, 132, 133, 136, 138–140, 144–147, 149, 151, 152, 154, 156n11, 162, 174–179, 182, 183, 185–187, 190, 194, 196, 204, 205, 207, 209
Text Grammars, 56, 185
Thatcher, M., 170
Times, 200n2

U

UK, 7, 9, 15n7, 47, 92, 106, 118, 120, 179, 181, 188
United Nations Monitoring, Verification, and Inspection Commission (UNMOVIC), 99, 151
United Nations Security Council(UNSC), 6, 82, 94, 98, 114, 122, 151, 156n3
United Nations Special Commission (UNSCOM), 98, 99

V

Values, 7, 17, 25–28, 31, 48, 58, 78, 100, 106, 107, 117–119, 123, 125, 134–137, 139, 140, 142, 143, 152, 153, 162, 165, 166, 205, 207
Van Dijk, T. A., 2, 8–11, 19, 27, 28, 37, 39–41, 44, 48, 59, 60, 65–78, 79n1, 109, 111, 119, 121, 132, 133, 138, 139, 143, 150, 154, 175, 176, 178, 183, 193, 204, 205, 208

W

Walpole, R., 108
War on Terror, 93, 125, 126, 128, 130–132, 155
Washington, 91, 125, 144
Weapons of Mass Destruction (WMD), 13, 92, 95–100, 107, 125, 131, 136–139, 145–147, 149, 150, 155, 180–183, 196, 198, 207, 209, 210
Westminster, 173, 210
Wodak, R., 2, 3, 14n1, 30, 57, 59, 60, 63, 64